WAR CHILD

Life 1

By

Annalisa Count

ISBN-13: 978-1-9164060-3-2

While all the stories in this book are true, some names and identifying details have been changed to protect the privacy of the people involved.

CONTENTS

ACKNOWLEDGMENTS

I would like to say a big thank you to my daughter, Susie, and granddaughter, Emma, who have supported me throughout the whole of this book. Without their help this book would still be a handwritten notebook sat upon my kitchen table.

Thank you to Martin, who showed great enthusiasm in driving me to Germany and researching facts and events and keeping me company through the long process of writing this trilogy.

Annalisa Count

Jessie J

Her story so far.........

ANNALISA – WAR CHILD

(a trilogy)

Part One

Annalisa was born in 1930 in Germany. Her life story is a colourful spectrum of events from growing up with a Jewish family and its tragic ending to walking across Europe to avoid capture by the Russians. Her idyllic existence as one of the favoured children in Germany kept and taught in a private sanatorium, and Hitler visiting their new home before the loss of everything and being left with just a pram to transport all of their belongings. Her loss of innocence is poignant in these years, as is her smuggling peanut butter and jam sandwiches!! Part One ends with her now 19 years of age with just a suitcase, travelling to England after the war to start a new life…

Part Two

Annalisa describes her rise to riches and wealth and her subsequent fall. The fashion industry where Annalisa and her now-husband Alf become lingerie manufacturers and mixed with the fashion world. From Biba, Canarby Street to Dorothy Perkins and the wooing of buyers. Annalisa has three children and even with a nanny, cook and cleaner they still do everything for their children. Part Two describes the hard work, determination and love for her husband and family. This book ends sadly on the sudden death of Alf whilst loading a stocking stand onto a van with Annalisa now age 56.

Part Three

This book starts sadly, with Annalisa trying to overcome her grief and rebuild her life again. Her massive value for life and how she overcame two types of cancer. How she meets her next husband Martin and their helter-skelter of living life to the full. Becoming well-known designers of lingerie to the biggest sex chains in Europe. Moving back to London and their eventual move to Spain.

Still with as much of a thirst for living as in her twenties at age 83, Annalisa joins a modelling agency called Ugly and works on shows like; Never Mind the Buzzcocks, Jessie J's music video and Channel 5's programme, 'Outrageous Brits'. Alongside this, age 86, Annalisa has taken up the ukulele and now plays in a band in Ely where she is currently living and writing.

Chapter 1

As she tried very hard to open her eyes and focus on faces bending over, her immediate thoughts were, *Where am I? Is this heaven or hell?* Slowly it became clearer to her she was coming out of an anaesthetic. She had wished, not for a million dollars, but that she would survive a second operation to treat cancer. Now the faces became clearer, nurses busying themselves with checking the various drips and other items connected to her body.

A voice asked her, "How are you?"

She replied, "I think I am all right, nothing is hurting." Now she was able to make out the kind face of a nurse.

"I am Nurse Carol, in charge of your wellbeing. Please tell me, what would you like me to call you? Anne or Annalisa?"

"Anne will be fine," was her answer.

"You are a very lucky lady. You survived the operation well, and a little later your surgeon, Dr. Avortri, will come to speak to you. In the meantime, if you are in pain, you are holding a little button in your hand, when you press it a strong painkiller will be realised into your body to repress the pain."

Now she remembered that something was put in her back before the operation. She looked up to the clock, saying 7.10pm. She went in at 1.10pm, what have they been doing to her all these hours? Drifting in and out of sleep, which seemed to last hours, she realised that her surgeon was trying to speak to her. "Annalisa, wake up, I have got something very important to tell you."

What a lovely man; from her first examination she trusted him at once. Within seconds he was joking with her and making her laugh. He spoke a few words of German and broke the ice with her.

What struck her most of all, was his friendly smile, on a black face, with big dark eyes and the most perfect row of teeth. Not the tallest of men, and a little on the chubby side. His perseverance in treating the cancer, made it possible for her to speak to him.

"What is this important news you've got to tell me?" she asked.

"My dear Annalisa," he started off. "I managed to cut out the tumours (three), and I can report I got a 100% result."

She wanted to jump up and down, and kiss and hug him, but all the tubes made it impossible to do so.

"I had to cut quite a bit away and leave you with a bag which I will remove in six months' time, when all is healed up, and you have got your strength back. Also, I hope you have put on a few pounds," he said with a twinkle in his eyes. "I know you ladies like to be slim, but ladies of a certain age look better with a few pounds more."

He must know that she was seventy-nine, one off eighty? She sank back into her pillow. She did not hear 'bag', and 'another operation'; all she heard was '100%'. Whatever next, she would think about it tomorrow. This has always been her strength, to put anything unpleasant away for the next day to think about or deal with. Gratefully, she pressed her little button and went back to sleep.

The next few days she spent halfway between consciousness and sleep. Sacha her first-born son, Steve her middle son, and Susie her daughter visited.

But she was not able to fully appreciate their visit, her body must have been full of drugs to supress the pain. But on day two, her mind was clearing. She was only allowed a couple of drops of water to wet her tongue. She could now understand how terrible thirst must be if there was no water available. Other than this problem, she had no real pain, her little button saw to that, and she slept some more. The nurses could not have been kinder to her, fussing and checking all the time to see if all the pipes and drips were working. Looking around she saw five more beds, all occupied by elderly ladies, except her immediate neighbour who was in her twenties. In her mind, she herself was only thirty or forty, but never elderly. Her life so far had been full of good and bad times, not leaving time to get old. And perhaps this was why neither up or down had called for her. Quietly, she said, "Thank you, God, for my life."

It seemed that only yesterday she played with her friends in Essen. Her thoughts went to her mother and her family. Klara, her mother, only five foot, a little on the plump side, with the energy of a dozen

3

men. Brown hair and brown eyes framed a pretty round face. Klara had never known any parents. She was left on the doorsteps of a Catholic convent. She used to tell Annalisa that life for her had been very hard in the convent.

When she was only eight years old, she already had to help in the kitchen, and scrub the bare stones in the convent. At the age of fourteen she was given to a farm family to help with work. If life had been hard in the convent, it got even harder for her. Her working hours were from early morning to late at night. She was the last to finish, as it was her job to wash up after late dinner. Sundays were her worst nightmare. She had to attend church in the village, a few kilometres away, and then run all the way back to make it for lunch. Many a time she did not make it and had to go hungry. There was only one elderly aunt who felt pity, and sometimes saved food for her.

At the age of fourteen, she was moved again. This time to be the domestic help to a Jewish man and his two sons. All her life she tried to figure out how come Jewish, not Catholic, but never learnt of the connection. The Jewish man's wife had died in childbirth. Now she was not only a domestic but a nanny as well. Her employer was a very caring man of about fifty years old; his name was Moses. To Annalisa, she had only known him as Opa – Granddad. For the first time in her life she felt safe and wanted. The boys – the eldest, Jacob, took to her immediately, as he could relate to this pretty young girl. He was a tall, dark-haired, good-looking boy of fourteen years. And then there was the youngest, age six. A very pretty light-haired young boy. But as soon as she spoke to him, she realised he had a learning difficulty, his name being Solomon. He kept asking not once, but over and over, what her name was.

Later on, Moses took her to one side and explained, that it happened at childbirth, his learning difficulty, but she should treat him as normally as possible. This was not hard for her, he was a nice good-looking boy, and very polite. And so she became Mum to the boys, and settled into this Jewish household. Moses worked in Essen in the wholesale meat market, Monday to Friday, and would leave very early in the morning to work. Klara needed to take the boys to separate schools. Jacob to a grammar school, he was a clever boy, and Solomon (Sal) to a special school. After that she could do as she wished. She was over the moon with her new position, she was being treated as an equal and was eventually loved by all.

As the years rolled on, she went to visit the convent, and was told there might be a stepsister. Moses had told her that on weekends she could do as she liked, being her free time. Eventually when she got the address from the nuns, she wrote to her stepsister. She lived about thirty kilometres away by train. And on one of her free weekends, after leaving meals prepared for the family, she set off to meet her stepsister. She also had grown up in a convent and had no knowledge of her mother and father other than that Klara was her stepsister. The nuns were just not going to tell them their history. Millie was older than Klara, but had stayed single and was extremely happy to find a relative. And so most weekends Klara would make the journey to visit her sister.

Chapter 2

The year is 1928. Nothing much had changed for Klara. Jacob had finished university and was working as an accountant, but still living at home. Moses still worked in the meat market, only now Sal would help him. He had grown into a nice young man, but retained the mental age of an eight-year-old. He regarded Klara as his mummy and would cling to her at all times. He could not understand why people were teasing him and laughing behind his back. Klara tried her best to shield him.

Klara still visited her stepsister every weekend. The train would be full with commuters, who worked in the city and then travelled at weekends to the surrounding villages. After a while she recognised a few of her fellow travellers who were commuters. Amongst these regular people, she had been watching for a week a handsome man, six feet tall, getting on the train. But however much she hoped, he never entered her carriage. This particular Saturday she was looking out of the window to see if she could spot him getting on. However, there was no sign of him. The train guard had blown his whistle and as the train started to move, she spotted him racing up the steps. She quickly opened her carriage door and he jumped into the compartment as the train started gathering speed. They were laughing as they nearly fell on top of one another. Klara's thoughts were, *Gosh, he is even more handsome close up*. His blond hair, already thinning with bits of red in it, had blown in the wind. But his clothing was immaculate; suit, shirt and shoes – a snappy dresser.

When they stopped laughing he introduced himself, and asked her why she made this journey every week.

"I am visiting my stepsister, she has no other relatives. Her stop came up," was her answer.

"How about you?"

Before she could answer him, her stop came up and she had to say goodbye. As if in a dream she went to her sister, telling her about the encounter. Millie had long given up on meeting a man, and was very bitter. "Don't make anything out of it," she told Klara. "At that age they are all married and he was probably going home to the wife."

Never had a week gone by so slowly. Even Moses noticed the change in her and wanted to know. She told him of the brief encounter and that she thought he was so handsome. Her mind was only on Saturday and seeing him again. Finally, Saturday came and she saw him standing on the platform with a big bunch of roses. Her heart sank as she saw the roses, her mind at once thinking they must be for a girlfriend. But as he spotted her, he waved and rushed to her as if they were old friends. "These are for you," he said, handing her the flowers. She nearly choked; no one had ever given her flowers. She also had long given up on finding a husband, the same as Millie.

And so a love story began, till the day he died. Emil told her why he was on this train every week. He also had a very hard time in his growing-up years. He was born into a family of wealth. They had a roadside restaurant and a hotel in a small village called Haslinghausen. At the back of the hotel set in its own grounds was a villa for the family to live in. His father also had a coal business, delivering coal to all the surrounding villages. As he grew up his father put him to work at an early age to help with the coal deliveries, ignoring his schooling. He liked his drink a lot and by the time Emil was fourteen his father was an alcoholic. Many a time he would lay in the back of the cart, drunk, while Emil humped about the heavy sacks of coal. But he knew no better and was happy.

World War One, 1914-18, had finished and life was very hard for everybody. Very suddenly, Emil's mother died. His dad was hitting the bottle harder than ever before. How he managed to find a new girlfriend in his state was a mystery to Emil. Worst was to come; in no time, he married her. Emil was heartbroken, but there was nothing he could do about it. With having a new wife, Emil assumed that his dad would stop drinking, but no. For the young lad it was very hard to keep it all together. His stepmother took an instant dislike to the boy and girl of the first marriage. And within nine months or less, a son was born, a little stepbrother to Emil. Emil liked him very much, but his stepmother did not want him near her son. His elder sister became the domestic and nanny. Many a time she cried on his shoulder for the harsh treatment she was receiving. In quick succession, a further son and daughter were born.

His father's drinking took its toll and he died, not before signing all his worldly goods over to his wife. Her first task was to close down the coal business. It broke Emil's heart to sell his faithful horses. Emil assumed that now he would help with the running of the hotel and restaurant. But he assumed wrong.

Now eighteen years old, his stepmother told him that there was no more room for him at home. She had arranged with friends of hers in Essen, for him to live with them until he could find work and lodgings. Essen, a very large city in the heart of Germany, known for its coal production and heavy industry, is called the coal pit of Germany. In years to come it became the armament production city of Germany. With a heavy heart, he packed his bag to leave Haslinghausen to go to Essen. However little he liked his stepmother, it had been his home. As he only knew about coal he became a coal miner and settled down for a life on his own.

Every weekend he would still go to his sister and stepbrother and sisters. Emil, now aged thirty-nine, had also given up any thought about marriage. He was doing well, with his lodgings and his fierce love of a BMW motorbike. After the meeting with Klara a short courtship evolved, but it was not long before Emil asked Klara to marry him. Emil had been to Moses' apartment a few times and met the family, and they got on very well. Klara, unable to tell Moses for a while, finally broke the news to him about getting married and leaving. Sal must have understood what she was saying about leaving, and threw himself onto the floor and screamed and cried uncontrollably.

Moses looked at Sal and Klara. "Is this really what you want?" he asked. "This is your family; you know nothing else other than to be with us."

"But how can I please all of you and Emil?" she asked him.

Moses' reply was, "Emil moves in with us and we will be an even happier family."

When she told Emil about the proposal he was only too happy to oblige. He had been in lodgings all these years and yearned to be part of a family. And so, they got married in a half Jewish and half Protestant church wedding.

The Catholic Church was creating no end of problems for Klara with regards to her birth. Klara decided to take on Emil's faith and become a Protestant. A strange couple as they walked down the aisle, Klara in white, all of her five foot one, and Emil in his morning suit, towering with his six-foot frame.

Emil settled very quickly into his new family, to live happy ever after? Emil, having been a bachelor all these years had developed habits of which Klara totally disapproved. One of them was, on payday all the coal miners would head for the nearest pub and get merry. Working in the coal mines was a very dirty, hard job and this was their way of letting go. She was not against him having a pint, she objected him coming home with a big dent in his pay packet. There was only one way to stop this – she learned to ride his beautiful BMW motorbike, an enormous achievement for a woman, especially this little woman. But her drive to succeed overcame any obstacle, and this drive Annalisa inherited in later life from her mother. Of course, a lot of teasing went on from the other coal miners, when she stood at the gate with the bike to collect him. But he ignored them, as he was quite happy to let her rule. Anything for a quiet life.

The next addition to the household arrived one year later at 8.45am, April 24th 1930. Emil had gone to work as usual but by 7am Klara knew that this was the real thing, with heavy contractions. Moses took her to the hospital and got in touch with Emil to tell him what was happening. Klara produced the biggest baby born for a while in the hospital – a girl weighing 13lbs. The nurses could not believe that this little woman was able to deliver such a heavy baby. They asked her, what did she eat? Klara, in the nine months prior, had a constant craving for Jaffa oranges and of course, as Moses worked in the market he would bring them home by the cartful. It was not only oranges; he would bring home an abundance of all foods. There was never a shortage of food in this home. As he sold all the good meat first the leftovers were generally the fatty cuts and therefore when Klara made soup you could stand a spoon in the fat. Emil liked it that way, saying how it was good for you. As he lived to seventy-nine years of age he was proved right.

Emil made it to the hospital, complaining bitterly. Typical, being a woman Annalisa could not wait three more days until it was his birthday. He was over the moon with his little darling as he held her, and his little darling she became. If they thought that they could continue with their lifestyle of going dancing and riding bikes, little Annalisa soon proved them wrong. This little bull always wanted to be where the action was. No, no, not the quiet life for her. But she was a very lucky girl to have two uncles, a granddad and a mother and father to spoil her. And spoilt she became.

Emil and Klara used to go dancing and out to restaurants a lot. But one night when Moses could not keep the baby quiet he told them that he would babysit during the day but at night-time, he needed his sleep. Therefore, they needed to find an alternative and a way to enjoy themselves, baby and all. The alternative was a side car on Emil's beloved BMW motorbike, where Klara and baby would be happy. As long as Annalisa could remember they were on the road, always going somewhere that involved restaurants and an enjoyment of life. Germany was tolerant of children in restaurants and other perceived grown-up places. Life was idyllic for this family but many a time they would get wet in the side car, so eventually a new side car complete with roof was bought.

The next few years there is little to remember. Except for one Christmas when she was given a beautiful porcelain doll. However hard she tried to like this expensive toy, she couldn't like it and would have much preferred a scruffy teddy bear.

Klara never mixed with the other coal miners. She always pretended that they were better. They also did not live in the same part of town. Klara was the epitome of a German hausfrau – 'Cleanliness before Holiness'. Her doilies stood up by themselves due to the amount of starch and if Annalisa or anyone would leave anything lying about, the world would come to an end. But all of them would let her rule and enjoy the benefits of a lovely apartment. One day she came out to call Annalisa in and one of her neighbours commented, "To whom does that little girl belong?

She fights and outruns any of the other children."

Keeping quiet, her thoughts were that Annalisa would be all right in life.

Chapter 3

Six years old, it was a big day. A school day; all spruced up with a big white bow in her hair, she was taken to school. Annalisa looked up to the ugly, stern face looking down on her and her immediate thoughts were, *I want to go home now!! I don't want to be here.*

"As long as she behaves," the teacher said, "we will get on all right," and with this comment Klara left Annalisa in the classroom. Thirty-eight children were then allocated their desks. Therefore, at least she wasn't alone as thirty-seven other children looked just as bewildered as she felt.

Klara collected her at the end of the day and asked Annalisa, "How was it?"

Annalisa replied that she didn't want to go there ever again, she looks like a witch. Klara knew she had trouble on her hands, as the teacher said to wait a few days and see how she felt. But Annalisa wouldn't; even the biggest bag of sweets and goodies didn't improve her thoughts. Things did not improve. In fact, they got worse. Annalisa's parents became regular visitors at the school to be told that their little darling had misbehaved again.

The day of the first school report arrived and instead of a figure 1-5 (1 being very good) in behaviour, the teacher hadn't even given her a grade as she had been so bad, just a comment with many reprimands. The rest of the grades for academic results were satisfactory. Annalisa had never seen her parents so disappointed. Even Granddad put his penny's worth in.

Annalisa promised that she would try harder to behave but it didn't work. She became quite moody and withdrawn and she stopped eating. A few months later with this still happening, Annalisa's parents called her into the parlour which was only used for best. They told her that they had decided to move away; however, her granddad and uncles would stay behind. She was happy to be leaving this school but was unhappy about Granddad and her uncles being left behind.

Being a little girl, she didn't realise that her father also wanted to move as they had never lived alone without someone else being around. So they happily moved to the posh quarter of Essen. Klara was in heaven. They had a spanking new sparkling apartment with an indoor bathroom.

The following week, after they had settled in Annalisa went to her new school; all three arrived apprehensively. After introductions to her new teacher everyone sighed in relief. From a stern old face, they now stood before a young happy face. This teacher won her battle with Annalisa with her first smile. Klara and Emil started to relax and life became good again.

Emil worked every day as a coal miner, still. Klara

created a lovely home and Annalisa excelled at school. After work on a Friday they would all get spruced up in their Sunday best and go into Essen's town centre and eat out. Klara always bought a cigar for Emil to enjoy after dinner. Anyone seeing these three would never think that Emil was only a coal miner, as Klara would not have been happy about this. The weekends would see them going off on lovely bike rides and of course, for coffee and cake, an old German tradition.

One particular Sunday Klara had dressed Annalisa first in a beautiful pink organza dress and Emil had the bike parked out front. As Klara was getting ready Annalisa went downstairs and Emil shouted to her not to go near the bike. Of course, to Annalisa that was a red flag in front of a little bull. She climbed on it and Klara arrived, and with a look of horror shrieked at Annalisa, whose dress was covered in oil. The dress cost 45 marks. For the one and only time, Emil marched Annalisa upstairs and gave her a hiding.

The time arrived for Annalisa's second school report. They wondered before opening the report whether the move had been worthwhile. They opened the report together and three faces lit up. A gleaming report described how hard Annalisa had worked and how her behaviour was excellent. Her grades were all 2s except for one 3 in religion. Her proud parents were very happy. Klara happily showed off the school report to all and sundry, boasting about her clever little girl.

However, this great life changed when Emil again called Annalisa into the parlour and told her that they had to move back to the centre of Essen. Annalisa's heart sank at the thought of going back to that horrible school she had left, and asked why they had to move. Emil said that Granddad was very lonely, which was one of the reasons. However, the main reason was that a coal miner's wages could not keep up with the demands of paying for their lifestyle. They promised that she wouldn't have to go back to the same school and as she had missed her granddad she felt that maybe it wouldn't be such a bad move.

Union Street starts in the centre of Essen and finishes in Segerott which is in the suburbs. It was a poor environment, like a slum area. Klara always insisted to everyone that they lived on the posh end of Union Street. The house was a four-storey building that had been divided into eight apartments. They moved into a ground-floor apartment which had three bedrooms, a large kitchen and lounge. Klara and Emil bought a lovely bedroom suite for their little darling and a brand-new piano which went into the lounge. Bath time was once a week where the three of them would walk over to the public baths; the alternative was the iron bath in the basement. Life, although poorer, was peaceful. Grandad would bring over an abundance of food again. Annalisa started at her new school, which was all right. So their lifestyle continued as before with weekends on the bike and work during the week.

Annalisa then went to go to her first piano lesson with Emil. Annalisa looked horrified on first impressions, as another old spinster looked at her, but luckily this one was nice. Thereafter, once a week she would go to piano lessons. There was never any thought of this young girl walking through the big city. She also had a friend called Ruth who she would go swimming with after school every day. Annalisa loved swimming and even got a medal for endurance swimming.

One day when Emil did not need to go to work, their beloved leader Adolf Hitler visited Essen. Every street was jam-packed with people in a very cheerful holiday mood. When he finally passed them in his car they were in a good position and they all went berserk with cheering. Politics, religion and sex were never much discussed in their household. All Annalisa knew was that he was in charge of the country. What she saw was a very smart man in a beautiful uniform standing up, waving from his car. Grandad and her uncles did not come; Annalisa did not know why.

On the other side of the hall where they lived, was a young couple with a baby. Although only eight years of age, Annalisa used to babysit for them. Mrs Shenkler explained to Annalisa that her husband was away in the army. Nobody had ever seen her husband and everyone wondered what he was like. One evening when they were all having dinner, Emil said that he had seen him sneaking out of the house when Emil left for work at 5am and the secret came out, as the uniform he wore showed that he was in the army that built the roads. Annalisa didn't understand why this was so awful. But apparently, he was under eighteen and married with a baby.

Emil agreed that all youths should do two years in the Youth Army. Hitler said on the radio that Germany needed a good road infrastructure and healthy youth. Therefore, all boys aged between sixteen and eighteen, built roads for Germany's prosperity with a shovel and lots of hard work.

Also, at school there was a big emphasis on sport.

Again, the preaching was that healthy bodies create healthy minds. Annalisa liked sport but apart from swimming she didn't excel in anything else. A few times she was asked if she would like to join the Hitler Youth. Even though she went on a couple of occasions it did not become a regular thing as her parents were not that keen on their strong ideas.

Very close by to where they lived was a big fairground, and many a time Ruth and Annalisa would roam around there. On one of these afternoons they watched a group of soldiers throwing balls to win a china lion. One soldier won one and he asked Annalisa if she would like it. Annalisa said she would and gave it to Klara for her birthday. However, Klara told Annalisa that she was not happy for her to go the fair anymore, as more and more soldiers were hanging around there in their spick-and-span uniforms.

One morning, Granddad and her uncles were very upset. They heard about some books being burnt and synagogues being stoned; an uprising by a party who did not like Jewish people. It was 9th November, 1938. Grandad did not go out on this day, they were too frightened. Apparently anybody who was Jewish would be threatened by gangs in brown shirts. When Emil came home from work he went into the centre to see what it was all about. He was horrified when he saw all the shop fronts smashed, with glass littering the streets and the synagogue doors hanging open. They had tried to burn the beautiful murals in the synagogue; they found it unbelievable that anyone could want to do such a thing.

This was supposed revenge for a Jewish person murdering Ernst von Rath. It was called Crystal Night (the night of broken glass). On this night ninety-one Jewish people were killed; 30,000 Jewish men, a quarter of all Jewish men in Germany, were taken away to camps where many died, and 1,668 synagogues were ransacked and set on fire.

Annalisa could not understand what it was all about as they lived with Jewish people and could not understand why they were thought of as different. But life was hard and after that day things changed. Grandad and her uncles were constantly afraid. The harmony of their lives became replaced with talk and worries about where this would go. Emil said they should have a meeting to discuss this. They all sat in the best parlour, and when they were all seated Emil said that he had been worried about where things would go and was worried for their safety. Grandad said he could not leave Solomon (Saul) as he only had a mental age of ten and could not cope by himself, and no country would want to accept him. Whereas Jacob was a trained accountant and should try to leave and only return if things got better again.

Shortly after this meeting, Jacob left and emigrated to America by himself. They took him to the station to say a very sad goodbye. Annalisa cried as she loved her Uncle Jacob and couldn't understand why he had to leave. Jacob promised her he would be back before she knew it. But little did they realise, on that day, that their idyllic life had started to end.

After work, when Emil came home he would listen to the radio. It kept stating that the Jews should get out of Germany as they were not wanted. Grandad's life in the market became more and more stressful. Saul was constantly harassed by the local boys. At twenty he was tall but with his mental age of eight he couldn't cope with the fact that suddenly people he knew were now going after him. Solomon had a financial worry too, as the best meat was not sold to him anymore, but to the Arian Germans. Klara was made to sew yellow badges onto their clothes so that everyone could see that they were Jewish.

Annalisa was doing well in school and was getting to the age where she could apply for a scholarship to go to the grammar school or high school. High school was not a possibility even with a scholarship, as the financial contribution was still too much and with Solomon not able to contribute as much now, they agreed that Annalisa should try for the grammar school scholarship. As always, her parents said, "You can do anything if you put your mind to it." Emil would not allow the word 'can't' to be used. Maybe you won't be able to do something well, but you can still try to do it.

As the time went on, on one of their outings to a big park in the city with a swimming pool and a ten-metre diving board, Emil would say, "You can jump from there," and of course Annalisa would stand there, terrified, looking down, but she still jumped.

The day for the exams then came at the local school. Her friend was applying for high school whilst Annalisa applied for the grammar. She managed to finish first and the teacher said to the parents, "She will do well in life, but try to tell her for the real exam to go a bit slower, but make sure that she doesn't make any mistakes."

While they were waiting for the date of the exam life was becoming more and more difficult for

Grandad and Saul; even some of their neighbours were putting up their noses because they lived with, not near, Jewish people. The radio would talk and talk, more and more each day, that the German people should be proud and they should defend their nationality against anybody who didn't agree. So good was this daily doctrine that most of the German populace were swept along with this belief.

Opposite the apartment was a cinema. On each Saturday Annalisa and her friends loved to go and see the latest cowboy films. As they knew her, she was occasionally allowed to go in to see the grown-up films. She loved films, acting and dancing. To look at the maharajas of India, with their bejewelled elephants and beautiful women, dressed in their finest silks and diamonds, made her wish that one day she would be on the stage too. On the downside the news reels became more aggressive towards non-Arian people. Any gathering where the beloved Fuhrer might be, was heavily organised propaganda. Which young boy or girl would not be dazzled by the might of the army in their spick-and-span uniforms? They all believed that Hitler would make Germany strong and powerful.

The three of them got ready to go to the grammar school for the important entrance exam. Grandad also gave Annalisa a big hug and said she would be fine. As they entered the hall Annalisa could not believe how many children were there. She felt a bit better when her dad gave her words of encouragement. Then they left her to it. She looked around and everyone looked as worried as she did. But she felt positive and felt it would be ok.

The exam was a blur and she could not recall much about it apart from the fact it went ok. As usual, a reward was justified and when Annalisa was collected, off they went to their favourite coffee shop for cake and coffee.

The radio started to churn out reports about how other countries misunderstood Germany's position, and then on September 3rd 1939, that their beloved Fuhrer had sent troops on the 1st of September into Poland. They then liberated all of the land taken away by Poland after the First World War. Of course, everyone was deliriously happy that an injustice had been rectified and Germany was once again whole. All the news reels in the cinemas showed cheering, happy people. However, all the saboteurs were rounded up and sent to work camps. No one was that bothered or interested in where these people were sent. Everyone just assumed that Hitler knew what he was doing and no one questioned how they were treated or looked after.

Grandad became very worried as some of his oldest friends were also taken away. He asked Emil worriedly where it would all end; they had done nothing wrong.

Some good news came when a letter arrived saying that Annalisa had passed the entrance exam. She was expected to attend middle grammar school. Klara told as many people as she could as she was very proud that her daughter one day would go to university. Emil very proudly reiterated that she was capable of anything she wanted to do.

On Sunday, off they went on the motorbike to Dusseldorf to celebrate. However, this happiness did not last for long, as a letter arrived for Emil and Klara to go to the office of the Nazi Party. Emil was very worried and wondered what it was all about, as they never had anything to do with politics. When they returned from the meeting Annalisa became really worried as her mother had been crying. Grandad asked, "What is the matter?" but Klara could not talk as she was so upset.

Emil told Grandad to sit down. "The Nazi Party have told us that we are not allowed to live with you or Saul anymore. If we do, we will all be put into prison," which Emil could not let happen.

Klara started to cry again. "I don't want them to go." And then Annalisa started to cry as well.

"What were their exact words?"

"You and Saul can live somewhere alone but not with any Christians."

They decided to talk again the following day as they had been given one month to sort things out.

Klara made a lovely dinner and they sat in the best parlour to eat. After dinner, poignantly, Annalisa was asked to play the piano. The outcome was inevitable. Moses and Saul have to leave and try to find a small bedsit nearby so that Klara could still cook and look after them.

They found a small bedsit. Annalisa and her friend found it fascinating when Klara went to bring them food and to clean for them. Nearby was an office block with a jump-on escalator; when it was level with the floor you stepped onto the floor and then jumped off when it reached the floor you wanted to be on. The two of them played on this, going up and down whilst

Klara would clean. Grandad and Saul were always pleased on a daily basis to see Klara and Annalisa.

Emil could not understand what was happening even though there were very strong feelings in the coal mines, as everyone was swept along with this feeling that Germany was the greatest and nothing would change this.

In very quick succession the news came through that Holland, Belgium and France were invaded. And the glory of it all was shouted from the rooftops. Of course, some of Germany's young men who died were not mentioned.

In order to increase money, which was tight, Klara took in a new lodger. Walter arrived with his belongings and Annalisa took one look at this gorgeous young man and was besotted. He was 5ft 11, with beautiful black hair, blue eyes, and a smile that dazzled. He quickly became a part of the household. Walter had just finished university and was employed in communications.

At school Annalisa was doing all right; there was only one subject, English, being taught by another grey-haired spinster, that bored her. She generally managed to achieve a grade 2 in her subjects, apart from English which was a 3. Having Walter in the house was great and even if she really didn't need any help, she would ask Walter anyhow. She started to have daydreams about marrying him when she grew up.

Klara had found another hobby. In the yard shared with all the other tenants she got Emil to build a shed. There, she kept rabbits for food. Emil was never one for DIY so the cage was built but was a bit rickety.

Before long there were about thirty rabbits. One rabbit became Annalisa's pet. It was one-eyed but she loved it. One Sunday as they sat down for dinner, eating rabbit of course, Annalisa realised it was her pet. Walter had helped Emil catch a rabbit and not knowing it was Annalisa's pet, had taken that one. She cried for a long time as this was the first time something close to her had died.

Klara demanded cleanliness in her home, however, one day they all started to itch and eventually they realised that something was in their home. It turned out to be chicken fleas, as the people who lived in the apartment above them kept chickens on their balcony. After a few arguments, they were told they had to put the chickens in the yard in a cage or have them destroyed. They were put in the yard; the pest control people then descended to fumigate their apartment. All the doors were taped up and they were not allowed to go in for several hours whilst the poison worked. The people above were also done.

For Grandad and Saul, life continued to get worse. Especially Saul, who now had a new problem, as with all the teasing he became very emotionally disturbed and became incontinent. This was very hard for Grandad to cope with. But Moses knew that if he put Saul into an institution he would not live long. So Klara had to wash the bedclothes each day, lugging them back and forth to wash by hand. On one of these journeys one of the neighbours whispered to Klara that the Gestapo were watching the flats and not to go into Moses' flat if she saw anyone lurking around. She told Moses, at a prearranged time, to put a big ornament on the windowsill for her to see and know that all was all right. Such a foolish game but most people still believed in good and evil. But Klara did not tell Emil about this and she continued with her daily routine, checking and worrying as she cooked and cleaned. She never saw anyone and started to relax, thinking that this neighbour must have been exaggerating.

One evening when they sat down for dinner, Walter told them that he had found a girlfriend and asked if he could bring her around to introduce her. Annalisa sat there, wide-eyed, not believing that it was true as she was going to marry him in a few years.

The girlfriend came around on Sunday for coffee and cake. Klara and Emil thought she was a very nice person and they got on well. But Annalisa was having none of it; she sat there, sullen-faced, glaring at this girl. Walter asked if she was all right and although she wanted to scream at him, just grunted back in reply. "Don't take any notice of her," said Emil. "She is in one of her moods."

After a very short courtship Walter told Emil that he would be leaving them and moving in with his girlfriend. Annalisa, mortified, ran to her room, shut the door and cried her eyes out.

He then left and another lodger appeared on the scene. Where Walter had been polite, this new lodger called Franz was stocky, red-faced, and was rude. He also had a large appetite and ate masses. German tradition was that food is placed on the table and everyone helps themselves. However, when Franz arrived Klara had to start sharing out the food otherwise he ate the lot. Things became so bad that in the end Emil asked him to leave.

Around this time Klara started to have stomach problems and started to spend many an hour in bed.

Number three lodger then arrived – a Dutchman called Hans who was polite and a good-looking man. He told Emil that he worked from home repairing watches. Which wasn't a problem, but he was very secretive, even locking his bedroom door when he went to the bathroom. He even did his own cleaning, which although it suited Klara, was a bit strange. As time went by they started to get suspicious and wondered if he was a spy as he was away a lot, never saying where he went, and when he was back, being secretive. However, apart from that he was the perfect lodger.

Saturday began as usual; Emil was at home, about to clean the bike in order that they could all go out. But first he had to do something else. With it being January, the weather was very cold. Christmas had been and gone, with Klara making it as nice as possible, but gloom lay over the household like a blanket. Moses and Saul did not come for Christmas as they were now too frightened to come out. It was the first time in twenty-one years that they had not been together for Christmas. They had not had any news about Jacob either, which made it worse. On this Saturday, the three of them were going to see Moses and Saul. Emil had started to bring them logs for their fire as no one would supply them directly. This was for their small fire in the middle of their bedsit, with their beds around it.

Moses had a very bad cold; luckily Klara had managed to contact a Jewish doctor who would come and see him, as Arian doctors were not allowed to look after any Jews. Emil loaded the logs into the side car with Annalisa sitting on top of the logs and Klara behind Emil. As they got nearer, ambulances and police cars were rushing past them. Emil parked the bike a little way from the commotion and told Klara and Annalisa to stay there and he would find out what was going on, as he was less known then them.

A small crowd were standing around Moses' apartment and asking what was going on, a man said, "A couple of Jewish fellows, a father and son, have done themselves down and nearly burnt the house down."

"How did they do that?"

"They taped and nailed all the doors down so that no one could get in, then built the fire up until the fumes got to them."

Another man shouted, "Good! Two less to worry about."

The police started to question people in the crowd and Emil left quietly before they could question him. He ran the last bit, shaking, and shouted to Klara and Annalisa just to get on the bike immediately. He drove home as fast as the bike would go, anything to get away from the scene. Once they got home Emil swallowed down a large glass of schnapps and his shaking started to stop. He then calmed down and told them the horrible news. Klara broke down completely as Moses had been like a father to her and his children her brothers. Annalisa also felt very sad as they had been like her granddad and uncle. This happened on January 10th 1941. Annalisa was ten years old.

On Sunday Klara said to Emil that they needed to

find out where the funeral would be. Emil then told her that they had committed suicide and the police were involved. And for once, he spoke to Klara in a harsh voice, forbidding her to have anything more to do with them. He told her that she had tried her best but now she would be putting their lives at risk if she did anything further. Klara agreed and sent a silent prayer instead. Emil knew that this was right as rumours started to fly about that Jewish people were being treated badly and as he could no longer help Moses or Saul, his duty must be to his family.

A short time later they got another letter from the Party headquarters telling them that they wanted to see them. This time Emil was more than just worried and it kept going over in his mind. Did they know that they had helped Moses and Saul? His mind in a turmoil, he dreaded what might happen as they might send them to a camp for helping the supposed enemy, and decided that he would leave Klara at home and go by himself.

A very arrogant man behind a desk told him to sit down and he sat down with quite a few other men. An SS man then told them all that Germany needed their vehicles for the war effort and they must bring them to a set place in order that they could be confiscated. His beautiful bike and side car would be gone forever; he could not believe it. A few of the men meekly objected but were quickly put down. As much as it hurt Emil to lose his bike, he was also relieved that it was his bike they wanted, not him. He told Klara; she took it very hard as to her it was a status symbol, as not many people had their own transport. Owning a car was only for the very rich but a motorbike was still rich. Again, though, they were led by the propaganda and they were told that if they started saving now they would quickly be able to buy their own car.

On the news reel a happily smiling family sat in the first vehicle on the production line. Saturday came and they had to say goodbye to their beloved bike. The thought that his gleaming pristine bike would soon be a camouflaged green made him wince. The money they received went into their pot for this new car. After all, it would only be a couple of years that they would be at war.

When they got home, more bad news. Hans, their silent Dutchman, said that he was going back to Holland and must leave at once. He paid Emil a month in advance and was then gone. This convinced them that he was a spy. Their apartment seemed so quiet as the three of them just sat there. But Emil would not have this and told them to put their glam clothes on and they would take the tram to their favourite place. It was an experience to go by public transport and it was also different to come back to an empty apartment. This did not last long as Klara persuaded Emil to buy a dog. Klara fell in love with this long, white-haired Alaskan dog which she named Spitz. It became her shadow and followed her everywhere. It was a beautiful dog but poor Annalisa's chore was that when the dog had diarrhoea she had to clear it up!

Chapter 4

There seemed to be a bit of a lull; the war was going well according to the news reel. As all of the fortifications were being built on the frontlines of France and Holland, not a mouse could penetrate. Then in the east, Hitler had already made a pact with Russia for non-aggression in 1940, whereby Hitler seized half of Poland, Estonia, Latvia, Lithuania and Finland. There was a big exchange of goods between Russia and Germany. Russia supplied millions of tons of grain and oil in exchange for technical goods. There was a mention that Hitler's deputy, Hess (they wrote *Mein Kampf* together in prison), had flown to England apparently in order to tell Churchill about an invasion into Russia. This was dismissed as the ramblings of a traitor. Not even Stalin took this seriously. But on 2nd June 1941, they were told that Germany had invaded Russia. How this had been kept a secret was an achievement in itself. In 1,250 miles of frontier from Estonia to the Black Sea, Hitler managed to hide and place 148 divisions of men, 80% German, 14% Romanians, 22% Finnish, three Italians and a Slovakian. Three million men, 60,000 vehicles with Emil's motorbike probably amongst them, and 3,350 tanks. To most Germans and even Stalin, this came as the biggest shock.

Over the next few weeks news reels would shout that the Russians had planned to invade Germany, hence Hitler's decision to invade first. But Hitler wanted to have all of the riches of Russia, from grain to oil, for Germany. The last train from Russia crossed the border 21st June 1941, nearly two weeks after the invasion!! It was impossible to understand the enormous scale of the war.

Emil occasionally would murmur that Hitler had gone too far. No one could conquer Russia, as Emil had been through it all before in the First World War. But he kept these reservations to himself as he would have been branded a traitor otherwise. For the three of them, they started to enjoy having the apartment to themselves until once again another letter arrived summoning them to the Party office. By now they were terrified, wondering what else they could want. They were informed that as their apartment had three bedrooms they needed to take in three foreign workers. Also, Klara had to start working in the Krupp factory that made most of the armaments for the war, for six hours every day.

Their new lodgers arrived – three Italians who spoke no German, and Klara and Emil spoke no Italian. The language barrier was not the only barrier; they ate so much food that it caused issues. Klara found it very difficult to make ends meet. She became quite often ill with her stomach problem and Annalisa, going on for twelve, was expected to help around the house before and after school. Many a time she would camp outside a horse butcher at 5am in order to reserve their place in the queue for horse meat, and then Klara would see to the men and then relieve her at 8am when she needed to go to school. Annalisa became a good cook, very quickly making an excellent roast horse meal.

On one occasion when Klara was again ill, Annalisa made pea soup with thick sausage in it. She hadn't peeled enough potatoes so the soup was very watery. In her panic she poured in semolina to thicken the soup. Fortunately, for once the Italians were happy and thought it was delicious. The apartment was generally not a happy house. The Italians appeared rude and would moan about everything.

Annalisa still went swimming with her friend Ruth until Klara got home at 4pm. She then had to help with the cooking and cleaning until the four men would come home. She also had to do her homework afterwards.

*

Autumn arrived. As Russia was not prepared, Germany conquered vast areas of territories. All that the Russians could do was pour people at the Germans, which they had in abundance. Pictures showed Russians piled high in front of defences.

October 1941 came and Klara had been sick for a whole week. The doctor confirmed that Klara was pregnant. Annalisa had no clue how this could happen as there was no sex education at school and it was never discussed at home. The only good result was the doctor told Klara to stay in bed for the next three months, as she was by now forty-one years old and there was a higher risk of her miscarrying. For any doctor to let this happen would result in lengthy paperwork and a black mark against his good name. Hitler wanted every child to be born in order to protect the Arian line and keep it pure. The doctor contacted the Nazi headquarters. Emil did a little dance when they left and it had taken his utmost self-control at times not to hit those ignorant, selfish men.

Klara rested and rested, which was very hard for her to do. Her fright of the consequences if she miscarried was a bigger issue than looking after the home. Between Emil and Annalisa, they managed to cope. It was far better than having dreadful lodgers.

As the autumn was lovely in Germany, with beautiful sunshine, the opposite started to happen in Russia. Torrential rain and cold turned roads into rivers of mud. Progress by the German army was getting slower as mechanised vehicles got stuck and the army had to revert back to horse power. This gave Stalin a break in order for him to reorganise his troops. Up to then all they heard about was one victory after another. The German army managed to be within 200 miles of Moscow by 31st August. In its path it had taken 720,000 men prisoner, and destroyed the 3rd, 4th and 10th Russian armies – 6,500 tanks destroyed and 1,800 field guns. But Germany, as well, had suffered heavy losses; 100,000 men died – more than all the men in the previous countries they had conquered. However, much surprised was the German soldier by the ferocity of the Russian soldiers' fighting. They were writing home saying that they fight like caged animals to the bitter end and do not mind dying for Mother Russia. There were three ultimate reasons for this. First, their love for Mother

Russia, their homeland. Second, the brutality of the German army itself; Hitler's orders were that any prisoners remotely connected with the Bolshevik army would be shot immediately. But not least, any prisoner making it back to their own lines was also seen as a traitor and treated as such. If given a chance they would shoot the prisoners before taking them back to a camp.

Fear was so great on both sides. Stalin himself imprisoned his daughter-in-law for two years. His son Yakow was captured by the German army and put into prison. He died suspiciously there without any reason given. A letter was sent from Hitler to Mussolini about the sub-human fighting of the Russian soldier.

Annalisa noted the terrible treatment given to the Russians. They were considered second-class people. A friend of theirs wrote home. He came across a column of prisoners six deep as far as he could see, in a stinking mess, left in rags, that barely resembled human beings. So ill-equipped were the Russians that they quite often didn't even have uniforms.

On September 1st 1941, the first shell was fired on Leningrad. Having liberated Latvia, Lithuania and Estonia from the Russians, they were greeted as friends. Also, Finland helped the German army to drive the Russians out of their country. But they stopped at their own border. They refused to help with Leningrad which was a mere forty miles away from the German lines. This was the turning point for the Russians.

On September 6th 1941, Hitler gave an order. The assault on Leningrad was stopped and Moscow became the priority. He must have thought rather than feeding a whole city, he would starve them into submission. The siege of 900 days began. Statistics show that one and a half million people died in this siege. At the home front, everyone started to knit, sew, anything in order to keep the troops warm. Russia's winter fast approached and the German uniform was no defence against the torrential rain, ice and snow that followed. Many soldiers lost toes, hands due to frostbite. All schools were mobilised to collect blankets, warm clothes and shoes. The children sold postcards of film stars to make money.

Klara did her best with trying to sew as she rested. She would sew rabbit furs into blankets. She had enough rabbits for their food and the rest were sold. Annalisa never adopted another one as a pet. Life was ok. Being only the three of them, it was quite easy to look after themselves and their apartment. Klara felt a bit better as the pregnancy progressed. The doctor would check her regularly, and of course Spitz the dog was by her side day and night.

Chapter 5

Christmas was a low-key affair whilst remembering Saul and Jacob. The whole nation felt sorry for their soldiers. So far away in a country with such hostile weather. They all baked, cooked and send as many parcels as they could. While Germany tried to celebrate Christmas, bitter fighting went on between Russia and Germany. Whilst the German soldier was becoming battle-weary due to being ill-equipped and stretched, Stalin ordered his fresh Siberian troops to defend Moscow. These 578,000 soldiers were clad in fur-lined boots, jackets and white over-tunics. Used to harsh winters, they could lay outside for days in the snow. Civilians, 470,000, from children to old men, dug ditches around Moscow. Stalin himself remained in Moscow. The temperature dropped to forty degrees below and there were 113,000 cases of frostbite with 14,000 amputations reported on the German side. One of Emil's friends returned with all of his toes having been frozen off.

On December 5-6th, the Russian army attacked. Also, America entered the war after Pearl Harbour had been attacked, and by January 1942 had driven the German army back by fifty miles. Hitler was so outraged that he dismissed two of his field marshals and thirty-five corps and division commanders. But the Russians did not have it all their way. The small towns behind the lines had been fortified and the German army had the advantage and left the Russians out in the cold.

1942 did not start well. The army in Africa was being beaten by the English troops. Big fat Mussolini, another ally; Emil and most Germans could not understand how Hitler could be bamboozled by this windbag. After all, their idea of fighting was to put the Panzers in reverse gear. Hitler had to help him on all fronts, especially Greece, much to Hitler's annoyance. But Goebbels (their propaganda minister) could dress up any defeat as a victory, and they believed him. Another apparent victory was the bombing of all of England's industrial targets by the German air force.

Walter visited one day; he had enlisted in the navy and looked very handsome in his uniform. Annalisa's heart was beating so loud she was worried that he would hear. His friendship with his girlfriend was not in the best of shape, as he told Klara. Annalisa's thoughts still remained that when she grew up she would marry him. But on another visit by his girlfriend, his U-boat was destroyed and everyone died. Annalisa could not cry in public as no one knew that her heart had been broken.

March 1942 arrived and the impossible happened. The first bombs fell on Essen, the reprisal to the bombing of England by Germany. This could not be. *How could Hitler let this happen?* the German people thought. But in quick succession, 28th March, Lubeck was hit and the city lit up like a firecracker. Cologne was the next target for the English air force. A thousand bombers attacked; 2,500 fires were reported – 330,000 buildings were destroyed and 469 people died. The low number of casualties was due to the high number of air-raid shelters that had been built.

Back in Essen one of these ugly buildings was around the corner from their apartment. Annalisa never went in one. But Emil would use it if necessary. Of course, they were all trained to recognise the different sounds of the sirens and supplied with their own gas masks. A device was fitted to all radios which would make a ping-pong sound even if not turned on, which would report enemy aircraft approaching.

Klara was nearing the end of her pregnancy and Annalisa still had no idea. Approaching twelve years of age, she still had no understanding of how babies were made. Emil was home when Klara's contractions started and promptly got the doctor; a speedy journey to the hospital followed.

Annalisa watched her mother in a white gown on a trolley being wheeled away. She thought her mum was going to die and cried her eyes out in fear. When Emil and Annalisa got home without Klara, Spitz sensed that something was wrong as he hid himself behind the couch and would not come out. The next day they got the news. June 22nd, 1942, a little girl had been born. But all was not good. Emil was taken away by the doctor when they arrived at the hospital to be told to prepare for the worst. The baby came into the world a mere 800 grams – less than a bag of sugar. With other complications, she was put into an incubator. Klara was also ill and remained in hospital for another four weeks. But little Ingrid, as they called her, was a fighter and each day she got a little bit stronger.

Finally, after visits every day for four weeks, Klara came home and baby Ingrid was allowed home two weeks later. She was a lovely, helpless little doll. As she was so tiny she had to be fed on the hour, every hour, twenty-four hours a day. The stress on all three of them was tremendous. Emil also had to work harder as every ounce of coal was needed for the war effort. One consolation was that coal miners were given two and a half times the food rations. The meat ration per person was 450g. Farmers had no ration cards and were envied for living it up. The black market started to flourish, with coffee being the number one currency. Soldiers who were stationed in the other occupied countries would send fur coats and clothing home. But no real hardships occurred. Life was all right until the end of 1942, until the RAF started nightly bombings. Essen was a priority target as Krupp produced 80% of all armaments.

The daytime bombing was not successful as too many aircrafts were being shot down, but there was no definite target for the RAF. The aim was to destroy the will of the German population. Literally, large areas of the city were just flattened. Klara was so frightened that they made a decision to shelter at night in the main station air-raid shelter and to return home in the morning. So, every evening the pram was laden with sleeping bags and food. The journey to the station took half an hour. Annalisa counted each and every step down into the underground and there were seventy-two. Emil and Annalisa would carry the pram down whilst Klara would carry Ingrid. The underground was so busy with people and soon a pattern would emerge. Families staked their own places where they would rest and sleep. A feeling of camaraderie could be felt as they were all in the same boat.

Emil would go back home, and when the air raids would start he would run around to the local shelter and then leave to go to work at 5am. In the mornings, everyone dreaded finding out that this time it was their home that had been destroyed. It was also hard on Annalisa to lug the pram up seventy-two steps by herself. Then to find a path through the day's ruins. By the spring of 1943 this had become a way of life.

Emil started to feel ill on quite a few occasions. At first the doctor assumed it was stress. However, after a thorough examination they discovered dust on his lungs – a common ailment among miners. Further tests were done to discover the extent of damage to his lungs. Whilst this was happening Ingrid, slowly, was putting on weight. She was still on regular feeds and would be handed around people in the shelter to be fed. This gave Annalisa and Klara a couple of hours' sleep. Ingrid thrived on all this attention.

5th March 1943, the journey to the shelter was made. This night was particularly ferocious. In thirty-eight minutes the RAF released 138 tonnes of bombs over the centre of Essen – 168 acres of homes were destroyed and 30,000 people became homeless. The news of the onslaught reached them in the shelter and they were told to stay put as it was not safe to go above with all of the fires raging and the buildings collapsing. Klara and Annalisa were very worried about Emil. Whether he was in the shelter or, as he sometimes ignored the sirens and stayed in the basement, in his home. As the hours passed, more and more people arrived to collect their families. Emil then appeared and Klara cried out in relief. They hugged fiercely, holding on to each other. Slowly Klara realised he was not at work, which he never missed. Heartbroken, he told them that their apartment had suffered a direct hit and was totally destroyed.

"You are safe, that is all that matters," Klara said.

He had luckily spent the night in the shelter, not in the basement.

The ugly purpose-built shelter had withstood direct hits whilst every building around it had been flattened. It stood defiantly against the vengeance of the RAF. Finally, they emerged into daylight and the scene that greeted them was unreal. Where multi-storey blocks had stood, now rubble greeted them. Big craters gaped in the roads before them. Ambulances tried to get the wounded to the hospitals and civilians and the army desperately tried to help those people trapped. The air was thick with smoke and dust. Normally a twenty-minute journey, over one hour passed before they could get to their destination. One could not call this home, as it was once. An unreal sight greeted them; the four-storey block, which had taken a direct hit, had fallen into the road and a large crater awaited them. However, to their amazement, at the top of this huge amount of rubble stood Annalisa's piano. Through the tears, they burst into uncontrollable laughter. The devastation around them stretched on forever. Loudspeaker vans tried to tell the people where to assemble, and that they should make their way there.

German efficiency; within a few hours the army

and civilians had cleared sites, erected tents and taken names, in triplicate of course, to get a clearer picture. They were handing out food, blankets and dealing with minor injuries. They were then allocated a place in a large sports hall to rest.

Over the next four months 1,052 aircrafts dropped more than 4,000 tonnes of bombs. The RAF lost 872 bombers between March and July, 1945.

Emil found the stress difficult to deal with and a doctor gave him a sick note. Annalisa's school had also taken a direct hit and lessons stopped for the time being. Then a notification was given to them that the grammar school, with all of its pupils, was being evacuated. This was exciting news to Annalisa, to go away from this constant bombing and looking after Ingrid, and Klara when she had her stomach attacks. Packing was no problem, as all they had left was what they stood in – all else had gone. However, Klara went into action and between bartering and begging she managed to get enough clothes together for Annalisa to go away. Annalisa felt a little bit guilty leaving Klara to cope with Ingrid. But Ingrid was now nine months old and out of the danger zone. She was still a very small little doll, but was growing.

Annalisa thought back to a year ago when she was upset and decided to break away at the ripe old age of eleven. Without telling, she went to the train station and got a ticket to the only place she knew about. This was where Klara had worked as a young girl on a farm. Klara had kept in touch and would often visit. When Annalisa arrived at the farm they could not believe their eyes, that Annalisa stood there by herself. They immediately notified Emil and Klara. When Klara came home from work she was beside herself, but when she got the telegram she calmed down.

In the meantime, Annalisa thoroughly enjoyed herself. For the next days, she stayed there. She would go with the farmers, who she called Uncle Heinrich and Auntie Gertrude, to the fields. No tractor, but they had a lovely set of horses to plough the fields. Amongst the horses was a black stallion that worked very hard. He would lead the other horses to pull harder. But away from the team no one except Heinrich could touch him. Annalisa was told to never go near him. But once again, there was the red flag. He did not look so forbidding to her and one day when he was put in the stables, she sneaked in, climbed up on the side and mounted him. Heinrich caught her and was petrified that at any moment the horse would rear up and hurt her. But to his amazement the stallion stood peacefully like a lamb. However, she got a good telling off and was made to promise not to do it again.

By the weekend Emil, Klara and Ingrid arrived to collect their runaway daughter. They were so happy to see that no harm had come to her that there was only a token telling off. However, this time, when she was going away it would be with her parents' permission. They were to go to the Black Forest in South Germany. Away from all of the bombings and hardship.

The platform in Essen was heaving with all of these children. Mostly boisterous, but there were a few who cried about leaving their parents. Annalisa thought it was a great adventure and was looking forward to it. As they waited, long-distance trains stopped to take on and let off passengers. Looking at the dining and sleeping cars with their still beautifully dressed passengers, Annalisa stood there dreaming that one day she would travel on one of these trains to faraway places. Finally, the train arrived and in orderly fashion, they boarded. All Annalisa could think about was freedom; she wanted to shout it from the treetops but had to settle with shouting it internally. Three teachers went with them but had their own compartment.

As the train started moving along, the devastation became clearer. But mile by mile into the heart of Germany, away from the industrial areas, the scenery started to change. Green meadows where cows peacefully grazed met her eyes. Spring was in the air and everywhere she looked trees were in blossom and lambs could be seen with their mothers. The contrast between the two places was unreal. The atmosphere in the compartment also changed; laughter and singing became louder and became the norm.

A few hours later they arrived in Freiburg, a larger town in the Black Forest. The contrast was immense. Houses with beautiful murals adorned the streets, with flowers everywhere. The styling of houses was also different; they had large overhanging roofs. This was in order to protect the houses in the winter from the snow. But this was not their end destination. A large convoy of coaches was waiting to ferry the 300-plus children to their final destination.

In orderly fashion, of course, everyone was seated. The Black Forest is one of the most beautiful parts of Germany. The drive was like a picture postcard, not mountains but rolling hills and fir trees – a painter's paradise. Fast-flowing but shallow streams cascaded down the hills with crystal-clear water.

An hour later they arrived in a small village with the customary fountain in the town centre. Annalisa was not impressed. Surely this was not the destination, this small village with a few houses and even less people. She was a city girl who loved the hustle and bustle – this was not it!

After collecting their suitcases, this long line of children started walking. A small pathway led them between the fir trees downwards. These fir trees were enormous and had stood there for a long time, and were very daunting to Annalisa. There was little laughter or talking by the children as most were quite frightened. And Annalisa realised why they called it the Black Forest. Down the winding path they went for about twenty minutes. Then, a miracle. An area the size of a few football pitches met them, bathed in sunshine. On the patch of grass were about four white, gleaming buildings with a stream running through the centre. It used to be a sanatorium for the very rich.

It was for the super-rich when they had mental illnesses from counting all their money. Even though the good furniture had been removed, the place oozed money. Everybody was ushered into a large dining hall where a great warm meal was waiting for them. Slowly the atmosphere changed to happy, laughing children again. The sanatorium had been converted to house them all and one by one they were allocated their own dormitories. A little way separated from the main buildings stood the mill, or control house, next to the stream. Annalisa plus about sixteen other girls were allocated there. The little house had five bedrooms, one taken up by a teacher. In Essen, the last couple of years had been hell; this was heaven on earth. Blissfully, they went to their beds and soon fell asleep.

The next couple of days they were allowed to settle in, relax and explore. Every day just got better and occasionally Annalisa wondered whether this special care and treatment was given to all of the children. Or, as they were the elite in education, were they being groomed for the future? But Hitler had always shown that he loved children. Arian, of course. So they started their studying, sport and pleasure. A first-class equipped room with swimming pool greeted them. Great emphasis was placed on sport. 'Healthy bodies create healthy minds' was the slogan.

The dining room doubled up as a cinema where films mostly of victorious troops were shown. Annalisa was still constantly worried about how her mother, father and baby sister were doing. But letters soon started to arrive reassuring her that they were fine. Call it good or bad news, it was how Annalisa interpreted it. Emil had been for another visit to the hospital and was declared unfit for work and the army. The dust on his lungs was above 50% and only lots of fresh air would help to heal and prolong his life. So he became retired in his mid-fifties, with a very good pension. They had also been allocated a large room with a small bedroom on the ground floor, in a small town near where Emil was born. The war had not affected it and their life was the same as before the war. The rooms led out onto a small garden that they shared with other residents.

Emil started to go for long walks and slowly his health improved. Klara, as usual, managed to make the one room like a home to the best of her ability. Ingrid was also growing but at a snail's pace. With her mind at rest, Annalisa felt that she could enjoy herself.

To Annalisa this was one of her happiest moments. There was only one fly in the ointment. Annalisa's bedroom, over the next few weeks, started to smell. All the cleaning by the girls did not help. Eventually they found out it was one particular bed and girl. At the age of thirteen, this girl still wetted her bed at night. For a while the other girls helped to wash and dry these sheets. But after a while they had to tell the teacher. She was moved to the main house and under doctor's orders eventually she stopped bed wetting.

As the weeks went by they were taken on an outing to Freiburg. This was so exciting; to be in a large city again, the noise and smell was overpowering. The day went by far too quickly but they made many memories. However, there were also sad days when bad news came to the school, when either parents or families, etc., had been killed in the war.

The war continued whilst they enjoyed their isolated solitude. The main cities continued to be bombed at night. Hamburg, Berlin and Cologne were their favourite targets. But however many bombs were rained down on Germany, the people did not lose their spirit. Bomber Harris, England's general, had to admit to Churchill that the war would not be won by air. What affected German morale more than anything was the disaster of Stalingrad. Stalingrad, named after Stalin, situated by Russia's mighty river, the Volga. Stalin gave command to the newly installed Chuikov, who, later on, led the army to conquer

Berlin. There is no land after the Volga, which meant that not one German soldier would cross. Under his command he had 55,000 men and only eighty tanks to defend the city. Facing him were 100,000 troops and 500 tanks, and later increased to 200,000 soldiers. General Paulus was amongst the German generals after Rommel, one of Germany's best-loved generals, with a status of a film star.

Annalisa and all of the school were selling photographs of Rommel and others to make money for the war effort. His task was to take Stalingrad and start his offence on August 23rd 1942. But for no known reason, it was delayed until September 13th. Stalingrad was a city of 500,000 that manufactured a quarter of all Russian tanks. In the week's delay, General Chuikow had managed to increase his men, with specially trained troops like the SAS in England, trained in house-to-house fighting. On Paulus's first attack, 600 planes dropped their bombs and 40,000 people died, but however hard the German soldier fought they could not gain any ground.

By mid-November, after eighty days of hellish fighting, even the dogs and the rats swam across the Volga to escape. One soldier wrote home that German tanks were idle through lack of fuel and to protect the engines they were covered in straw. The mice liked the warmth of the straw and gnawed their way through the electrical wires. So when fuel finally arrived the tanks would not start. The temperature dropped to below forty degrees during this stalemate. But General Chuikow had not been idle; his army had increased to one million men, 13,500 heavy guns, 900 tanks and 1,100 planes to start his counter attack on

November 19th.

Paulus realised that he could become enclosed in a trap by the Russians. He pleaded with Hitler to withdraw. But Hitler would not hear of it. Paulus' loyalty and obedience stopped him from disobeying his orders. Most of the troops in the front line were Romanians and they fled when the attack came. This left 250,000 in the trap when the Russians encircled them. Paulus continued to plead with Hitler to try and break out. Hitler listened to Goering, who said the air force would help to relieve the army.

There were only two airfields in range, but 165 transport planes would need to land with supplies each day to achieve this. If one third of the planes got through this was high, with not only the Russian guns but the severe weather conditions with dense fog. Worse were the wounded laying near the runway on stretchers during the day and then put back into the building at night. Hope crushed for another day and another chance of escape – 1,280 Germans died of frostbite waiting to be rescued, 400 horses were slaughtered, and the daily ration was two ounces of bread with a bowl of soup.

In January 1943, Russia offered Paulus the chance to surrender but he refused. A soldier wrote to his wife, "Forget me if you can but never forget what we have endured." Hitler made Paulus a field marshal and never in Germany's history had a field marshal surrendered. His choices were to fight to the death or commit suicide. However, he did neither. He surrendered at the end of January and other units followed.

The cost was that 750,000 soldiers died. Only

5,000 soldiers saw Germany again. The hatred for the prisoners was so great that few managed to make it to the prison of Siberia, and if they did then they died there. Most German people believed that Hitler deserted them in their greatest need. It was a very sad ending, they felt, to a great man and his soldiers. Hitler, however, called Paulus a weakling and a traitor. Paulus, as a prisoner, turned against Hitler and helped the Russians, and stayed in Russia.

The Russian survivors who had also suffered greatly, were all given medals for their bravery.

Chapter 6

By summer time, Annalisa and her friends had goals set for them. Along the fast-flowing, deep stream, were an abundance of blackberries, and strawberries were found. Each day after lessons they were sent to collect these fruits. The reward for returning a good harvest was a bar of chocolate. However, the girls just enjoyed the fun of splashing through the ice-cold water to pick the fruits. Unfortunately, all good things come to an end. By the end of August they were informed that all of their parents had been rehoused and were out of danger so they could return home.

Annalisa had not really missed home that much, but had missed her parents, so was pleased at the prospect of seeing them again. Some of the other girls had suffered badly with home sickness and were jubilant when they were told about going home.

Klara and Emil decided that they could do with a holiday, so they communicated with the school, who then allowed them to come and collect Annalisa themselves. All three arrived in the little village. Annalisa went with a member of staff to welcome them. Klara and Emil were both overcome with pleasure in seeing their daughter looking so radiant. Ingrid looked on, at age one, not really remembering her big sister. Annalisa was so relieved to see her father, as when she had left he had looked so haggard; however, with the new home and country air, he looked his usual dapper self again.

Emil and Klara stayed in a small bed and breakfast in the village. The next few days were lovely, waking and just enjoying each other's company again. Annalisa went up and down every day with a member of staff to see them. The only problem was Ingrid's nappies, as she was not at the stage of using a potty, so Emil ended up outside the village on a daily basis, washing the nappies in the stream. It was good that as it was summer they dried beautifully in the warm August air. They also managed to come to the school for one day. This was quite a feat as Ingrid had to be carried all of the way, as she wasn't walking yet. Klara gushed over the facilities where all of the staff made them feel very welcome. A great big lunch was enjoyed, which made Klara praise them even more. There had been times where they had worried that Annalisa might have made it sound better than it was, but now that they were there they could see why. However, Klara was promptly ill the next day after indulging too much.

One day they visited Freiburg. Klara was in her element again, drinking coffee and visiting many shops. But the day of goodbyes came for Annalisa; she had been very happy there with all of the teachers, and had got on very well. So many friends had been made and sadly were all going off in different directions. She sighed and cried when she said goodbye. With a small suitcase, she walked for the last time up to join her parents and Ingrid. As usual, the train journey to her new home was excitement in itself.

On arrival at their new home, Klara told Annalisa to close her eyes as they had a surprise for her. She led her into a room and told her she could open her eyes now. Annalisa could not believe her eyes. Klara had managed to buy a second-hand piano. Annalisa gave them big hugs full of happiness. When the excitement died down she looked around the rest of the house, the room was fairly large and Klara had managed to make it quite pretty. At one time it must have been someone's lounge, with the patio doors leading onto the garden. Klara had also managed to get her cottage industry going. In the garden was a cage and twenty-odd rabbits. Keeping these lovely creatures was easy. Nearby was a factory selling canned food and meat cubes. Klara collected the leftover vegetables from the factory to feed the rabbits. Of course, there was the good cabbage and potatoes that she kept to one side for them to eat. Again, Klara was able to feed her family.

The next week was spent getting Annalisa back into a school and finding a piano teacher. Having achieved that, they started to settle down into their new routine. But again, a higher force dictated that their life would change. Another letter from the Party arrived asking them to come and see them. How they hated these letters. All four of them arrived at the office, all spruced up in their Sunday best. But to their surprise, whereas in the past the staff had been arrogant, this time they were greeted with a smile.

Apprehension must have shown on their faces as they were told it was good news for them. They had been selected for their newly built houses and they had their own apartment. *What and where?* Emil wanted to know. The town was called Xanten, by the Rhine. He had never heard of it but eventually they found it on a map. Xanten was near the Dutch border with 5000 inhabitants. They asked when they could move in and were told as soon as they wanted.

As they had few possessions; moving was not an issue. The only issues were the rabbits and the piano. Klara asked Emil how they could manage, as due to the high level of rationing of petrol, nobody wanted to know. Emil thought his sister who lived in the nearby town could help. His sister Else and her husband had built up from a small factory employing about twenty people, to a workforce of eighty people. They manufactured wheels and other iron goods for the trains. They definitely had profited from the war. Emil, cap in hand, asked his sister whether they could take the piano to their new home, but the sister refused, stating they had no fuel for this. Instead, she offered to buy it for a small amount for her two children. Emil had no other option so the sister promptly, a few days, later collected the piano. Klara vowed never to speak to them again. Annalisa was also very upset; she had practiced hard and was getting quite good at it.

Their few other possessions were packed, with the rabbits being put into boxes to be carried to the station. This took a couple of journeys, using Ingrid's pram as transport. It was a common sight for people to be at the station with all of their belongings. With a lot of good-hearted laughing and joking, everything was finally loaded onto the train. They were not alone; the train was already two-thirds full and it hadn't even started on its long journey. The journey was very sad as they travelled through the bombed-out cities along the way. But they were alive and on their way to a new home so they felt hope.

They finally changed trains for the last part of their journey. The weather was warm and the scenery changed from war-torn cities to flat farmland scenes. Cows grazed in lush meadows and horses galloped about. There were no signs that the war had ever reached this area. A very peaceful scene that made them feel less anxious. They started to look forward to yet another new chapter in their lives.

*

Xanten railway station was as boring in architecture as all of the houses they could see. But an old van had been laid on for them to take them to their new home. The station was a twenty-minute drive away. They rattled off with all the rabbits, boxes and possessions. Along the way, the place was immaculately clean, with well-swept roads and paths. Time appeared to have stood still in this town. Along the cobbled high street there were still water pumps for the people. In amazement, they looked onto this scene as the van rattled on into the woods, and then they arrived. A large site had been cleared to make way for ten wooden barrack-style buildings. They were not pretty, but functional. Each building had three front entrances with two flats on either side, on a raised ground floor and the same on the first floor. In the basement was a large separate area for storage. There were 120 flats waiting to be filled by about 500 people.

Klara was not very impressed as she felt it looked like a large prison. As they climbed about six steps towards their new apartment they smelt how clean and fresh it was. Upon opening the door their first sight was a large, airy, open-plan lounge furnished in light-coloured wood with an aga in the corner for cooking. A nice settee and dining table with a wall unit was already there. Klara was overcome with joy and again, tears of joy this time came. Annalisa rushed into the bedrooms which, again, were furnished, and she got to share a room just with Ingrid. The second bedroom was of course for her parents. They also benefitted from running water, unlike the village which still used the pumps. The whole apartment had been designed to give a light feel and that is what they needed after all of the grime and destruction they had witnessed. They felt happy and ready to start yet another beginning.

With winter looming the war was not going well. Even Goebbels found it difficult to convince the people that all was all right. But as always, Germany continued to work hard; the bombing by the big American bombers did not achieve the anticipated results. Due to their size, German fighter planes were causing large casualties and daytime bombing slowed down in the next few months. However hard all the cities and factories were hit, production carried on. To the family it came as quite a shock on their first night, and every night after this, to hear this burring horrible sound of the V-1. It seemed like 1,000 planes descending on the cities. Xanten lay in the direct pathway to the Ruhr cities. How grateful they were to not be there and their hearts went out to the people who were.

Annalisa had a disappointment; Xanten had a grammar school in the Catholic convent. In no uncertain terms they were told that as Annalisa was a Protestant she could not be accepted. In time to come they began to realise how bitter the local villagers were towards the newcomers from the cities and their different religious views. They had been quite happy without the invasion of foreigners from the cities. Annalisa started to feel this attitude more and more, living there.

The other option for a grammar school was to travel to Wesel or Kleber, which was 30km away. However, transport was difficult and another factor was that Emil was now a pensioner and money was getting short. It was therefore not possible for Annalisa to go to a grammar school and she was enrolled in the local state school. As Annalisa had inherited some of Klara's snobbery this did not go down well. She had worn with great pride her velvet beret to show that she was one of the elite, and now that had been taken away from her. There was only one consolation; the teacher took an instant delight in having a clever girl in her class. Little did she realise that they were nine months behind in their teaching and Annalisa appeared even more clever.

They settled into their new lifestyle. Klara busied herself making the apartment feel like a home but apart from that did little else. When they used to go to the air-raid shelter in Essen they would take a suitcase. In it were Klara's trinkets, china and precious memories. Now they were displayed in the apartment in all of their glory. Emil, again, had to make a cage for the rabbits. This was not a problem as living in the woods, materials were not an issue. However, he got more and more worried about the bombers flying over them every night. He felt that sooner or later bombs would fall on them. Xanten had finally had a siren installed to warn them about the aircraft. He said to Klara that he wanted to build an air-raid shelter just in case. Even though he wasn't that great at DIY he built this shelter and was in his element doing it. After all, he had not worked for thirty years in the coal mines not knowing what he was doing.

Klara loved the idea as it kept him busy, and she could boast to the neighbours about her clever husband. She helped him to get all of the neighbours together to explain the idea and it was greeted with enthusiasm. They all helped to make this shelter a reality; even little Ingrid helped with her bucket, carrying earth. They dug from the basement out into the woods, being spurred on by the siren going off every day and night. After all, they had been through it before and knew what could happen. The local town people were laughing and saying, "What could you expect from these crazy city people?" Little did they envisage how many lives it would save.

Once more, a Party letter arrived, and again they were worried. There was to be an inspection of how all the refugees had settled in. Along came the Party people in their spick-and-span uniforms. They were very impressed with how they had all made their new homes nice. There was talk that once Hitler had inspected the defences in France, he himself might come by. A few weeks later another letter arrived;

their apartment had been picked as the best and the news reel people would come and film it.

Klara started to clean and clean as the day drew closer. The excitement grew in the settlement. Even the town's mayor was expected. At lunch a couple of limousines arrived with high-ranking officers and supporting soldiers. The German news reel people had already set up their van. The town's dignitaries lined up to greet them and the tour started. Emil and Klara's apartment was one of the last to be visited. Klara was beaming with pride as she was presented with a large bouquet of flowers and a certificate for having the best-kept apartment. Annalisa and Ingrid were then asked to go into their bedroom. Annalisa took hold of Ingrid as she held her favourite toy. Lots of photographs were taken of them as Klara had scrubbed them clean and they looked like the epitome of German good looks. Annalisa, with her long blonde hair and light green eyes, which should have been blue for perfection, and Ingrid with her sprinkling of blonde hair and blue eyes. Emil was also interviewed about his work in the mines to help the war effort. When they were leaving, he told them about the shelter and they were impressed by his ingenuity, as the six-foot-tall generals stooped into the shelter with their sparkling clean uniforms.

Hitler had supposedly been delayed inspecting other areas, which was a disappointment but the day was still considered a great success. Indirectly they helped in supporting Goebbels' wartime propaganda displaying how well the poor bombed-out victims were looked after and cherished. Even though they were a pebble in the overall suffering that was going on.

The war was not going well. Annalisa's hero and everyone else's too, Rommel, fell out of grace with Hitler and was blamed for losing them Africa. He was replaced with another general – Jurgen von Armin. Rommel became sick with jaundice and returned back to Germany in March 1944, never to go back to Africa. The defeat and turnaround of the war was due to Montgomery. In the previous battle at El Alamein, Rommel was faced with overwhelming odds. The German losses were horrendous. Allied losses were 1,750 killed and sixty-seven tanks destroyed. At one point Rommel only had sixty miles of fuel left for his tanks, whereas the allied forces' supply was endless. Their main supply line was through Malta, where every ship and gun was employed not to let German army supplies through.

In the last couple of weeks before the end, General Armin faced an enemy of 380,000 men, 1,200 tanks, 1,500 guns and 3,000 aircraft. He himself was down to 170,00 men, 130 tanks, 404 aircraft ammunition for only 400 field guns. His retreat became a shambles. Boats were systematically destroyed by the allies and the largest aircraft flying, which could hold an infantry company and twenty tanks, became easy pickings for the RAF as they were so slow and cumbersome. Only one quarter of Germans would make it back to Germany. On May 12th 1943, General Jurgen von Armin surrendered to Montgomery.

The Christmas of 1943, by now most people had been affected by the war, if not bombed out, having lost loved ones. On the food front things were rationed, but with the black market ripe it was easy to get other provisions. The most ingenious recipes were dreamed up. Annalisa's favourite, marzipan, was made from semolina. Every scrap of land was used to grow something. One of the saddest things to happen was that Klara's friend would pick mushrooms in the wood; everybody assumed she knew what she was doing but unfortunately she ate a bad mushroom and later died.

Klara's knack for making friends extended to Gunter, a soldier, and thirty Russian prisoners that he looked after. She felt sorry for the prisoners of war; they did not look ferocious, as Goebbels had painted them. It was the opposite; their clothing in rags and a look of hunger on their faces. Gunter and two other German soldiers took these soldiers to the farms to work. On the way back he would stop for a cup of imitation coffee from Klara. Whilst he was not looking Klara would sneak out and give food to the Russians. This became a daily occurrence.

Annalisa also had some good news; she got on so well with her teacher that she asked Klara and Emil to see her. Their immediate reaction was, what had their little darling got up to now?! But their faces soon brightened up when the teacher asked if they would like Annalisa to become a teacher. Teachers and all of the professions were thought of as the elite. She explained that a letter had arrived from Hitler to put forward their best pupils for teacher training. Unfortunately, Emil said their funds would not support this, but the teacher explained that if Annalisa passed the exam it would all be free. They were delighted and at least the years of paying for the grammar school would have been worth it. Annalisa was over the moon when she was told. Klara, of course, told everyone she could find about her clever little girl.

A few weeks later, a letter arrived saying that Annalisa had been selected to attend a pre-training course of one month, and an exam to be enrolled into the teacher training college. The college was situated in Elten, so close to the Dutch border. Annalisa was in seventh heaven; even some of the town's people started to talk to her, as the news had been printed into the local paper.

Things in Xanten and the surrounding countryside started to change. First the occasional bomb was dropped, which might have been left over from the visits over the cities. But slowly these bombings became more regular. Emil and helpers started to work to exhaustion to finish their shelter. By now it could hold 100 people; standing lights were installed, using electric when it worked or paraffin if not.

There was talk that the enemy was trying to land in France. Most people still said, "Let them try, we will give them a good thrashing." But were they dreaming? With what? Invalids and old men? All the leftover good troops were in Russia, but even with daytime bombing by the Americans and night-time bombing by the English, morale was still good. Civilian casualties were at their highest, but still factories managed to produce.

Questions were being asked by the allies themselves as to the fairness of these mass killings. Air Marshal Arthur Harris, in charge since 1942, eventually told Churchill that the war could not be won by air power alone. Between November 1943 and spring 1944, 147 bomber planes were lost and 1,682 bomber planes were badly damaged. The Ruhr targets, starting with Duisburg oil-producing plants only twenty-five miles away from their homes, to crop armament factories in Essen. However, locations en route were also selected for the invasion to come. Xanten was in the flight path and Emil and Klara had jumped from the fire into the frying pan. Emil and Klara became sick with worry as to what would come next.

A bit of good news came though. Annalisa's teacher training would start in April. That kept Klara busy, trying to find a couple of new dresses and other items that she would need. Annalisa's prized possession was a jacket made out of rabbit furs and high brown boots given to her as a present from Emil. She would turn fourteen whilst she would be away. She was not the tallest girl yet, only measuring in at five foot, one inches in height, however, she carried herself with confidence.

But in that year she grew to five feet, four inches. The dresses that Klara had made for her turned into mini dresses. Once more, Annalisa was very happy and went off to teacher training. Klara was very proud of her daughter and shed her customary tears. Annalisa had to come home to attend her confirmation. What a pitiful handful of children attended; only her and a couple of boys. However, one of them became a good friend of hers.

Fitting in was easy, with all the other girls and boys, especially having other boys there. The college was an old, quite dark building, unlike the splendour of the sanatorium. But that all did not matter; achieving the end goal was important. The actual lectures were easy for Annalisa; she had never been the quickest but her willpower to understand got her there.

At weekends, they were allowed to go into the local town. She felt so grown up going out for coffee with her friends. The four weeks went by far too fast and then, again, she returned hoping that she had passed and would be accepted.

The talk back home was about the Russians getting closer. The Russian army, by now had regained more ground, extending more than halfway beyond the 1939 Russian-German border. But the worry in Xanten was more about the invasion. As they were situated next to the Rhine it would become a fierce battlefield, as they would not want the Russians to gain access to the heart of Germany. Everyone knew something was up as equipment and soldiers started to pour in. However, in the woods where they lived they were not too badly affected. It was like Klara said, a prison without bars; the war could pass them by and forget about the little community hidden in the woods. But they didn't have this luck.

Klara became more and more friendly with Gunter and the other Russian prisoners. She started to tell Gunter about where they lived and he also told her about Thüringen, and his family's business. Thüringen, as of that moment was untouched also by the war. Once or twice he mentioned that they could flee to his parents for safety.

Emil, by now had completed his shelter. An ugly building where every bit of wood had been used. Now they started to hoard food and necessary items like blankets in order to survive, if required, several weeks. Emil had been there in the First World War when he was the same age as Annalisa was now.

Maybe his knowledge was not with the fighting, but more about the shortage of food afterwards. He used to say a loaf of bread cost 1,000 marks – worthless paper money.

The bombing started to increase at such an alarming rate that the sirens remained on most of the time. But even though they were getting ready for the invasion, deep down they still believed that Germany would win and the enemy would perish on the beach. Goebbels had film-star status with his amazing propaganda to make the masses believe. Field Marshal Rommel was in charge of the field defences in France and the whole line stretching from France to Spain. He wanted to plant two million mines.

June 6th 1944, there was talk of a special bomb which would destroy enormous areas in one go; apparently, some sort of water was needed. But some of the factories that produced this water had been destroyed. Emil kept wondering where they would drop this bomb. A plan to take up Gunter's offer started to sound very appealing. Emil's biggest worry would be whether they would call him into the Volkssturm which is the equivalent of Dad's Army. All around, from the sixteen-year-old youths to men older than seventy, and every woman and child, had to help with the war effort to defend the Fatherland. Eventually Emil had to report to the Party office and join the Volkssturm.

Learning how to use a gun would prove to be a good lesson. Because of Ingrid still being too fragile, Klara was not expected to do heavy work.

The spring of 1944 proved to be a disappointment. June was wet with drizzle or rain most days. It was nice in the woods in the sun, but in the rain it became quite a dismal place. Even trying to take the pram into town along the muddy roads became a problem.

On June 6th, the invasion started but it was played down. After all, the enemy had tried before and not succeeded. Everyone thought that they still would win. Due to the bad weather, not even the hierarchy was prepared for that day. A large contingency of generals were away from the beaches; even Rommel was with Hitler in Berlin and informed only by the next morning, cursing how stupid he was not to have seen this coming their way from Britain. Little did he realise that 950,000 US troops had been assembled. The landings on the beaches proved to be the bloodiest of battles. Over 5,000 ships and 150,000 men were launched across the English Channel. Bodies were piled up against the sea wall to the extent that General Bradley considered calling the invasion off. But General Taylor spurred the men, saying that to stay is to die, to live is to go forward. Lord Lovet led his commandos in with his personal pipers. Caen, a strategic town, was only taken after one month of fierce fighting.

Cherbourg, a main harbour, fell on June 25th, which was a great blow to Hitler. A thousand aircrafts bombarded Cherbourg – 1,800 soldiers died, 15,000 were wounded, and 40,000 became prisoners of war. The harbour became totally unusable with mines blocking all access.

All the German people heard was that their defences were holding. Even though the allied forces broke through, no land or airfield was gained. In July, Churchill was worried that the war would become a replay of WW1.

Emil started to relax a little as the allied forces were not making much progress. The idea of leaving was shelved for the moment. A letter arrived saying that Annalisa had passed her exams and was accepted onto the teacher training programme. Her starting date was September 1st 1944. Jubilation in the household was great and of course a time for coffee was found to celebrate. They also had their new weapons arriving.

The V-1 was launched July 13th to fly to London. Again, Xanten was in the flight path. The sound of the doodlebug flying overhead on its mission signalled that all would soon be over. About 500 bombs fell on London on the first day. Another 6,750 doodlebugs were sent with 2,420 falling on London. The casualty figures amounted to 6,000 killed and 18,000 injured. Goebbels milked this for its propaganda. More new weapons were promised to help win the war. However, all was not good with the hierarchy. Field Marshal Gerd von Rundstedt resigned on July 1st apparently with ill health. His replacement was Field Marshal Hans Gunter von Kluge, not too familiar with fighting on the Western front. But the next shock came when Rommel was injured by a British fighter bomber when his car exploded on July 16th. Then on July 20th an attempt was made to assassinate Hitler, but the Fuhrer survived with only minor injuries. Most Germans had a tear in their eyes. How could something like this happen to their beloved Fuhrer?

Hitler now distrusted all of his generals, including Rommel. Erwin Rommel committed suicide soon afterwards. A sad end to one of Germany's finest generals. He was Annalisa's hero and she cried when she heard the news.

But all was not good with the enemy; they also lost one of their generals – Lesley G. McNair.

The weather became worse through July; days of rain and fighting in these conditions whilst receiving heavy losses, and the Americans' spirit started to wane. However, they were still getting closer to them. Under normal conditions the enemy was only a three-hour car ride away. Plan B of leaving and going to Thüringen was brought forward. The final point came in August when the news came through that the teacher training programme had been suspended due to the war. This was one of the biggest disappointments to Annalisa. Emil said to Klara, "We will wait until September but if things get worse we will leave earlier."

August was a beautiful month. Finally, the rain stopped and the sun started to shine. However, it proved to be one of the worst months for fighting. German losses were horrific and the front came closer and closer. The wounded who managed to make it back suffered trauma from all of the fighting and they called Normandy a hell hole, where for hundreds of yards the dead were left; not a tree, house or animal could be seen. In the last battle 10,000 Germans soldiers died, 50,000 became prisoners, and from fifty divisions only ten remained.

Gunter had been in contact with his parents and they assured him that they would be happy to have Emil's family. The bombing became more frenzied and they spent more and more time in the shelter.

Klara's stomach condition became worse, the main reason being the irregular meal times and the constant worry of it all. The decision was then made that they should flee from this nightmare. Many of the other neighbours and townspeople had already left.

Little Ingrid was now two years old but made very slow progress. On a visit to the hospital a small heart defect was noted. But it was not life-threatening.

For them to leave they could only take the minimum of items. The plan was that if required, Annalisa and Emil could return and collect more. Klara cried a lot when she said goodbye to Gunter.

By now there were very few hours in any day when the RAF were not harassing anything that moved. But once in Duisburg, even though the town was a big bomb site, the trains still ran. They finally got on their train and the relief was immense. It had taken so much effort to get the pram and all of their possessions onto the train, as it was full to capacity with refugees and soldiers. Everyone trying to go somewhere where they hoped sanity still existed.

Ingrid proved to be an asset as everyone felt sorry that such a small, fragile child should be caught up in this chaos, so space was made for Klara and the pram.

The train rumbled on and the landscape started to change from horror to untouched countryside; a sigh of relief came over everyone. No one worried about how uncomfortable their perch might be, every hour travelling was another hour away from destruction. When they finally arrived, taxis were waiting and Emil told the taxi driver the address. A small grin appeared on the taxi driver's face but quickly was replaced by a polite smile. At the address in the middle of town, a large iron gate led to a house several hundreds of years old. All around rubbish consisting of iron, furniture, and anything of any apparent value, lay around. All four stood in disbelief. Steptoe and son lived in a palace compared to this. The house also sheltered the horses that pulled their carts. Dogs were running towards them, barking their heads off. Klara wanted to turn around and leave but Emil told her to hang on.

After a while a man appeared and with a big smile on his face, welcomed them to his house as his son's friend. If the outside was a shock to them, looking at the father, things got worse. They could not guess his age but old clothes hung off him and he had a three-day growth of stubble on his face. But he was so friendly, ushering them into his house, that they were led in. The doors and ceilings were low and Emil had to duck his head going up the staircase. The room had the largest stove Klara had ever seen and it took up a third of the room, tiled to the ceiling with seats around. Coal was shovelled into it and when cooking was done it went into the same place on trays.

The ceiling was low with black beams and Gunter's mother sat in the middle of the room at a large table with a pretty girl who was about eighteen years old. The mother found it hard to get up, weighing over twenty stones in weight. But again, with a big smile of welcome on her face. The girl was introduced as Gunter's girlfriend and was in the last stages of her pregnancy. Gunter did not know about her having his baby, as it might worry him.

They were asked to sit down but this also was a problem as the floor dipped into the middle of the room and the chairs would slide into the middle as well. Klara was not sure at this stage whether she should laugh or cry. But their genuine friendliness and eagerness to do something for them won Klara over and she accepted the situation. A real cup of coffee, not war-time imitations that they had had for the last couple of years, was offered, with freshly baked bread, salami and cheeses. Ingrid also had fresh milk to drink. After food and drink they all started to feel better. They could not hear enough news about their darling son. And Emil made sure not to mention the bad situation where Gunter was. Why make these simple people worry when no known outcome was guaranteed?

Their next problem became their sleeping arrangements. The whole house was the one sitting/cooking/dining room with only two bedrooms and an outside toilet. There was a stable used for the horses and it was agreed that the girlfriend, Victoria, would sleep in the main room, and Emil and family would take her room. The room was so small and messy that Klara was unable to hold on any longer. She said to Emil, "What a fibber. Gunter painted a picture of a palace and it is a hovel not really fit for anyone."

Emil consoled her and took her by her hands and led her outside. He told her to stand still and listen.

"Listen to what?" she asked.

"That is the point. Peace and quiet, and we are all alive. No aeroplanes, no bombs, just the birds singing. Tomorrow we will think again. But tonight we have a roof over our heads like the manger." This made Klara laugh and harmony was restored.

Nearly all the towns were flooded with refugees. Erfurt was no better, where they stayed. It was a small, unimportant town surrounded by beautiful fir woods on gently sloping hills. They had a good night's sleep without worry. Annalisa and Emil woke up and had to find their way down the rickety stairs to find the outside toilet. They then checked out the adjoining yard; if the front of the house was bad, the back was unbelievable. The rubbish was piled high. Chickens and ducks ran about, scraping the ground for food. Two big German Shepherd dogs roamed around on long sturdy steel chains. They were amazed that the dogs were needed for security as why would anyone want to break into here? Emil said to Annalisa that they had to get Klara out of here otherwise she would go crazy seeing this. Annalisa was in total agreement and they decided that after breakfast they would go into town to see if they could find a better solution.

Klara had fed and cleaned Ingrid and was busy chatting to the two women. Emily, Gunter's mother, and Victoria were busy cooking scrambled eggs and bacon. A full stomach pacifies even the grumpiest of people and Klara became more mellow and said things were not too bad. Herman, Gunter's father, went to harness the horses. If all around them was chaos and dirt, the horses were kept in beautiful condition and even the stables were spotless. Herman spent all of his time with them and they were his pride and joy.

They all went to the town hall and asked for help with their predicament. At each reception desk they spoke to, sympathy could be seen on their faces and they promised to sort something out. With this organised, they then went for coffee and cake. Klara did not want to go back to the squalor so with only one option, she rolled up her sleeves ready to clean!! Klara kept saying that she had known quite a few lazy women but Emily takes the prize.

Every day Emil and Annalisa went to the town hall hoping to wear them down and get them better accommodation. They were worried that when autumn ended, if they had to spend the winter there, with another baby it would be dire. By October, good news arrived and they had been found new accommodation. It was a two-bedroomed large apartment and they were pleased with what they saw. Their bedroom was large, with two beds, a further put-you-up bed and still space for Ingrid's pram. There was a large kitchen-lounge area which would be shared with another couple who already lived there. It was exquisitely furnished to a high standard. The owners were not too keen that they had to have lodgers but it was the law that they had to take in refugees.

All forms in triplicate were signed and dated in order that they could move in as soon as possible, Klara being over the moon with happiness. Suitcases were once again packed for their short journey to their new apartment. Having installed Klara and Ingrid, Emil and Annalisa went back to Xanten to bring back their last few possessions and any food they had. The trains again were overflowing with people moving from East to West, running from the war, everyone trying to find a place of safety whilst large quantities of soldiers travelled, joining up with their units. Everyone was worried but there was still a sense of comradery and togetherness, and still the false belief that everything would be all right. However, the closer the train approached the Ruhr and seeing the devastation from all of the bombings, doubt could be seen to grow on everyone's faces and the quiet in the carriages grew. Day after day, with all the destruction they still managed to maintain the railway.

The closer they got to Xanten, the more the continued harassment of the RAF on anything that moved showed, with the destruction from the machine gunning from the low-flying planes. Emil couldn't understand why there were no German planes to stop them and he was worried that it had been a stupid idea to come back. They decided to go and get what they needed and get back as soon as possible. When they got back to Xanten their apartment was still neat and tidy and they wearily put their heads down that night. Quite a few people had left and whatever the news reel showed, people had stopped believing that they would be saved if they stayed there. Emil worried that they didn't have enough men let alone machines left to fight the enemy.

February 27th 1945, Canadian troops conquered Kalkar in Hockwald which was only twenty miles away from Xanten. How long, would be proven in a couple of weeks. As usual Gunter was busy taking his Russian prisoners to work. Emil said hello to the ones Klara had befriended and given food to. By now they spoke a little German and were telling Emil that soon they would be free. The English are coming. A lot of things would happen before then but every person needs to have hope. Gunter was very worried they would turn on him, as there were thirty prisoners and only three Germans. "As soon as I smell a rat I shall shoot the lot of them," he boasted. How strange that war brings out the worst in people when they try to survive, as he was a kind and gentle person who the prisoners liked.

The air-raid sirens were on more often than off. Emil's shelter proved to be very useful; although it would not survive a direct hit, it provided some sort of safety. Whilst Annalisa packed away the most precious of Klara's collection of figurines, Emil went about to see what was going on. While they were in their barracks in the woods little news reached them. However, as he got closer to Xanten and the main road the picture that greeted him was of disbelief. The roads were saturated with cars and people fleeing, herds of cows being driven away from Xanten by soldiers, and in all this mayhem the German tracks with soldiers tried to go in the opposite direction in order to rejoin their units. As he watched all of this a thought came into his mind. If he could get one of these cows his family would have enough meat for a long time.

He went quickly away, back into the woods before one of the planes shot him, as waiting in the open was suicidal. He told Annalisa of his plans.

"How are we going to kill the cow?"

"I will get Gunter to shoot it as he is always talking about shooting something. This way, he will get some practice."

In the morning they both went into Xanten equipped with a thick, strong rope. The view that greeted them got worse. The smell of death hung in the air, dead animals rotting by the wayside. Soldiers were still driving back an assortment of animals, anything that could be forced into going with them was made to go. Both felt a bit like lions on the prowl. After several attempts to put a rope around a cow's neck, they finally managed. However, a sergeant had seen what they were up to and in no uncertain terms told them they would be arrested if they tried again. But luck was on their side. Planes were coming over and dropping bombs on the roads, with people panicking and diving into the ditches. The animals started to stampede with soldiers shooting at the planes with their guns. When there was a clear period everyone tried to move along; the actual road was cleared of burning cars and the doctors attended to the people shot.

Emil said, "Come along, Annalisa. It is now or never. See that bunch of cows slowing down? Let's run and get one before the soldiers round them up."

Nearer and nearer they got to this bunch, and finally put a rope around the neck of one of them. Pulling and pushing, they walked away with the thinnest cow of the bunch. Nobody took any notice of the pair with their cow and finally they got back to the barracks. After resting they then went to find Gunter. His face was full of gloom and worry, not the usual happy soul.

Emil asked what was wrong. "Why aren't the prisoners working?"

Gunter said the unbelievable had happened with the landing in Normandy on 15th June 1944. "My orders are to take my prisoners back to a prisoner of war camp. Then I will have to rejoin my unit to fight. I had hoped not to fight anymore as all is lost already."

"You had better not let anyone hear you talking like this as there are still a lot of Hitler supporters left. They would make sure that you would be strung up if they heard you."

He persuaded Gunter to come to the barracks with his gun. The cow was standing peacefully next to a tree. First the cow had to be coaxed to go down into the basement. Neighbours came to help and with a lot of pulling and pushing, this was achieved. Emil held the rope tight whilst waiting for Gunter to shoot the cow in the head. But Gunter, who had boasted about shooting the Russian prisoners, was shaking so hard that he was unable to pull the trigger. Time after time he tried but would break down in tears. "I can't do it," he sobbed.

Emil then took the gun from him and shot the cow cleanly through the head, and it collapsed immediately into a big heap. Emil ran outside and promptly was sick himself.

Luckily, a neighbour who had some knowledge of butchering said that he would help to cut the cow up. But time was not on their side and everything took a long time to do. The bombardment had increased tenfold and spitfires fired on anything that moved and dropped bombs.

Later on in the day, Gunter rushed around. "Emil," he gasped. "I had to tell you. I have to go immediately to fight in France."

Emil asked what was going on and Gunter said, "It is nothing like Dunkirk. Many more have landed."

Emil wanted to know if the defences were holding

but they were told nothing.

"The Russian prisoners are being taken to a camp with two of the soldiers whilst I go to the front with the other soldier."

Emil told Annalisa to make sandwiches for the two Russians who were their friends. *Poor things,* Emil thought. *Will they make it to the camp? And if so, what then?*

Emil slipped them the sandwiches, making sure that no one had seen them doing it, and said goodbye.

"Tell my parents and girlfriend that I love them when you get back to Thüringen," Gunter said, and then they were gone.

Chapter 7

The news people were very coy. Hitler was still ranting and raving about a speedy victory but slowly the story was unfolding – 1,000 and 10,000 had landed in Normandy. The actual figure was 150,000 men with thousands of ships; 2,000 paratroopers had landed behind enemy lines, trying to keep the bridges intact. So, this was the story of the livestock being driven back and the enormous movement of soldiers towards Holland, Belgium and France. Whilst they were worried about their food supply thousands had died on the beaches of Normandy.

All Emil kept murmuring to himself was, "What a futile war. All these young men at eighteen years to die because of one man's ideology." But Emil had to keep these thoughts to himself. Tomorrow he had to put all of his energy into sorting out the carcass in the basement. "Annalisa, you must keep the stove on and cook the meat to preserve it. But when you hear the planes run down into the shelter."

How many times she had to put the meat to one side and run into the shelter, she could not remember. It felt like a big game of Russian Roulette and this was not a game, but live ammunition. However, eventually they managed to fill all the containers they had. The neighbours who were still about also had a share of the meat. The basement looked like something out of a horror movie, with the empty rib cage and skin laying down there with blood everywhere.

The planes still continued to harass them, the big formations going to the cities whilst two or three planes would keep the pressure up on smaller targets. Very occasionally, at nights they heard doodlebugs flying towards England.

Emil built a little cart to put behind the push bike in order to pull back the belongings. By now trains out of Xanten were no longer running and their nearest train station was 40km away. Whilst every effort was made to keep the main rail-lines intact, the smaller ones were eventually destroyed by planes and bombs. However, food was still getting into the shops and they bought what they could to bring back to Klara. After a week, they were ready to make their move. The news became very patchy as to how the enemy was doing. All they knew was that each day things got worse. They could hear the big guns firing in the distance.

Emil and Annalisa worried that any day now, they would be caught up in the fighting. Where there had been heavy movement on the roads in the last few weeks, now it had slowed down to a trickle. Most army vehicles went at night for safety and the refugees had mostly gone. Emil had finished his cart that worked but he would never have received a medal for craftsmanship, DIY not being his strongest point. He would always say to Klara, "I go to work all day to provide. Get a craftsman in to do what I can pay for." Emil proposed that they leave in the morning. Annalisa wanted to know why they would leave in the morning and Emil said at least they could see the potholes and craters and try to avoid them.

Ingrid's little tin bath was filled with the jars of food and a further two suitcases and rucksacks filled with the rest of their possessions. They only had Annalisa's push bike between them so one would ride whilst the other walked. Annalisa wanted to clean the apartment but Emil said, "Enough, time to go, as it probably will not be standing when or if we come back."

As they set off they felt that walking was almost better than riding with the cart on the back. There was one blessing; this part of the country is as flat as anything, with no hills – heaven for them on a push bike. But progress was still very slow; the road was very empty and the atmosphere was eerie, with Spitfires flying overhead, prowling for targets. They ended up spending more time hiding from these than walking on the roads.

It took over two and half days to reach Duisburg railway station. Loads of wheeler-dealers waited near the station to buy anything people were unable to carry and take with them. Annalisa's push bike was sold for a miserly sum. It was not chaos in the station, but a saturation of refugees and soldiers.

They worried whether they would get onto the train with all of their luggage. Emil said, "Let's be optimistic and just look helpless when the train arrives."

It was impossible to get into the doors but one

carriage full of soldiers took pity on them. They shouted, "Come on, Granddad, lift your stuff through the window," and all of their luggage. But when it came to the baby bath, even the strongest of the soldiers winced and they wanted to know what was in there!! Finally, they got it all in and then they had to get through the doors, with a lot of good-natured pushing. In later years when it was impossible to find a seat it became Annalisa's job to do so.

The soldiers were more than happy to have Annalisa amongst them. The train gathered speed and wanted to get away from all the bombing, and even packed to the hilt, managed to speed away. They sat on top of their luggage; people were everywhere – sitting, standing, lying. A sigh of relief came over them all. Emil said, "I told you we could do it, you just have to have the will and determination and a big shovel of luck to succeed, my Schatzi," and gave Annalisa a big hug.

Singing and laughing started to erupt in the carriages, for in this moment they all started to feel safe. As the train went into the heart of Germany where it was still intact, there was an air of relaxation. They watched out of the windows as cows grazed without a care in the world and gleaming houses glistened in the sunshine. The soldiers, however, were going to the Russian front. This would probably be their last piece of respite.

Then Emil and Annalisa reached their destination. Time stood still as taxis still waited to take them to their final destination.

Klara and Ingrid were overcome with relief when they drew up in the taxi. Klara cried out how she had missed them and worried about them when they heard all of the bad news going about, but Emil said, "I told you we would return."

Emil asked how things were and Klara said, "Life has been ok. A bit cramped in the one room, but I made friends with the landlady and we came to an understanding as to when I use the kitchen. It will be worse with the four of us but at least we are together and alive. Tomorrow we can sort things out and try to make it easier."

Sleep came easily to Emil and Annalisa that night as they felt more secure than they had for a long time.

However, life had not been easy for Klara, as although Ingrid was now two years old she was still demanding. Even now, she was underdeveloped and needing feeding every three hours and as for walking or potty training, Ingrid didn't want to and was carried everywhere. She liked to be played with and taken out in the pram. This, then, was how Klara spent her time. She also had stayed friends with Gunter's parents and so life once more settled into a routine. Annalisa became like a second mother to Ingrid and looked after her a lot. The one blessing from the lady of the apartment, as soon as her husband would go to work she would get ready to go out herself. Where she went all day, nobody ever found out. In the evening she would rush back and make sure she had a meal ready for husband on the table. Therefore, this was the time Klara avoided using the kitchen.

Emil's first task was to visit Gunter's parents and give them his messages. By now Gunter's girlfriend had given birth to a little girl called Kaite and

Annalisa would occasionally babysit her for money. They had only one letter from Gunter in the last month and that had been about how hard the fighting was in Russia.

In the next few months Emil helped in the scrapyard as Gunter's father was getting on. With regards to the war, all they knew was what the news reels were telling them. The cinema always had a lot of news reels telling them how well the army was doing. Emil would talk to himself, saying how they must think they are stupid, as he knew they were being driven back from Russia, lost in Africa, getting closer to crossing the Rhine, and coming up from Italy. "With four fronts to fight it is no wonder if we bleed to death."

Annalisa still loved going to the cinema and would dream that one day she might see herself on the screen, or go to all of the exotic places they showed. India was presented as a land of beautiful people with their maharajas covered in precious jewels. Hitler himself had a soft spot for India. Annalisa did see herself on the screen but that would be sixty years later on. As for the distant lands, this happened much earlier. Most people don't realise that German people dream of faraway places; it is their escape from everyday life's expectations and contemporary German music would be about this.

Life was still pretty normal; if there hadn't been the news and ration books, the war still seemed faraway. But with each week the illusion was shattering. Autumn turned to winter and being in one room, it was far easier to keep warm. Food was all right with ration books and whatever extras they could get on the side. However, everyone knew that it would only be a matter of time before the war would reach them again. Only this time there was nowhere else left to run to.

By now, spring arrived and in April, the day started pretty miserably. The bombardment and gunfire was close by and they knew that it wouldn't be long before the Americans took over their town. They had no idea what to expect apart from what the German news reels spoke about which was always the same about the rape and brutality of the Americans.

Emil could not decide what to do. This would be the fourth time that they would have to run. But where could they run to? They were already deep in the heart of the German forest. He glanced down at his little family; his beautiful, wilful, fourteen-year-old daughter, his fragile, tiny wife, and his helpless baby daughter who was just starting to walk. His wife's health had never totally recovered after being made by the Nazis to go through with her final pregnancy. Ingrid was born just weighing 2lbs and it had taken all of Annalisa's strength to help her mother and baby sister to survive.

The thought of what the Americans might do to his little family forced Emil to make up his mind. There was only one decision and that was to run again. Emil and Annalisa made their final journey into the under siege town in order to buy anything that they could eat. Whatever they were offered, Emil just shrugged, gave a smile and took it, saying, "You never know when it might be useful."

The town was a riot of noise and overwhelming chaos. The German army were still pulling out local people, accusing them of being from the Collaborators, and shooting them. The other locals naively clung on to the belief that they would still win whilst others were desperately packing up their belongings and trying to leave. Ambulances came screeching through the streets, dropping off wounded soldiers and returning to the front like a crazy clockwork toy gone mad.

Emil and Annalisa tried to blend into this chaos, only making themselves visible to those who had food to offer. What was left, they bought; tins of anchovies, garlic and other weird combinations. When they had nothing left to offer or buy, Emil and Annalisa loaded up their old pram up with their goods and slowly, avoiding everyone, returned to their house for their last night.

Emil watched as his family finally fell asleep. For him, the night carried on. The air was heavy with smoke, gunfire and the gentle continual sound of rain dripping on the trees. His mind whirring away, his decision, as always, weighed upon him. Not the luxury of deciding mundane matters like what shirt to wear but decisions on what road to take and whether that would mean another day they stayed alive, or if the decision was wrong, their death. The Americans were attacking their town but the Russians were also decimating resistance on their path to taking Berlin. Finally, as a weak, feeble light shone through the grey, wet clouds, dawn broke and the time to run arrived.

Silence as they loaded the pram up with all they could carry. The pram became their focus. Baby Ingrid sat amongst anchovies and pans. Klara's delicate hand rested on her daughter's pram for support and the other shrugged the tears away from her eyes. Her years of having the best front parlour room, where the piano would be played by Annalisa and her visitors would enjoy their finery, were long past. Looking over at Annalisa, she gave a sigh. Her daughter, age fourteen, was growing into a beautiful woman. Her eyes were deep brown which contrasted with her rich blonde hair. But when Klara looked closer the beauty of youth had been replaced with the burdens of responsibility and bitterness of seeing too much death in one so young. Emil then looked over to Klara and hesitantly stated their route. With a nod of acceptance, they left behind another home and went.

They walked against the tide of people escaping the Americans. People looked in disbelief as Emil made his family walk through the town and then into the woods beyond. The people walked towards Berlin, never believing that it could ever fall, confident that Hitler would still prevail and win.

People train for marathons, people enjoy fitness sessions at the gym, people enjoy going out to restaurants and dining in style. People enjoy hiking through forests using the best Nike has to offer. Emil only had one thought – one foot in front of the other. He spurred them on metre after metre after metre. As the sound of gunfire started to fade his shoulders started to relax. They looked back down into the valley and by late afternoon the town was shrouded in hazy smoke and it sizzled as the rain gently fell. Klara shivered as the cold started to seep into their bones and minds. Even with the shelter that the pristine fir trees tried to provide, the cold invaded their bodies. Ingrid started to cry softly as her feet ached so much and the cold drained her of hope. City people forced into basic survival, each mile made it more apparent.

As the light started to fade a blessing of massive proportions happened. An abandoned hunting lodge for the aristocracy appeared. Locked up and abandoned, it felt like manna from heaven. Klara worried that they would be punished for breaking into this lodge but war changes all rules and survival becomes the new law.

The lodge belonged to a very wealthy person. The walls were mounted with trophies and within an hour they had managed to get a fire going in the ornate fireplace. The heavy wooden shutters kept the cold and the horrors of the day out and eventually they all managed to fall asleep to the sound of a fire crackling and giving off a beautiful warming heat.

"Clarchen, we have found Shangri-La. We will not go any further, you would be joking to suggest this. Here we are and here we will stay."

Relief flowed through Klara's body. A few days' respite, not having to run, or hide. With a lighter heart, they opened the heavy wooden shutters and let the light gently warm up the rooms. The lodge was like a treasure trove of warm blankets, cold weather clothes, bottled food and even a bicycle greeted them. The lodge was an isolated building amongst a forest of densely populated fir trees. No one would easily find them and as such, their worries eased a little.

A moment out of time where Emil would call Klara 'Schätzschen' (darling), Ingrid would happily play on the floor, Mutti (Klara) happily busying herself arranging everything and Annalisa preparing their unorthodox dinner of anchovies and bread. The guns were distant and the sound less intense, but never gone, and eventually the sound stopped as they won.

The town Erfurt fell to the Americans on April 11th and by April 13th the concentration camp had been liberated. Vengeance and retribution were the new gods. Any German person was either a Nazi, an officer, or a sympathiser. No German could possibly be innocent or have finer feelings; they were the enemy down to the babies like Ingrid, or Annalisa, who had her youth and innocence stolen from her.

Chapter 8

Life for our four was pretty idyllic with the lovely mountain air at Hunting Lodge. Emil busied himself cutting up as much wood as possible. Klara wanted to know, "Why, Emil?"

"There might be times when we have to stay indoors. At least we'll be warm," he told her. He also fortified all the doors and windows, a little bit like on old Western film, expecting the red Indians to attack. He oiled and cleaned all the guns, even showed Klara and Annalisa how to shoot.

"What are you expecting?" Klara again wanted to know.

"We are here on our own and there will be no law and order for a while now the town has fallen, and we have more than most people, especially the concentration people."

Next came the question of food.

"Come, Annalisa, tomorrow we'll try and get some supplies."

His basic training for handling a gun was half a dozen hours in the Dads Army. They needed real food. The city dwellers faced the fact that they had to try and kill their own food.

Early morning came, a mist hanging in the air. The fir trees looked pretty dark and uninviting, as they ventured into the woods.

Before leaving, Emil did tell Klara to lock herself in, and not open the door to anyone. He told Annalisa to move very quietly so as not to disturb the animals. But after hours of searching, trying to find something to shoot, the unhappy pair went home. Klara tried to hide a grin.

"I'll prove you wrong tomorrow," Emil commented, as he had noticed her grin. "Have you seen anybody?" he wanted to know.

"No, not a soul."

"We do one more day in the woods, and then I sneak down to the town to see what is going on."

Klara was terrified by this suggestion; if anything were to happen to him, how she would cope?

The next morning was another one of those days when staying at home was a better idea. But the pair set off again into the woods. Annalisa was terrified; every sound was alarming.

"Come on, don't be such a baby. There are no wild animals in the woods, they are more scared of you, than vice-versa."

Emil always treated Annalisa more like a boy than a girl. She was walking two feet behind Emil when she heard a rustling noise. Scared as she was, she turned and looked down into a pair of eyes. Her scream must have woken the whole wood up, as she ran an Olympic mile followed by a pig. Emil tried his best to keep up and also to shoot. This was not easy as Annalisa was in the line of fire. After what seemed like a lifetime, he managed a shot. He had hit the pig, which was squealing louder than Annalisa. "For Christ's sake, quiet!" he shouted at Annalisa. The pair were still running, but the pig started to slow and eventually crashed down. Emil had only managed to hit it in the backside. One more shot and it stooped squealing.

Annalisa was shaking and crying at the same time.

"Come on, Schatzi (darling), look how well we have done. Mother will be proud of us; it was always to prove something to Mother."

She finally stopped crying, and looked down at this hairy brown shape, this time laughing with relief. Looking at it properly, it was a fair size, too big to be carried. They went back to the lodge to collect a wheelbarrow. It took all of their strength to lift this thing into the wheelbarrow, but they eventually managed to do so, and the two hunters returned with their quarry. Emil joked and said, "We'll hang the ears on the wall between the other trophies, or shall we do the whole head?"

Klara hugged the pair, filled with joy to see them back safe and sound, as she hated every minute of being left by herself. Little Ingrid also had a look at the animal and tried to poke it.

"So Klara, what are we having for dinner tomorrow? I suppose pork?" Emil asked with a twinkle in his eye.

The next day brought more drizzle and rain than all the days beforehand, and it was cool, which was in their favour.

Mother took promptly to bed. With all the stress and excitement, her old stomach problem reared its ugly head. She suffered a lot with this.

"Come on, Annalisa," Emil said, "it is up to us to sort this pig out." They had already wheeled it into the basement. Being half built into hill, the basement served as a natural fridge at all times. Emil sharpened the knives to the utmost. Annalisa's task was to get this brown hairy thing hair-free. Being a city child, her knowledge of butchering consisted of handing money over the counter.

She boiled water and scraped away until all the bristly hair had gone. By now her arms were hurting and unable to do more. But they had to carry on. The big stove was lit and every available saucepan readied. Emil told her to hold the head, when he slit the pig open. What a mess came out, to the extent that she had to run outside and be sick. "You are a simperlich (weak girl)," Emil teased her. "In theory we should keep the skin to make sausages, but we won't bother."

After cleaning this thing and separating it into two halves, it more closely resembled a form Annalisa had seen in the butcher's. Emil carried on separating it into pieces to be cooked.

Upstairs, the serious boiling and frying began. They were lucky; with what they found in the basement and their own jars from before, they were all now filled. What a beautiful smell wafted over the whole lodge. What could not be put into jars was put into a big barrel with salt. The remains, Emil took into the woods for the wildlife. Finally, when evening came, they all sat down to their first meal of roast pork with potatoes and vegetables. How this tasted was indescribable, and they munched away until their tummies were as big as the late pig.

Candles out, and four exhausted people went to sleep. If it would not have been for the fear of the unknown, life was pretty idyllic.

By now they had been in the lodge for a couple of weeks, and Emil decided it was time to find out what was going on below. "Do you really need to go?" Klara asked.

"We must know what is going on," was his reply, and the following morning he dressed like a farmhand, in old clothes, to sneak down.

Klara started crying. "If anything happens to you, what are we to do?"

"You wait a while and then go down and find someone in charge, but it will not come to that. Now Annalisa, I rely on you to look after Mother and Ingrid."

She felt like saying, 'What about me? I am scared too.'

But, off he went.

The rain had finally stopped and the sun tried its hardest to peep through the clouds onto the hills, which made for a picture-postcard appearance. Klara busied herself, cleaning and making the lodge look pretty. She was a stickler for cleanliness and tidiness. To leave even the smallest thing lying about would arouse her anger.

It was not long before Emil returned.

"I am so happy you are all right," Klara said as she hugged and kissed him. "Tell us the news. "How come you are back so quickly?"

"I never made it into town," he said. "Halfway down there is a small cottage and I thought I'd better ask if they had some news. I am glad I did so. Yes, the Americans have taken the town, and put up a curfew. Anyone leaving the town limits or found outside the town limits would be put into prison. The other thing they said was, hordes of ex-camp prisoners are roaming the countryside, taking revenge and plundering easy targets. We have to be, more than ever, ready to defend ourselves. Never leave any door unlocked, all shutters except one closed, and never ever leave Ingrid outside alone to play."

So, our lovely sanctuary became our prison. Only once did they hear noise, a war far down the hill, a bunch of people. They did not spot them as the lodge was hidden from view.

After fourteen days of this self-imprisonment, Emil decided to try again to get some news. "This time I'll try to get into town. We have to find out what is happening," he told Klara. "Stay inside and be extra careful, and I will do the same."

He spoke to the people down the hill, and was told that the curfew was still on, but law and order were starting to return.

As he ventured further down the hill, he could hear trucks and car noise. And all of a sudden, he came face to face with the enemy. A jeep with a couple of soldiers roared past him. He had dived into the nearest ditch, to avoid being seen. By now he was shaken. Had he done the right thing? They looked pretty normal and after a while he decided to press on. Eventually, he got very close to town and could no longer duck and dive. He decided to bluff it out, looking like a poor farm worker in his old clothes and cap. Nobody took any notice of him. What greeted him as he got closer to the centre of town? Utter chaos.

The town itself had not suffered too much. All the heavy fighting had been in the surrounding area. The streets were full of American transport vehicles, and it seemed they were not sure where to go next. Soldiers were sitting on top and anywhere there was room, smoking and laughing as if they were on a family outing. Uniforms looked as if they had slept in them with shirts hanging loosely over their trousers. He was muttering to himself, "Surely this bunch of hillbillies was not able to concur our armies? What in heaven's name had gone wrong?"

In comparison, a German soldier without the buttons on his shirt done up, would probably get him a sharp reprimand. Discipline and cleanliness were the first requirements of the German solder. As he pressed on he was fascinated by a bike and sidecar, and started studying it. How he missed his own. Where was it now? One of the young soldiers shouted to him, "Lovely machine, Granddad." He spoke a few words in German. Emil tried his best to demonstrate, that before the war he also had a bike and sidecar.

"There, have a smoke," the Ami said, and tossed him a pocket of cigarettes. "You got a family, Grandpa?"

"Yes, a girl of fifteen and another of two and a half," Emil told him.

"Here, have some chocolate and a tin of milk for them."

Emil could not believe this. Were these the people who supposedly were raping and plundering Germany? He thanked him and said his goodbyes and carried on. Next he came upon a queue. A queue meant food, and he joined. The queue was for a baker; he had managed to bake a few loaves. After an hour queuing, he got his two loaves. Things were looking up, at least he was not going back empty handed.

Not many shops were open, and most had empty shelves. However, his survival instincts told him to concentrate on flour, sugar, lard, and baking powder. *This must be better than the odd loaf of bread. We can make our own until things get better.* He told himself he deserved a drink before starting back. On the table next to him, sat a young fellow with his hand in plaster. "Did you help with the fighting?" Emil wanted to know.

"No, I fell over an ammunition box and broke my wrist. So much for the fighting."

"Was it very hard?" was his next question.

"Yes and no. Up to the town, it seemed to be foot by foot, but then the town was vacated very quickly, as they did not want to be involved in house-to-house fighting with a lot of damage to the town."

As it was getting late, he thought he better start on his journey back. He had forgotten that he had rucksacks full of food. Every step was an effort, carrying these full rucksacks. His breathing was given him trouble from the job in the coal mines – it had affected his lungs. He wanted to lie down and rest for a while, but he knew Klara was very worried. At last, after a few hours – it was pitch black by now – Emil spotted the lodge. He gently tapped a secret tap on the door. No light was showing, at least Klara had listening to him. Klara opened the secret locks and bolts and smothered him with kisses.

"I must go away more often," he joked, "with such a welcome."

"Tell us all the news, and what are the Americans like?"

"I cannot believe the state of the Americans. Very friendly, but sloppy in comparison to our armies," was his reply.

"And what about other news? Are our soldiers driving them back and winning?"

"I don't think there is much winning going on. Morale amongst the people is getting low and most are worrying that we are losing the war. But enough of war, look all at all the goodies I brought back. Tonight, we have a feast, but from tomorrow we still have to cut further with rationing our food. The shops are very empty. I was lucky not to have been caught on this visit. We must try and find another way to find food. Also, the shooting is out, that can be heard for miles."

So life went on, as if there was no war and they were on another planet, without even a radio. Ignorance was bliss. Even with rationing, after a while stocks were beginning to run down. The only thing left was plenty of the pork. Emil decided to make another visit to town, to see if there was any change. The people in the cottage on the way down, told him that the curfew was still on and the Americans were getting meaner when they caught someone breaking it.

"And how about the war? How is the news there?"

"Not so good," he was told. "They are gaining metre by metre on their way to Berlin. Weimar fell April twelve, followed by Dresden and Munich. However, Heidelberg, our oldest university town, fell with very little damage."

"And what about the new weapons we were promised?" He knows time is running out. He said his goodbyes and carried on.

Yes, there seemed to be more soldiers on the outskirts of the town, and he had to do more ducking and diving, to avoid running into one of these patrols. His problem, also, was being a man. Any able man was eyed with suspicion, as when the German army left, every man able to carry a gun was forced to go with them. Even young boys of fourteen, still believing in the dream, volunteered.

The town was getting itself more organised, not the shambles it was before. American transport flowed freely, which meant that the Americans had conquered much more ground and were well on the way to Berlin. He had hoped that the shops were also a bit more stocked up, but the opposite had happened. More had closed altogether and those open had not much to sell. The ration books he had, were not worth the paper they were written on. He asked one of the shopkeepers what the problem was. Quite simply, the Americans had confiscated all the food, and were not releasing any. What was this all about? *They seemed friendly enough, are they trying to make us weak and starve us to teach us a lesson?* he thought. It was impossible that all the food had gone.

He saw people running to one shop and so did he – it was bread, beautiful bread. He managed to get two loaves of this yellow-golden bread. It turned to be made from sweetcorn, and had no taste at all. The other things he was able to buy, were swedes and carrots. His pride and joy were two pounds of salted herrings, and several pounds of milk powder, which made him jump for joy.

For a short while they carried on as normal, but after another visit to the smallholding below, he was told that it was soon all over. "The Russians have entered Berlin from the east and the Allies from the west." Unbelievably, the dream of a great Germany was ending soon.

"And what about our Fuhrer?" he asked the farmer.

"They'll probably string him up if they catch him. He is held up in his bunker in Berlin, still spuming out that the new weapons are coming. Our soldiers are still fighting to the last man, those who did not want to fight or desert, shot or hanged."

One thing was for sure, every German was terrified of the Russians; their stories of brutality towards any German were unbelievable.

Several days later he, again, set off to town to gather news. What greeted him confirmed his worst fears. Berlin had fallen. Hitler, his wife Eva Braun, Goebbels, with six children, all had committed suicide, and Germany had surrendered, May 7th, 1945.

The atmosphere in town was of jubilation by the Americans, riding on their jeeps, blowing horns, drinking and laughing. All German people had their heads down in disbelief. After all the suffering, all the people and soldiers who had died, the destruction of Germany. What had been achieved? More so, what or where next?

This was the second time Emil had lived through a war. His thoughts went back to the First World War. If it went the same way as then, Germany would be in for a rough ride. The laughing and merrymaking by the Americans, started to become noisier as drink was passed around. Some people were in the street and he knew that only a spark would escalate this situation into a major brawl. Not to be caught in this unhealthy situation, he hurried back home.

"I am so glad to be back home," he murmured to Klara.

"And I am so happy to have you back safe and sound."

They were eager to hear the news, and their faces dropped, as he told them the war was over. After a while, as the news sank into Klara that it was over, no more dying, she said, "As the fighting has stopped, we should celebrate. Let's face it, we were of late fighting a losing battle."

Looking at it from that that angle, yes, she was right to be happy for today.

"From tomorrow onwards there will be a few hard years ahead of us, I have seen it all before," Emil told them. "Money will not be worth anything, and eventually we will lose all the money we saved all our lives."

"What are we to do?" Klara wanted to know.

"Well from tomorrow onwards we have to buy, beg, or steal any food we can lay our hands on if we don't want to starve. Time is still in our favour while there is a curfew on. Annalisa, tomorrow we go to the surrounding villages and beg for food from the farmers."

They started very early on their quest to walk to the nearest village. To save time and avoid being detected they walked on the destroyed railway lines. Six hours of very hard walking brought them to the outskirts of the first village. Both of them were near exhaustion and unable to do more. But Emil spurred Annalisa on. "Just a few more metres. If we see a haystack or some shelter, we try and sleep a few hours." He spotted a small shed and went in. Inside were only a few sheep, and both collapsed in a corner.

Annalisa was the first to wake up. Outside was still dark, she had no idea how long had she been sleeping or where she was. Emil was gently snoring away; she shook him. "Wake up, Vati. It is time to start," she kept saying.

Emil was unable to move for a few minutes. "Every bone in my body is hurting," he complained.

"You should see the size of my blister on my foot," was her reply.

The time was five thirty; the farmers would be up, being early birds. To their best ability they tidied themselves up. The first knock on the first door was the hardest, begging for food. But it is strange how people bond together in times of hardship. Everywhere they asked the farmers and village gave something; the least, a thick slice of bread. Their bread was at least eighteen inches across and ten inches thick, one slice enough for a whole day.

After a few hours of begging, they had a little rest by the village pond. Children were chasing the ducks and also bringing something out of the water.

"What have you got there?" Emil asked one of the kids.

"Duck eggs," he replied. "They lay them in the water."

"Annalisa!" he shouted, all excited. "Go in there and get us some of those eggs, and while you're at it, a nice duck would be nice."

Here we go again, were her thoughts. But for a while she also became a child again, forgetting their hardship. She took off her shoes and splashed around in the water with the other kids. It was not easy to find them, but she found six beautiful duck eggs. As for a duck, these ducks knew how to duck; neither she nor Emil managed to catch one. But after their little rest it was back to knocking on doors. Their rucksacks and bags started to fill up nicely. Things which were not in the shops anymore, like goat's cheese, black pudding, sausages, smoked bacon, apples and much more.

One kind farm lady said, "Come back later when I have made dinner and have some with me." This was an offer they could not refuse. Eventually their bags were full, and any more would be impossible to carry. They made their way back to the farm for dinner; both were so exhausted, nearly not able to eat. But a good cold wash in the yard woke them up. The farm lady had done herself proud and cooked a hearty stew with lots of meat and sausages. She was telling them that both her sons and husband been fighting on the Russian front and she had not heard from either. She also gave them a room for the night. Before going to bed, they thanked her with all their heart, saying, "Hopefully your sons and husband will return safely."

"And I hope a kind person will look after them," she answered.

Very early morning, they started on their way back. Both had the same thought – *How are we going to manage?*

Emil wanted to know how Annalisa was feeling.

"My blister has burst and blood is running into my shoe, and my back is no longer my own, hurting like hell," she told him. "And how are you managing, Vati?"

"I am totally exhausted and my chest is hurting. But the good point is we still have quite a few body parts working," he joked. "I have been thinking, let's try the road, what there is – it is still better than the railway planks. If anything comes we have to hide in the ditches. As they were coming to a steep hill they heard a lorry coming towards them, clanking and puffing along. Smoke was coming out from the side.

"Vati, look, it is on fire."

"No it is not. It is running on a gas conversion fed with potato peels, letting out this horrible smelly smoke."

Milk churns were clanking away on the way to the village. "Interesting," Emil murmured to himself, "looks like the Amis are letting the milk lorry through."

"What are your thoughts?" Annalisa wanted to know.

"Well it comes from the town empty, loads up and comes back this way. What use is that to us? You know nobody is allowed to give a lift. Well we won't ask, we just take." A plan was forming in Emil's head. "Listen carefully, Shatzi. We are at the bottom of a very steep hill, as it rattled past us at no more than fifteen kilometres an hour. Laden up in the middle of the hill, it can do no more than three to four kilometres an hour changing gear. We lay in wait for him just before the middle and as he passes we run and jump onto the back. You run as you've never ran before and climb up. I will then throw the bags up."

It seemed a very long time before they heard, in the distance, the lorry returning. Like two hungry lions, as it came nearer they jumped out from the ditch, running with all their strength to get close. Emil pushed Annalisa up on her backside and hauled the bags after her.

"Oh my god." She felt the lorry speeding up and Emil was still dangling, trying to get a grip. "Vati, give me your hand!" she screamed. She was terrified they would be separated. She pulled on his trousers and hands and finally got him over the edge into the lorry. Both lay there unable to speak for a few minutes. It was heaven to lay there, not needing to walk, as the lorry puffed and clanked along. Of course, this wellbeing did not last long, as the next problem was getting off. No way could they jump off. There was no other way but to knock on the small back window.

The lorry came to an abrupt stop and Emil climbed down.

"What in heaven's name are you doing?" shouted the lorry driver. "If the Amis catch me, I'll lose my licence and livelihood and get locked up."

After a few minutes ranting and raving, he saw the state of them and simmered down. Emil explained the situation they were in, starving in the woods, and shortly they talked like friends.

"So you are in the woods?" the driver wanted to know.

"That's right," was Emil's reply.

"Can you get your hands on wood?" was his next question.

"How much do you want? I've got a whole wood for myself."

A deal was struck for Emil to bring firewood to an arranged meeting place, in exchange for milk and a few other goodies, and of course the occasional lift. These became many black-market transactions in the future. A definite date was set for the first as they said their hearty goodbyes, not forgetting a few litres of milk as a present.

Life was looking good at that moment.

"Mutti will be so pleased," Emil commented. He was a husband and a father, his whole life devoted to his family. They gathered up their bags which seemed lighter now, and set off on their last lap to home.

Klara, of course, had worried herself sick being locked up in the lodge, and her stomach problem had flared up again. But on their safe return it soon got better. She still had not seen any people about. And so, they survived a little longer.

Finally, it happened. The curfew was lifted and the people could move freely about.

"Our problem will start now," Emil commented. "They are all looking for food and shelter."

The food situation was getting worse by the day, with still nothing to buy in the shops. At the moment, it was not affecting them too much with their hoarding. Also, as they could move freely about, they got lifts from the milk lorry. Begging became harder, as many town people were doing the same.

From their outpost they could see everything going on in the fields below. Emil had been watching one particular farmer planting for a while.

"You are so absorbed in watching, Emil. What is so interesting?" Klara wanted to know.

"Can you see what he is up to, Mutti? He is planting something, but what? Potatoes, that is what."

"Well, what are your thoughts?" She could not quite follow where this was leading to.

"Later on, when he is gone we go and dig them up again."

"But that is not fair," Klara protested.

"Would you rather starve now so people can eat tomorrow?" was his answer.

When it started to get dark all four of them sneaked down to the field and dug up the potatoes. Precious potatoes. Even Ingrid had a little spoon to help digging, and she thought it was fun doing this. They worked very hard until midnight, and then carried their sack back to the lodge.

Next morning, the farmer was back to plant the rest of the field. Emil was watching as he stood by the part where they had dug up his potatoes, scratching his head as he realised what had happened. Emil had planned to go once more that evening.

They all got dressed to go down, when he saw a light shining. The farmer had put a guard with a dog on the field to protect his potatoes. Well, that was the end of the potato robbery.

One day when they were peacefully eating, there was a knock on the door. Everybody jumped. All the windows and doors were locked and Emil peeped out of the window. He saw a very smartly dressed man standing there. He opened the door to him. "Good morning," he said, "my name is Hans Schroder, and I am the owner of the lodge." There was a stunned silence for a moment to digest this revelation. Even Ingrid stopped playing; she knew by their faces something was wrong.

They had always anticipated that this moment would happen, and knew they could not have the lodge forever. The first one to recover from this shock was Klara. "Please come in and sit yourself down, Herr Schroder," and she offered him a cup of coffee. As she busied herself, making the imitation from corn which tasted dreadful, Emil tried to explain their situation.

"Herr Hohmann," he said, "I have not come here to make trouble." He looked around, seeing how homely Klara had made the lodge. "I am overjoyed that I was able to help a fellow countryman, and I must say how delighted I am with how well you looked after the lodge."

He was such a well-spoken man. About sixty-five years old and looking and speaking like an aristocrat.

"As far as I am concerned you can stay until you've sorted yourself out, Herr Hohmann, or can I say Emil? If you could bring some wood down to me in town, we call it a fair exchange."

They all thanked him and promised not to let him down.

When he had left, they all sighed with relief, to have sorted out this problem so amicably. When they first took over the lodge little did they realise that the felled wood would help with their surviving. It also kept Emil busy. Herr Schroder lent them a little cart, and Annalisa and Emil made their weekly trip to town.

Emil and Herr Schroder became good friends; he looked forward to their weekly visits. He was on his own, having lost both sons in the war, and his wife died of a broken heart. He always had a few goodies for them, especially Ingrid, as he spoke, heartbroken. "I will never have grandchildren with all of them gone."

One of their visits, he seemed not to be his usual self, very withdrawn. Emil did a lot of probing. "Come on, Heinrich. What is wrong?" he asked.

He finally said, "The allies have readjusted the occupation line, and we will come under Russian occupation."

The splitting of Germany had already been decided, as far back as 1944. There were to be three zones. This was to ensure Germany could never be strong again. However, the allies were not happy with the land the Russians wanted to have. Poland and Czechoslovakia did not wait until the agreement. They cleared whole areas of German people. Poland took, besides the old borders before the war, extra

German land, roughly the size of Scotland. The extent was that millions of German people were pushed into West Germany.

For a moment, Emil was speechless.

"Oh my god, this cannot be!" He gasped at the horrible news. "We have all been living in cuckoo land, hoping that soon life will get better. Instead we can look forward to more hunger, rape and plunder."

The stories which circulated over the years of brutality to any German prisoner they took, were so bad that quite a few committed suicide, especially the SS, if they had the chance, rather than become prisoners of war.

This was their retaliation to the brutality Germany inflicted on the Russian people. Among the German troops were special battalions of ex-prisoners to do all the dirty work. When Berlin was taken over, the Russian soldiers went on a rampage of rape and inflicting unheard hardship on the people. Even though things had improved and harsh sentences were handed out to the armies, it still went on.

Looking at Annalisa, Emil did not wanted to take this chance. With her blonde hair and good looks, she had grown into a young teenager, no longer a child. "When is this supposedly happening?" he asked Heinrich.

"In the next few months, that is all I know," was his reply.

"Come on, Annalisa. We have to get back to Mutti."

They hurried home with their little cart.

Klara knew at once, looking at their faces. "What is it?" she wanted to know.

"You better sit down for what I've got to tell you." And he broke the news to her.

"No! No!" she cried. "Not the Russians, they will kill us all."

"Not if I can help it," Emil told her, and held her in his arms. "Look, let's eat and sleep on it, and tomorrow we'll look at the situation with a clear head."

This motto stayed with Annalisa all her life – there will always be a tomorrow.

But sleep did not come easily, each one with their dreams of the nightmare to come.

After breakfast, Emil rummaged through the drawers to find a map of Germany. Working out the distance, it was at least 300km to get back to Xanten. He was muttering to himself and shaking his head. With no trains running or any transport working in this devastation, the only way to get back, was to walk. He looked at little Ingrid, not yet potty trained, and Klara with her stomach problems. It was impossible to attempt. For once, he was at a loss and became very depressed for a couple of days.

Eventually he went to see his friend Heinrich and poured his heart out with his problem. After listening for a while, he offered his advice. "Look here, Emil. I have a suggestion to make. The little cart which you use to bring the wood down to me, you can have it. With a few alterations, you can fix it. When Klara can no longer walk, she can sit or lay in it, and you pull it. For Ingrid, you've got the pram still. Only take food, everything else, you store at mine in the attic, and hopefully collect at a later date."

"You are the best friend. And what about you? You told me you have been in the Nazi Party."

"I am staying and too old to run. After all, they cannot look up or shoot everybody."

Emil was over the moon with this solution and rushed back to Klara.

"Are you sure we can do this?" she wanted to know.

He assured her, saying, "If Hannibal can come over the mountain with his elephant, so can we." He also had to believe it could be done as there was no other option.

Klara became very depressed, having to leave her last few possessions behind. Over the years she had collected priceless wall plaques and figurines. But as there was no choice, she started wrapping, and Emil set to work converting this cart. DIY was not Emil's strong point; he was a great believer, if anything needs doing, call in a tradesman. But after strengthening, and adding a new handle to pull the cart, it started looking like a possibility. He also added a board to put out for Mutti to stretch her legs.

Everything was oiled and cleaned, and at last, ready for the journey. Also, a miracle occurred – Ingrid started using her potty. Big deal, one would say, but there were no nappies to buy, and Klara had to manage with rags and then wash them. It was a very big deal.

Emil and Annalisa still took as much wood down to Heinrich. And also their few bits and pieces. He had been to Frau Horten and collected the things they had left behind there. Everything was stored in the attic. Herr Schroder came up to the lodge to look up and wish them well on their way. He took Emil to one side and gave him a gun and ammunition, just in case.

But it took until the next year for the 243rd army to conquer Xanten. The main obstacle was the Rhine, especially near Xanten where it was very fast flowing and approximately 500 metres wide. As kids, it became a Dare game – who could swim the shortest distance across this fast river? On 10th March 1945 Montgomery's army opposite Xanten attempted the crossing. They had tried at Arnheim and Emerick without success. Arnheim was one of the disasters of the war, the best English airborne division was wiped out with 6,642 English soldiers captured by the German army and 1,200 dead. Montgomery remarked that Arnheim was a bridge too far. Mother nature was also against the English as the mighty river defeated them without support. Further away in Ramargen, troops managed on 7th March to cross the Rhine. Hitler shot four officers at once for letting this happen.

The winter months were quite kind with the weather being warmer than usual. Being warmer than usual it rained constantly which indirectly helped to defend Germany as the roads turned into mud tracks. By December rain turned into snow and the enemy armies could not advance any further. The Hurtgen Forest near Xanten was about thirty square miles and it was fought over metre by metre with thousands of men dying because of it. Also, the bitter fighting in January in Reicwood was very fierce; Xanten changed hands seven times. There was not a tree left when the fighting finished. The surrounding areas of Xanten were fought over for over three months and by the end of it not a house was left standing. The crossing was made on 23rd March with English paratroops landing and destroying the last of the German troops by March 25th. The loss of life on both sides was colossal.

What a pitiful sight Annalisa and her family looked. They had a little cart and pram which rolled down the hill in order to get to the larger roads. These were still in a dreadful state after all the bombardment and fighting. The Panzers and heavy transport vehicles of the Americans made matters worse. Not one train was running, as when the German army retreated what was intact was blown up. There was no sense to it but thousands of bridges, anything and everything, was blown up. What they did not expect to see was the growing number of people on the roads. *Who are all these people and where are they all going?* Klara wondered. Emil thought they were just like them, desperately trying to get home. With every mile the quantity of people increased, which decreased their progress.

The reality was, all the people who had fled from the allies from the west to the east, were now fleeing the opposite way, from the east to the west. An estimated six million people were on the move. In addition, all the foreign workers, approximately nine million people, were on the move too, trying to get back. Italians, French, Dutch, Norwegians, Danes, etc. Then all the German people expelled from Poland alone equalled nine million, as when they conquered Poland they resettled it with the Germans.

The clever person was General de Gaulle, who put disputed land near France to a referendum and gave it back to Germany. But Russia agreed that Poland was in favour, that they would keep the east part of Germany, and didn't give it back. Then the prisoners of war were released from the camps, which then created a cocktail of twenty-four million people on the move in all directions.

The first day of walking was about twenty kilometres which would take them about three weeks to get back. Klara and Ingrid were feeling well, and they decided at their first stop when they passed some ruins, that the little cart was converted into a bed for Klara and Ingrid got the pram. Emil and Annalisa had to make do with the ground. Emil was still happy, though, as it was going better than expected. But it was only day one.

Emil also had made a secret compartment in the cart for their food. Therefore, once they had eaten they packed everything away and then Klara would sleep on top of everything.

The next day started quite well. Ingrid continued to use her potty. By the evening they came across a camp that was being set up by the Red Cross and UNRA. Everybody got a hot meal and for the frailer people, a bed to sleep on. Emil felt that luck was on their side and it was the best deal they'd had in a long time. There appeared to be little crime or fighting between all the different people. There was a camaraderie between them all. As Mr Churchill said, the German people were like sheep and would do as they were told. Which at the moment, was surviving.

The prompt action by the allies and Red Cross in

setting up these camps prevented epidemics. When they left in the morning they were given a note telling them where the next camp was, which was about 50km away. This would not be possible to achieve with all of the people on the roads, but it gave them a goal to aim for.

Emil worried that his cart and pram would not survive the journey due to the poor condition of the roads, as every village, town and city had the same stories of destruction. However, the weather was still with them and they still had each other. Klara's health seemed to hold out and with all the walking, she starting to become fitter and leaner. This little plump woman became a size twelve svelte person. However, Ingrid did not seem to grow at all and people would feel sorry for her. But Annalisa had filled out and had turned into a pretty young lady. Her main problem was outgrowing her dresses, which all started to look like minis, therefore she started to wear Emil's trousers which made her look and feel quite destitute.

Weeks later, they were still travelling and their positive thoughts started to desert them. The Red Cross and UNRA sites became lifesavers, for at least they could get something hot to eat and drink. If they were lucky Klara would even get a bed sometimes.

After about twenty-five days they finally reached the Rhine. If you closed your eyes you could almost smell the bloodshed, as if you counted all of the dead who had fought along the Rhine, it was one of the bloodiest battlefields of the war.

They had now entered the English zone after being in the American zone, and saw the difference between the brash Americans and then being greeted by polite, caring English soldiers. If they could help in any way, they would. They felt that finally they could start to relax a little and whatever lay ahead of them, they would be able to cope with. However, it still took another four days before they reached home – Xanten. The closer they got, the devastation became worse. Not a tree, house or animal had survived this futile war. Klara was in tears most of the time. Emil tried to cheer her up by saying they should be grateful that they had each other.

When they finally reached their beautiful wooden apartment, they looked on in disbelief at the total flattening of their place – all that remained was the basement. Klara now cried in total abandonment as this was her dream that they had walked back for. Emil said, "A pile of rubble should not get you down." Klara wanted to know what they should do and Emil said they needed to go into Xanten itself and look for shelter.

When they reached Xanten, luck was on their side. On the outskirts of Xanten, a three-storey house half stood, as if someone had taken a chainsaw and sliced it in half from top to bottom with half refusing to lay down and die. Emil found a way in from the back and opened the door for the others. One reception room was intact, however, the staircase was all gone, but at least they had one room which kept them dry. Once more, exhausted bodies lay down to sleep. They had accomplished what they had set out to do and were at least back in familiar surroundings.

Under normal circumstances most things look better after a night's sleep, but opening the door in the morning, all that greeted them was mountains of rubble where houses had once stood. Deep craters became the tombs of what were once homes where families had lived and laughed. Where roads had once been, they now towered above like man-made mountains of cement and brick. Klara felt very depressed, as she thought things would be better, but now did not feel quite so cheerful. Their food supplies were very low and they hadn't had hot food or drink for four days, and this became their priority. They ate their last bit of crusty stale bread and even though German brown bread lasts for quite a while, even this had seen its sell-by date.

Emil, positive as usual, said they could sort this too, and even managed to get Klara to give a small smile.

Emil left to see how the situation really was. He boarded the house up and told Klara that under no circumstances should she let anyone in. Annalisa understood the importance of Emil's words and knew that no one would get in whilst her father was away.

Emil could find hardly anyone about. Finally he came across someone and asked why it was so empty. When the allied forces conquered Xanten, the people who were left were put into a large camp twenty miles away. The ones that had fled. like this man. were only starting to slowly trickle back now. Emil asked if the man had stayed during the fighting, and he had. He explained how terrible the fighting was, as Xanten changed hands seven times. The German soldiers tried their hardest not to give one centimetre. So many died but he didn't know where they had all been buried. "Those of us who stayed hid in our cellars to survive."

Emil then said where they were staying, and was

told that this house belonged to a Protestant family and the church was looking after the property. Emil asked about water but Xanten had no running water, it all came from pumps either in the streets or in people's houses. A pump that Emil could use was by the cathedral. From all this devastation, the cathedral had only lost one steeple and had managed to survive.

Emil wanted to know about food.

"The Red Cross comes once a week to distribute some food and occasionally you can buy something."

Emil then went back to share the news with his family. They prioritised their needs and as usual, food was at the top of their agenda, as they needed to get something warm into their bodies. In order to do this, they needed a fire. Emil put something together with stones and wire outside, which looked like a very crude barbeque. Next, wood was collected and then they had a fire. However, in order to cook one must have a pot. This wasn't a problem as Emil had brought home German soldiers' helmets which were lying about, and converted one into a pot. This became a popular item on the black market for everyone to cook with. They still had some pork and potatoes and for the first time in ages they sat contentedly eating their hot meal. The finest chef in the world could not have produced a better meal, as this meagre meal was so appreciated by all, eaten under a roof, not the open sky.

The next day they boarded up their shelter and got ready to visit the Protestant vicar. He was very pleased to see them as the Protestant community was tiny in Xanten, Annalisa being the only girl on her confirmation with several other boys. He felt sure that

Mr and Mrs Honniker would only be too pleased if they looked after their house until they returned. This was a great weight off their shoulders and now the food problem became their focus. If all failed, then Emil said they would have to go begging again.

They went to their old apartment to see if food still remained in their basement. But what greeted them when they climbed down into their basement where they had killed the cow, all that was left was a few well-picked bones. However, there was a horrible smell as the potatoes and carrots and other stuff had been doused with petrol, they thought by the allies, and some soldiers had even defecated in hate over the food stocks.

They went back, empty handed and very down. The English occupation was less noticeable than the American occupation, as this time they were more or less left alone. But Klara, when she walked into town, befriended one of the soldiers. He was there to ensure that they behaved themselves and on another occasion, Annalisa went with her. He became a regular visitor and he only had a few bits himself, which he brought with him, but this made a big difference to them.

Their other problem was a lack of electricity, so he brought them a lamp, and this made a big difference as they could stay up later into the evening. When you ventured out at night the most amazing sight would greet you. The people who returned to their own houses would make their basement good enough to live in, and most German houses are built with a watertight basement to store food and other things like their bikes. As Xanten was below the water table they had to be extra secure to not let the water in. Because of this, the basements of these bombed out houses had survived quite well. At night the bizarre sight of makeshift chimneys and spots of light beamed out of the earth and rubble covered the rest. Bricks were no problem as the whole town was covered in them.

Chapter 9

Annalisa had a friend called Hannelore, who was a year older then her and was very streetwise. For when it came to men and sex, these were never discussed in Annalisa's household. Annalisa was therefore pretty naive. Her total sex education from her father was not to come home if she got herself pregnant. But she was never told how she was to get pregnant. Hannelore came visiting one day and spoke about her new boyfriend and how big his penis was. After she left, Klara hit the roof with anger and disbelief. How could she say that in her house? She said that she could not come in again. However, Annalisa wanted to know what all the fuss was about and found Hannelore, who told her all.

The English soldier, Robert, was still a frequent visitor and on one of his visits he asked Klara whether Annalisa could go for a ride to the nearest town in his truck as he had to collect something. Annalisa wanted to and Klara agreed. They set off and he was a very likeable fellow as a friend. After all, he was only a few years older than her. Once he had collected his boxes they started back. They drove through some woodland and he suggested that they stop and have a picnic, as he had some food and drink which was greatly appreciated. He then tried to cuddle and kiss Annalisa. However, he became quite insistent and pinned her to the ground. She shouted at him to let her go but he became more and more excited and had no intention of letting go, and started to rip her clothes off. She tried her hardest to fight him off and in her panic bit his nose. The pain made him let go of her and his nose bled profusely. He realised what he had done and tried his hardest to apologise to Annalisa.

Annalisa wanted to walk home but finally agreed to let him drive her back. Klara saw the state of Annalisa and asked what had happened but Annalisa was too ashamed to say. All she would say is that she never wanted to see Robert again. Hannelore said he had nearly raped her and told her to go to the police, who would deal with it as this shouldn't happen, and told Annalisa what love was about and that wasn't it. Annalisa did not want everyone to know and as her honour was still intact she wanted to just put it down to experience and forget about it. She was also upset with her mother for letting her go, as she felt that she must have had an inkling that something might happen. The outcome being that now their food became even scarcer.

Annalisa and Emil went begging, as they still had no food and were basically eating starvation rations of about 800 calories a day. For the allies this was one of their biggest problems, sorting out a supply of food. In Thüringen the farms had been left mainly alone, but in Xanten the opposite was the case as nothing had been left. No animals were in sight and if any farmer could get hold of a chicken or any other animal, it would be kept indoors under lock and key. The animals were so precious that the farmers would rather sleep outside and keep the animals safe inside. But however bad things were, the farmers would try to give whatever they could to help people survive. One of the last farms that they went to, Emil was asked if he would like to work for food. He was delighted to. They had problems with tools for planting and then no one to plant with them apart from the very old or very young. The rest were either dead or in prison camps, especially any soldiers in Russian hands. They had very little chance of returning.

So a deal was struck where Emil would work every day and get food in return. Every morning Emil would walk ¾ of an hour to the farm, work eight hours, and then walk back, but he was very happy that at least his family could now eat. Every evening he would return with two litres of milk. Half that Klara would use, and the other half was put into shallow dishes, skimmed off, and on Sundays shaken until it turned into butter. The buttermilk was Klara's favourite drink. Emil would eat at the farm and had only one complaint – that the sandwiches they made for him were liver sausage with treacle on top. He didn't mind the treacle, just the combination. But it was food and eventually he worked up the courage to tell them. He also brought home sugar beet, which they would then take to a factory which had just started again, and they would turn it into sugar and more treacle!! This factory was about 8km away but they had plenty of time to get there and back. If they were lucky they could hitch a ride as everybody still tried to help each other.

Unfortunately, just as they had settled themselves into a resemblance of normal life, the people who owned the house returned. Until this moment they had only encountered kindness, however, these people ranted and raved at Emil as if they had bombed the house themselves, when in fact they had made the house more secure. Emil tried his best to pacify them but in the end he went and fetched the priest. He confronted the priest with these people and asked the priest to tell them that they had asked him for permission. The answer from a man of god was the last thing they expected. He looked them straight in the face and lied, saying he had never given them any permission, and Annalisa felt a distrust and dislike for religion. It made her look at religion in a different light. The people insisted that they leave immediately and in a few hours, they had packed their few meagre possessions and once again were homeless.

Klara looked up at Emil and once again said, "What now, Emil? What now?"

For a while, for the first time, even he was speechless and demoralised, and had no answer to give.

Emil wanted to find somewhere with Annalisa whilst they left Klara with Ingrid. Eventually they found another ruin for shelter where three walls were standing, and part of the ceiling. This time they decided not to ask permission, just take possession. Ingrid and Klara were then installed into their new abode. Klara promptly had one of her attacks and Ingrid cried her eyes out.

It was up to Emil and Annalisa to clear out all the rubble and dirt, so at least they could put the bedding down for Mutti to lay on. After a few hours of hard work, they finally had cleared a corner, and once more four exhausted people lay down to sleep. But luck was not on their side; during the night it started raining, with thunderstorms raging. Rain was coming through every hole in the ceiling, and however hard they tried to move from place to place, they got wet. In the next few days, the weather did not get any better. All four huddled together to keep dry.

Ingrid started coughing and not feeling well. By now, a doctor had arrived in the town, and they took Ingrid to him. A makeshift hospital had also been set up.

"I am afraid she is quite ill," the doctor said. "She has got phomonia. I have to keep her here in the hospital." The doctor inquired as to their circumstances, and advised them to see the temporary town council for help. Saying goodbye to Ingrid, Mutti cried her heart out.

They went to see the people in charge. Two bedraggled people told them of their plight. They were not alone in this terrible situation, but German efficiency had taken over. Every house, barn, shed which had survived in any form, was listed in the town and countryside. Everyone had to share with their fellow countryman. They were told of a lady on her own, her husband still missing on the Russian front. She had a small holding about forty-five minutes' walk from town, which had survived. She had told them that she could only accommodate two people, but the council told them to go along, try to convince her to take them all.

Emil and Klara thanked them for their effort and went off to see the lady. Annalisa had to stay behind to watch over their few possessions.

This house was on the main road out of Xanten and pretty deserted, with not one car passing as they walked along. It had taken about one hour, when they spotted, on the roadside, this little house.

"My god, this is small," Emil commented. "You cannot swing a cat in there."

Klara took over and knocked on the door. A very nice woman in her thirties opened the door. Klara explained why they were there; she then asked them in. Her name was Frau Janson, and she made them a cup of imitation coffee. She explained, "As you can see, this house is very small and I cannot see where I can put four people. Believe me, I really want to help. Let me show you around."

The little cottage had one room either side downstairs; you walked through an inner room which housed the pump and a basin and then led to the back for the animals. And to their amazement, two cows were happily munching away.

"What about upstairs?" Emil wanted to know.

"I'll show you," Frau Janson replied.

Upstairs was only one room with sloping sides, only able to hold a small double bed. Klara had by now already become firm friends with Frau Janson. She had this knack for quickly making friends, but also, if they did not return this friendship in every way, they were cut off at once. She convinced Frau Janson that they would manage very well with the one room downstairs, and the other upstairs, until a larger place could be found. Frau Janson was still a little bit uncertain, but Emil said, "There must be times when you need a man to help with the chores, and I am willing in every way to do so."

Frau Janson, who had been alone for a long time, was pleased to have the company and help. She was a very efficient woman, who had managed amazingly well for being alone. She told them that her husband had been reported missing in Russia and her only child died of diphtheria.

When Emil and Klara left and were out of eyesight, Emil grabbed Klara and danced for joy in the empty road. "I told you things would get better again. Not only have we got a roof above our head, the farmer where I work is nearby, and I don't have to walk the forty-five minutes there and back anymore."

As fast as they were able to, they rushed back to Annalisa and their belongings. They also looked in on Ingrid; she was much better, her little face nearly back to normal colour. Before, it was all puffed up and a red colour. Mutti hugged her and told her, "When you are better and come out of hospital, we have a new home for you. It is small, but there are animals to care for and room to play."

She started to cry. "But when will I come out of the hospital?" she asked.

"It will take a while for you to be fully well," Mutti replied. "We'll come every day to visit you. It is up to you to be a strong girl and get better." Klara was holding back her own tears; she knew her little girl was a fighter. "Bye-bye now, Liebling (darling)," she said, and they left Ingrid in good hands.

Off they went to their new home. Frau Janson had used the one room downstairs as a kitchen and sitting room ready for them to move into, with a lovely big oven for cooking and heating. She said that she had a smaller oven for herself which she and Emil had taken out from the stable. For during the day there was a sofa, which doubled up at night as a bed for Annalisa. The three of them would sleep in the attic room.

Water needed to be fetched from the small middle room, which had the pump in it. There was a large sink to be used for washing, washing up, and all other chores. The weekly bath was to be in the shed where the cows and animals were. For this, water had to be heated then taken into the shed, to a large tin bath, and one by one they would have a bath in the same water. Being used to running water all their previous life, this was a culture shock to them. But to have a home again, nothing else mattered. The toilet was in the cowshed as well. A hole in the ground, but for the cows being there, nice and warm. And so, they settled in.

Ingrid came home a few weeks later, her usual happy self, liking her new home. Emil went to work every day and life once more was orderly. As the weeks went by, trains started running again, and electricity was restored in the big cities. Of course, Xanten was still in the dark ages with no electric and no pumps by the road. But even there, the road in the town centre was being cleared, with the craters filled in and repaired. Food was as bad as ever. Yes, they had ration books, but there was nothing to be bought. The family, as such, survived not too badly, as Emil worked for food, and brought the food home.

Klara started complaining that all her beautiful ornaments and china plates, her last precious possessions, were going to be lost forever.

Annalisa and Hannelore had become good friends, and were running around together. In one of her outbursts Hannelore suggested, "Frau Hohmann, why don't Annalisa and I go and get your things?" Klara thought this to be a brilliant idea.

When Emil came home in the evening, Klara could not tell him of her idea for the girls to fetch their possessions from Thüringen quick enough. Emil was not pleased with that idea at all and he protested. "So far we stayed alive and now you want to send them 330km away for a few lousy ornaments?" he shouted at her. "They are so young; anything can happen to them."

"Hannelore is eighteen years old and Annalisa nearly sixteen," was her answer.

As usual he gave in to her request.

Chapter 10

The year was 1946 and Germany was beginning to live again, to its best ability. Food was still the biggest problem and the black market started blooming. What little possessions people had left were exchanged for food, to the extent that cameras and other good items changed hands for miserly bits of food. As usual, the big cities were worse off. Klara's craving was for real coffee, and sometimes when Emil got eggs from the farmer, to please her, he changed two eggs for a soupspoon of coffee beans. The most ingenious recipes were dreamt of for cooking and baking. The only one Annalisa could remember was how to make imitation marzipan from semolina, as she had a very sweet tooth.

The Allied forces were very much stamping this out; anyone caught ended up in prison. To reduce the sentence they had to eat the wares they peddled. The unlucky ones who maybe had salted herrings or other delicacies served the sentence instead. In Berlin alone 3,000 thousand racketeers were rounded up in one day.

Emil also acquired the smallest battery radio. At last, they heard the news of things going on in the wide world. In their immediate surroundings, you could still not see one animal, all under lock and key. But crime as such, other than petty thieving, was unheard of. And so, the girls got themselves ready for their 330km trip to Thüringen. Klara made as many sandwiches for Annalisa as she could spare, and gave her a bottle of water.

Emil took Annalisa to one side to tell her something. "Look here, Schatzi, I am not happy for you to go, but you know what Mutti is like."

Oh yes, she knew what Mutti was like, and he stuffed money into her hands. They would have to pay for the trains and other items. Not that money was worth anything, but for certain things, money was still accepted. He also gave her the gun he had. "Don't tell Hannelore about it, this is purely for your protection, and only to be used in an absolute emergency. I hope sincerely you never need to use it."

The teenagers then set off, old in their minds, saying goodbye. Both were pretty in their own way; Annalisa with her long blonde hair, nearly five feet five inches, a very wholesome size 12-14, filled out in all the right places. She wore long brown boots and a multi-coloured rabbit jacket. Both had been acquired by Emil, and she was looking and feeling a million dollars. Hannelore, on the other hand, was very pretty, shorter than Annalisa – five feet three inches, and had short dark hair.

The backpacks had only the minimal items of clothing in, plus the food, to save space for the way back. It was a pleasure for the girls to carry so little. The first part of the journey was the hardest, as the trains were only running from Duisburg, about 60km away. Anyone with transport would give hitchhikers a lift because of the problem with no local trains or buses. The hitchhiking did not create a problem for the girls; anyone would give two pretty girls a lift and soon they got on their way. Anything was acceptable, mostly farm lorries ferried about. A car was a luxury beyond dreams.

"How are you?" Annalisa asked Hannelore.

"I am all right but my feet are hurting like hell due to the wrong shoes."

Finally they arrived at the railway station, changing a couple of lifts and walking, and so were the other thousands – all trying to get a train. After making enquiries the train was only running once a day, the following day. "Well let's find a spot for the night," Hannelore suggested, not an easy task amongst all these crowds of people. After deciding, they settled down to Clara's sandwiches and drink, and sleep, when they huddled up to each other.

The next day the quantity of people had dwindled when their train finally came. But still the train was full to capacity with people occupying every inch of room. It was the floor again, between kids and grownups alike. After hour upon hour of this agonising journey they arrived at their destination. What greeted them was a nasty surprise. All along the platform Russian soldiers were stationed, guns at the ready.

"Oh my god," Hannelore whispered to Annalisa. "What now?" she asked.

"Let's play it by ear," Annalisa whispered back.

They checked every identity card very slowly, most people allowed to go on their way.

Closer and closer they came towards the two girls. After looking at their identity cards, they were told to join the group on the left. A long time had gone by when at last all people had been checked and let go except for this group of 25-30 people. Hannelore whispered to Annalisa, "I am terrified. What will they do to us?"

There was no need for Annalisa to answer as a lorry came along, and all were told to climb into it. All of them were frightened, not understanding one word that was spoken. The soldiers looked very grim and nasty; there had been so many stories of rape and cruelty.

"I thought the Russians not to be here yet, at least that's what I have been told," Annalisa whispered to her.

A very rough command told Annalisa to keep quiet. The lorry rattled along for about 45 minutes, when it slowed down and came to a standstill in a courtyard. To Annalisa it looked like a prison, with large black stone walls. Again, another rough command and gestures to follow the soldiers. A very large room was their last command to be ushered into. Some of the women started crying, and the boys and men looked very bewildered.

By now it was getting dark as evening was approaching; no explanation as to why they were here. Annalisa pointed to a corner and told Hannelore to go for it, to sit down. They huddled together and, not letting the others see, had a bite to eat.

Other than one guard sitting at his desk and smoking his cigarette rolled with newspaper, there was nothing happening. Everyone made themselves as comfortable as possible. Hour after hour went by and evening became night. Some people started sleeping and the girls did the same.

Morning finally came with everybody looking exhausted and also hungry. One of the men who spoke a little Russian was told to be quiet. If anyone needed the toilet, a guard would take them. Around 10 o'clock some movement was happening. A very nasty woman, about 40 years old with very short cropped hair, in a soldier's uniform with lots of medals, appeared. She walked by the cage inspecting the animals, or so it felt. She shared a look with a soldier, gave him a command, and disappeared.

One by one they were taken away, presumably to be interrogated. As none of the people came back, the remaining still did not know what fate awaited them. Around 12 o'clock it was Annalisa's turn. Her mind was racing when she entered an office. She thought back to her first year in school; this woman seated behind a desk, was the image of her first teacher, or worse. She was terrified that she would find the gun. During the night she tried her hardest to push it somewhere, but there was always someone awake and watching. When she went to the toilet she was frisked there and back. And so it stayed well wrapped up in her knickers.

This woman took a long look at her without speaking. She did not look good, quite bedraggled; she had not washed for three days and had slept rough. Finally she spoke to her in perfect German, asking her name and where she came from and why she was here. During the night, Annalisa and

Hannelore had concocted a story that they could not find their parents in the west, and came to stay with an uncle. She probed some more but eventually was satisfied with the story. Next she wanted to know what she had in her rucksack and to bring it over to her. "Only a little food and some underwear," Annalisa told her. With a long stick she started poking around in it, but did not want to touch, as if Annalisa had the plague.

At last she stopped, not finding the gun. Annalisa's heart had also stopped. She told her to leave town immediately and find her uncle. This, she was only too happy to do, and rushed out of the room. Once outside she was promptly sick. But her worries were not over – she had to wait for Hannelore and prayed she would stick to the story.

An hour or so had gone by when Hannelore appeared. The girls hugged each other without speaking a word. Walking as fast as possible away from the prison, they now had to find the way to Herr Schroder. They had no clue where they were, but after making enquiries the town they wanted was about 20km away. The last of the stale sandwiches were eaten and once more they went on their way. Between walking and hitchhiking, their goal was in sight.

Knocking on the door, Herr Schroder could not believe his eyes when he opened up, to see two very bedraggled girls in front of him. "Is that really you?" was his question after recognising Annalisa.

"Can we come in and I'll tell you all about us being here?" she replied. He hugged Annalisa, as he'd always had a soft spot for her, and greeted Hannelore politely.

"We have come to collect Klara's bits and pieces, if that is all right with you."

"Look, girls," he said as he steered them into the kitchen, "first you eat, then wash and sleep, and tomorrow you tell me all about your ordeal."

In the morning when both girls had a very good night's sleep, everything looked better. Herr Schroder, what a lovely man, was busy in the kitchen making breakfast, with the coffee smell wafting through the air. He shared his meagre rations with the girls.

"How is the food situation now, Herr Schroder?" Annalisa wanted to know.

"Not a lot better," he replied. "I have several friends with farms – they help out. I have been shooting once, from the lodge. Being an old man, I don't need that much," explained Herr Schroder.

"That brings me to the gun, I brought it back to you," Annalisa stated. She told him all about the family, and their hardship to get back. "And what about you and the Russians? How are they treating you?"

"In general they behave themselves, keeping a lower profile than the noisy Americans. At present there are not too many here, but they seem to be increasing. They are checking everyone leaving town. As much as I would like you to stay longer, I suggest you leave as soon as possible. Yesterday I saw heavy cranes coming in and lorries with building material, I don't know what for. Maybe they are building a wall around us," he joked.

That made Annalisa's mind up, to leave the next day.

The little iron bath which had been left behind, was packed and repacked with Mutti's ornaments and china, so it would not be too heavy to carry. Herr Schroder suggested they keep the gun once more for their safety.

The next day, after a lot of hugging and kissing, they said their goodbyes, and promised to come and see him as soon as things improved. Little did they realise, this was not to be. Every step they took, they worried about being caught, looking out for any problems. When finally they reached the railway station, it was free of Russian soldiers. A sigh of relief came over them. It was getting nearer and nearer to the time the train was due to arrive, when out of the blue, a company of Russian soldiers arrived. Again, identity cards were checked.

"I am terrified," Annalisa whispered to Hannelore.

Again, several people were not allowed on the train, including our pair. Hannelore started protesting. "We have been checked before by one of the soldiers." But he refused to listen to this girl telling him what to do. He shouted something in Russian and shoved them towards the others.

Both lost their cool and started shaking and crying. This time there was no lorry, they were marched to the outskirts of the town and pushed into a large barn. Once inside they realised that there were already fifteen to twenty young people in there. An older man of about forty-five came forward, and introduced himself. "My name is Hans, and you are?" he wanted to know.

"Annalisa and Hannelore," they answered.

"Have you been here long?" Annalisa enquired.

"About four days," he replied.

"And what happens next?" Hannelore wanted to know.

"You will be taken to the next town and interrogated."

"But we have been there already. What are they looking for?"

"Be very careful how you answer, especially questions about the Hitler Youth movement."

For the present, there was no more to be done, other than find a place to sit and maybe sleep. They spread out their only blanket on top of straw, being plentiful in the barn, and sat down. The biggest worry was to hide the gun. In this large barn, easily done, and when no one was looking, they hid it between some rafters. That accomplished, there was nothing else to do other than relax. As Herr Schroder had given them sandwiches for their journey, hunger was not yet an issue. But they tried to hide it from the others, eating only a few bites.

"We don't know how long they'll keep us here." Annalisa spoke to Hannelore. "And this food has to last us."

Nightfall finally came, but not sleep. In the morning, Annalisa, one of the first to wake up – she had always been an early riser – watched the others sleep. Her thoughts were, *Will we ever get home?* and she regretted going on this foolish trip. Hannelore did not make her feel any better; she also had not slept well, she was the grumpy type in the morning. She did not want to be spoken to for an hour.

But conditions were not too bad, at least they were warm and had a few bites to eat. Also, there was water outside the barn to have a wash. Most people feel happier when they are clean. The girls prettied themselves up for their own morale.

Nothing happened for a few hours; some of the others who had already been interrogated, were allowed to go into town.

"We have to find a new story when our turn comes, as the old one will not wear," Annalisa said to Hannelore. "We will say that the uncle had no room for us, but gave us an address for more relatives, and this is where we were heading."

Hannelore thought about this for a while and commented, "That sounds plausible."

At last the waiting was over; a company of about seven soldiers came to collect the people from yesterday's arrest, to take them to the local town hall. Rough commands were given to follow, and they had to bring all their belongings. The town hall was not far away, as they marched into a flurry of activity. Where before, the Americans had been, there were now Russians, with their flag flying high above. The town hall itself had not suffered too much with the fighting and was nearly intact. A very large conference room was their place for the next few hours.

One by one they were called into an adjoining office. It was Hannelore's turn first to go in.

"How was it?" Annalisa asked when she returned a little while later.

"Not bad. The interrogator is very young and nice, as if they want to make a good impression. He did not give anything away, as to what is to become of us. I told him our story and he seemed satisfied with it."

Annalisa's heart was thumping away when she was called in.

What greeted her, was a small office with two desks in it. Behind the smaller desk, a female Russian soldier was sitting, and behind, a larger one – a Russian captain. "Please sit down," he said to her in perfect German, which threw her. He busied himself with some paperwork for a while. At last, he looked up with the most gorgeous blue Paul Newman eyes. He asked her to state her name and why she wanted to board the train. Annalisa choked on her words, as she looked into his blue eyes, to explain why they were here. He seemed to be satisfied with her story, telling her that it all had to be checked.

She plucked up her courage and asked him, "We have done nothing wrong, why can we not go on our journey?"

His reply was, "In a few days I will let you know," and he dismissed her.

She left as if in a dream. This gorgeous tall fellow, in his spick-and-span uniform with lots of medals, was the enemy. Had he worn the German officer uniform she would have believed she was dreaming. When all had been interviewed, they were given a note, that they could move about freely in town until 6pm. But if they tried to leave without permission they would be arrested and immediately sent to prison.

Outside the town hall the girls hugged each other,

so relieved to be free again.

"What do you think will happen next?" Hannelore asked.

Annalisa thought for a while, replying, "I think we will not be out of here for a while." She wanted to add, 'maybe never', but this, she thought she'd better keep to herself.

Back at the barn Hans knew everything; heavy discussions were taking place. Annalisa knew it was only hot air. She thought, *Let's play along for a while, and then make our own decision.*

A few days went by and the girls plus a few others were called into the office again. Annalisa felt a little bit more at ease, as soon as this handsome fellow spoke to her. It was a good thing that she was sitting down, as her knees were shaking. Not fright, but what then?

The female soldier brought him a cup of tea. He asked Annalisa if she would like a cup of tea. "Yes please," she replied. He told the soldier something in Russian and off she went. A long while had gone by, when she at last returned, not the friendliest of women, with her tea and an assortment of freshly baked buns. Annalisa could not believe it when he offered the buns to her. She was so overwhelmed by his kindness that she burst out crying. The last few weeks and all the hardship of time before, came out in this outburst. He came around from his desk, offering her a clean hankie, and held her hand to calm her down. After a while she stopped, drying her tears. The woman soldier had disappeared when she had this outburst.

He went back behind his desk, asking, "Are you feeling better now?" He showed genuine concern. All she could do was nod her head. Other than her father, no one of late had shown a lot of kindness; it was always expected of her to be strong.

"Now come on, Annalisa. Have your tea and buns and we'll start as friends. I know your name, mine is Yurie." He took off his jacket and sat there in his crisp white shirt, looking not at all like a Russian. After all the propaganda, not what she had expected; he should have two heads and ravage her. Russian black tea with a lump of sugar in your mouth, is an acquired taste, not the coffee she was used to.

The two of them talked like old friends, munching away on their buns. Nothing had tasted so nice before, after all the shortages of food she had experienced in the last few months and years. But all good things have to come to an end as he said, "Look, Annalisa, would you like to do this again? For now I have more work to do."

Would she like to do this again? What a silly question. But she must not seem too eager, as she nodded her head.

Hannelore in the meantime had been getting worried; her interview had not lasted more than three minutes. "Where have you been and what has been happening?" were her eager questions.

"Here have a couple of buns." She had asked to take them for Hannelore. "Woo!"

Hannelore was not impressed. "What is the matter with you, Annalisa? Are you simple?" she asked her. "You know what this is leading up to, or have I got to spell it out for you?" she said. "I think you don't tell anyone about this, as the others would misinterpret it as being friendly with the enemy."

"But—"

"There is no but. To most people they are still the enemy."

Chapter 11

Several days had passed, with the barn getting fuller by the day. Some people who promised to go back where they came from, were released, but the others worried about their fate. Hans was talking of all the people complaining together that they were free people. Annalisa was laughing inwardly. Complain? Not her, nor Hannelore. Once more, our two were called in, and the same ritual of tea, buns and discussions happened. God, was he handsome. Shame he was Russian, she could have easily fallen for him.

Yurie casually mentioned that in two days' time, he had to go to another town for work. Would she and Hannelore like to come with him? Of course, she'd love to come. She felt like dancing on the table for joy.

"I better pick you up on the outskirts of town, so as not to be seen by the people in the barn."

Hannelore was very worried by this proposal, but there would be two of them and only one of him. "He must be lonely and needs female company," she said to Annalisa.

She was counting the hours to see him again; deep down she knew it could only end in tears, but for the moment she was on cloud nine.

On the day of their outing both girls spruced themselves up, the best they were able to. Annalisa's long blonde hair was gleaming in the sun, complementing her one and only flowered drees. Hannelore, with her dark complexion and hair, looked nice as well. As usual, Annalisa's punctuality, they arrived at their meeting point half an hour early. When at last, they could not believe their eyes, an old shiny Mercedes Benz car drew up. Yurie was in civilian clothes, a very smart suit, white shirt and tie. If he was handsome in his uniform, he was even more so in a suit. With a twinkle in his eyes, he asked if they had waited long. Waited long? Red rag to the bull.

"No, we only just made it," was her reply.

"Then let's go on our outing."

Annalisa got into the front, and Hannelore into the back. If she closed her eyes, it was similar to being a child again, going away for their Sunday outing with Vati and Mutti in their BMW bike and sidecar. But this was even better; the Merc smelled of polish, and she wondered which poor soldier had spent hours cleaning it.

Seeing these three together, they all sparkled with their beauty and youth. Yurie was not what one would expect for a Russian, as he was tall, blond, with piercing blue eyes, unlike Annalisa, who surprisingly had deep, warm brown eyes that contrasted beautifully with her blonde hair.

Driving along the road, there was much activity with soldiers erecting wooden poles. Annalisa was quite upset when Yurie explained that they were making lookout posts to keep their part of Germany protected. Luckily he didn't notice the spread of red across Annalisa's face, as her angry thoughts were that Germany belonged to the Germans, not Russians. Hannelore, blissfully unaware of this, continued to chat to Yurie which gave Annalisa time to get her feelings under control before they reached the town centre. He dropped the girls off and said he would be back in an hour after he had completed his business affairs, and then he would buy them lunch.

As soon as Yuri left Annalisa asked Hannelore if she had noticed the building work, which she had, but didn't see an issue with it. Finally, the penny dropped and Hannelore let out a cry of dismay. "If they are making a border line, soon no one will be able to leave and we will be stuck on the Russian side. What can we do?"

"We must start to make plans, but quietly so no one can find out and stop us."

And then Yurie could be seen coming back towards them with a big smile on his face. "Did you have a good time? Did you miss me?" he asked.

Annalisa replied, "Yes to having a good time and because we were having such a good time we didn't have time to miss you, so no," and she smiled back at him.

He laughingly said that was fine as the hierarchy was just happy that he was keeping 'you lot' under control.

Annalisa cringed. *How dare he? We are free spirits.* He managed to find a small restaurant/hotel for them for their lunch.

"Can I order?" he asked.

"Yes please," was their reply.

Not a big choice, something in French took his fancy, which he ordered with a bottle of wine. It took no more than one glass of wine for Annalisa to start giggling, and they were all having a ball, forgetting all the hardship before and probably still to come.

More and more, Annalisa liked, lusted after this fellow. It seemed like hours later when they finished their meal, especially the main course, a sort of goulash, a bit chewy, but the sauce tasted like nothing they ever had before.

Driving back, Annalisa asked Yurie what sort of meat it had been.

"Oh that was not meat, it was snails. Escargot – a French delicacy," he told her.

Annalisa wanted to choke, but thought, *What the hell?* Hannelore, however, did not fare that well. She asked him to stop the car, got out, ran into the bushes and was promptly sick. As she did her business and wandered away, Yurie leant over and kissed Annalisa. It was the most wonderful experience for her, she heard bells ringing, with her heart on fire. Nothing like that time with the Robert the English soldier. This man was gentle and knew all the right moves. After all, he was ten years older than her, and must have had a few encounters in his time. If ever there was a time she wished for Hannelore to stay away longer, this was it. But the spell was broken on her return. For a while they travelled in silence, Hannelore feeling squishy in the back, and both Yurie and Annalisa deep in thought. Eventually Annalisa asked him where in Russia he came from, and how come his German was so perfect.

"Well," he started to explain, "I still live with my parents in Moscow. My father is Russian and has spent the whole of his life in the army but has now retired. However, my mother is German which explains my language abilities and looks." This was quite a bombshell and Annalisa was astonished as she had assumed he was 100% Russian. He had joined the army to please his father and follow in his footsteps. He asked if he could see them again the same time and place tomorrow, to which Annalisa replied, "Yes please, if we aren't able to continue with our journey," and Hannelore piped in from the back seat, only if there were no more snails!!

The next week passed without event except for Hans talking about starting a revolt over being kept in the barn against their will, but he couldn't work out how to do it, so it fizzled away and calm returned.

The next outing was even more wonderful than the last and Annalisa felt herself falling in love. Yurie, tentatively unsure of how she would react, asked her if she would go away with him at the weekend, as he was free for the whole weekend. He said obviously they would have separate bedrooms. In her head, she screamed, *Yes, yes, yes!!!* Clean sheets, a bedroom and Yurie to herself for a weekend. However, to Yurie she said that it would be lovely, but she needed to confirm that it was all right with Hannelore.

With her approval, they had a whole weekend away.

When they returned Hans demanded to know where she had been, but rebelliously Annalisa thought, *We are already restricted in what we can do by the Russians. How dare Hans then think he has the right to know my movements?* So she glared at him and just walked away. Little did Hans know that soon their barn, which had been quite a safe haven, would be overflowing with refugees passing on tales about fences and walls being built, people being sent to prison or Russia if they were remotely suspected of being Nazi sympathisers, or even soldiers returning as living, walking skeletons with horror stories of suffering and death on an overwhelming scale.

Hannelore felt very guilty for being friends with the, of late, enemy, and told this to Annalisa.

"Look, we do this one last time, going out with him," Annalisa commented. "In the meantime, let's explore the way out of here. If we wait any longer or for the others, we will be stuck in this town. After all, the Americans are only maximum ten kilometres from here, and freedom."

The next few days were taken up with getting their bearings and direction, to break away from this semi-prison.

"And what about Yurie?" Hannelore wanted to know.

"Look, Hannelore, let's not cloud the issue. He could and would arrest us any day, if he gets bored playing friends. He did not get where he is by always playing Mr Nice. Of course, in a different time and circumstances I would have loved this friendship to continue. The plan is set. After the weekend we try our escape. Not a murmur to anyone."

Saturday came and he was there in his gleaming

Mercedes Benz car. Annalisa's heart was beating so loudly, a wonder the others could not hear it. Outwardly she played it cool, but was very pleased to see him. They drove about one and a half hours to the next town, laughing and teasing each other. A small hotel came into sight; it had survived the war quite reasonably, with very little damage showing. A very friendly proprietor greeted them as long-lost friends, as if they were regular visitors. *Or was he?* Annalisa wondered. The girls showed their identity card, and Yurie as well. The proprietor showed no signs of surprise when he looked at Yurie, and ushered them to their rooms.

Heaven on earth greeted them, with two freshly made beds, and washing facilities in the room.

"Get yourself settled and then come downstairs for a coffee," he said to the girls.

Both girls jumped onto the beds, and bobbed about, laughing, forgetting that there had been a war on, and that there was a bleak future ahead for them. This was now; two teenagers enjoying themselves.

The rest of the afternoon was spent exploring the town, and then back to the hotel for their evening meal. A little pang of jealousy entered Annalisa's head; Yurie was getting a bit too friendly with Hannelore. But then, c'est la vie, this was probably their last time together anyway.

Yurie must have noticed Annalisa's look of disapproval, and from then on he could not do enough for her. The dining room was very cosy, with seating for at maximum about thirty people. This evening there were about fifteen people excluding them, mostly couples. As for the menu, still very limited, with one meat (deer) dish, and one fish. All three ordered the deer, cooked to perfection, and presented in a super way. With it, came a homemade wine.

Annalisa and Hannelore's experience of drink, up till now, had been very limited. In no time both girls, to put it mildly, were a bit merry. Annalisa wished the evening would never end. After the meal an accordion player arrived, playing all the best songs. Some couples got up to dance, and Yurie asked her to dance; she would love to. The whole atmosphere felt unreal with the music playing. She had a little experience in dancing; before the war Mutti and Vati used to go once a week dancing to various restaurants with music. Emil would whirl his little girl around the floor. After all, she was his little princess. She got up and Yurie held her a little too close, after a while. "You are the most wonderful dancer, I have ever danced with," she told him.

"How many have there been before me?" he wanted to know.

"Only my father," she replied.

He then asked Hannelore to dance to be polite. She was getting a bit tipsy, as the evening wore on. Definitely two was company, but three was a crowd.

"Do you mind if I go to my room? I am feeling a little under the weather, I don't want to spoil your evening," Hannelore whispered to Annalisa.

"That is fine," was her reply. "I'll take you upstairs." Looking at Yurie, she said, "I'll be back."

She made sure to have Hannelore well tucked up in bed, and on leaving already heard gentle snoring.

Yurie was waiting for her, smoking one of his Russian cigarettes. *Was he handsome,* her thoughts were, as he welcomed her back with those beautiful blue eyes. The accordion player had changed to playing very romantic songs, as they moved around the dancefloor. But one by one people said their goodbyes, until there were only a couple of people left.

"Schatzi, I think we also have to go to bed," Yurie whispered in her ear. "If you like we can have a goodnight drink in my room."

Of course she'd like that. Any minute longer with him, was heaven on earth. Annalisa looked in on Hannelore, who was fast asleep.

Yurie must have counted on her coming to his room; a bottle of wine was standing in a cooler, waiting for her. Another glass of wine made her feel very light-hearted, when he took her in his arms and gently started kissing her. A warm feeling came over her as he touched her. She could feel his manhood pushing at her, and she surrendered to him. With her inexperience, she really could not enjoy the moment of his climax, as he fell into bed, exhausted. *So this was it,* she thought, having lost her virginity. It had been all right, but not such a big deal as Hannelore had told her.

After a while he asked, "Are you all right?" realising that he been the first with her.

"Yes, I am fine." But by now the room started spinning, and all she could think of was to be on her own, to collect her thoughts. "I am going to my room, to be with Hannelore," was her reply. "I'll see you in the morning." A very passionate last kiss and off she went.

At least Hannelore was fast asleep, and no questions or talking needed to be done. She stood under the shower for quite a while, before falling into bed. It was good, still being a bit tipsy, sleep came easy. She was still the first one to wake up, her head throbbing from all that had happened to her; happy in one way, but also sad in another. She knew this was the beginning of the end. Hannelore started stirring, and at once wanted to know the gory details. She listened in silence when she told her about the night. "Do you regret what happened?" she wanted to know.

"Not at all, I went into this with my eyes wide open, agreeing to all, and happy that it was such a wonderful experience," she replied. "I will never forget him, but it is only a whirlwind romance. Of course, I regret that the time and place could have been different."

They got themselves ready for the journey back, when Yurie knocked on the door, asking if they were ready for breakfast. He'd see them downstairs. He greeted them, his usual smiling self, as if the night never happened. Perhaps it was better this way, there were no awkward feelings.

The journey back was a pleasure, with the car humming along on a near-empty road. Hannelore was in full swing, talking as usual, which made Annalisa happy to reminisce. On the outskirts of town Yurie stopped the car to let them out, but asked, "Coffee tomorrow, same place?"

"Yes please," was their eager answer. And then he was gone.

When they arrived back at the barn, Hans rushed towards them, asking, "Where in heaven's name have you been?"

"We went to see my uncle and stayed a couple of nights. Why? What is the matter?" Annalisa wanted to know.

They were surprised on arrival to see that everybody was in the barn and not outside, as the weather was nice.

"I tell you what the matter is, we are all under house arrest, until the commandant comes and speaks to us."

"But why? What for?"

"The reason being, a couple of undesirable people joined us. The soldiers came and searched the barn, and found a gun. But no one is owning up to whom it belongs."

The girls froze with fear. What would happen to them, if Yurie realised that it was their gun? Hans babbled on and did not notice the look of shock on their faces.

Hannelore could not keep quiet any longer, she asked Annalisa what they should do in a panicked voice.

"Right now, we calm down, pretend we know nothing and wait and see what transpires."

The atmosphere in the barn was one of gloom, everyone terrified about their future. A few anguished hours went by, when Yurie arrived with a group of soldiers, guns drawn. What, did he think they were criminals or still the enemy, this bunch of frightened scruffy people? His face was very stern, with ice-cold blue eyes. Gone was the twinkle of this morning. This was a totally different man as he made his way to the centre of the barn. Even his voice was ice-cold, as he asked the person to come forward to claim their ownership. Silence greeted his request.

"You all were asked on arrival if you had any weapons, concealing one is a big offence. However, I give you one more day to come forward. After that, it will be out of my hands, and I have to report this to my superiors." His eyes went from person to person. As he looked into Annalisa's eyes, there was no change, still ice-cold. She wondered how he would react to her under the circumstances.

"As a goodwill gesture on my behalf I am lifting the house arrest," were his last words as he left with his soldiers. Annalisa realised that this man would do nothing to hinder his career, their encounter being put into another file, maybe never to be opened again.

Hans and the others still believed that it was the last few undesirable gipsies. Again, the prejudice against different groups of people. Even so, they protested their innocence. Hannelore was shaking like a leaf and it took quite a while for Annalisa to calm her. Even so, she herself was in a state of turmoil. "What are we to do? We are going to be sent to Siberia," she cried.

"First and foremost, we must keep our heads and plan our next step," Annalisa told her.

They slumped down onto their blankets behind some bushes, to collapse with exhaustion, and immediately fell asleep. But, it was not long before they both awoke when the first sign of daybreak came. All around them was silence, except for the first birds making their daybreak calls. But something dreadful had happened to them during the night. They were unable to see, but in the night they had been lying in a patch of nettles! Their hands, faces, anywhere that had not been covered had erupted into a massive red rash which hurt and itched terribly at the same time. But they were so worried about their position that there was no time to worry about it.

"We have to push on." And they did.

They then heard faint car noises on another field. They both prayed that it would be Americans and please, please not the Russians again. As they made their way through trees and bushes, being careful not to be seen, following the sound, they then arrived at the edge of the trees. The sound was coming from below and what greeted them was a road busy with jeeps and trucks.

"We made it!" Hannelore cried.

"Not quite yet," Annalisa replied. "We still need to get down there."

It took some time to get the bath down the hill to the road below, which they achieved mainly on their bottoms.

"Now we have made it," Annalisa said, as an American jeep rushed past them.

They hugged each other and cried a little for the pressure that they had been under. For a while they sat by the wayside, when a jeep stopped. Some big Military Police. One got out and came towards them and in a deep Texas drawl he asked, "Where did you both spring from?"

She told him that they had escaped from the Russians.

"Well you had better hop into the jeep, let's get you both cleaned up and fed."

A sigh of relief came from both of them. They drove for a while when a sort of castle came into view, as they drove into the courtyard.

"This is it," said the Texan. "There will be someone shortly to take care of you."

The two girls thanked him profusely, being so overwhelmed after the last couple of days. A soldier came and told them to follow, where he took them to a big room full of camp beds. *This room must have been a ballroom in days gone past,* thought Annalisa. He told them to find a bed each and to get cleaned up and then the soldier would return in an hour to take them for some food. They could not believe what was happening to them. Was it all a dream? But when they stood under the shower, the water was real and felt so good on their nettle rashes.

The soldier came back as promised and took them to the canteen. "Will you remember the way back?" he asked. "Make yourself comfortable for the night and in the morning you will be asked some questions." This was not the German way; it would have been questions first in triplicate and then the rest!!

The food in the canteen was something else; they could not believe what greeted them. Fresh white rolls, hamburgers as large as side plates, fruit, soup, and lots more. "I don't know where to start," Hannelore said, "but I am sure I will manage to sample everything."

"You had better be careful, we have been on starvation rations and to overload your stomach will make you sick." But with all the good intentions they went overboard and they gorged themselves.

All of that was over. Hitler was dead, with all of his ideas leaving behind this chaos and suffering. *Enough dwelling in the past,* Annalisa thought. They were, at the moment, safe and whatever the future would bring they would have to deal with it.

During the day, the soldier returned to take them to the office. A lady captain and another soldier were seated behind their desks. They asked the girls to sit down and tell them a little bit about themselves, whilst they patiently listened. Most of their questions were about how the Russians behaved and what was going on with them. It was a very light-hearted questioning. They also wanted to know when the girls intended to move on. They were told they could stay on for a few days until they felt well rested.

"When you do want to leave there is a jeep each morning that can take you to the railway station."

After that, a doctor then came to examine them and to give them something for the nettle rash. Hannelore wanted to know when Annalisa planned to leave. Annalisa wanted to give it a few days to enjoy the hospitality and the food. As they were walking through the corridor it was easy to imagine the lords and ladies going to their various rooms. One place they were not allowed to go to was the tower. The Americans probably had their lookout placed there to see what the Russians were up to.

Whilst they looked around and explored they found a box of dresses and they both dressed up as lords and ladies, and their laughter could be heard echoing through the corridors. As usual, the soldiers chatted them up and a lovely rapport was established. In the library, a few books had survived and anyone could read them.

The rash, over the next few days started to improve, and the girls started to look their pretty selves again. One day, one of the soldiers told them that in the evenings there was music in the Great Hall and asked if they would like to go with him. That decision took less than a second to make. Of course they would come. During the day their only dresses were unpacked and hung up ready for the evening. A few of the other Germans in the dormitory showed their disapproval for mixing with the Yanks. "You are happy to eat their food and stay here." All Annalisa could say was that they were hypocrites. "You should all be happy to be alive and free." But still, only a few came to the hall.

What greeted the girls was laughter, discussions, a guitarist and trumpet player trying to get a few songs together. It was a lovely mix of males and females with a large quantity of female soldiers now dressed in their civvies. The soldier who had invited them rushed over to bring them over to his group of friends. Annalisa wished that she had paid better attention to her English lessons when she was in the grammar school. But then again, she didn't like that teacher. However, she still somehow managed and it was even handy to sometimes pretend not to understand. It was only soft drinks, which was probably better, remembering her last episode with alcohol. But still, she felt no regrets. The evening went on with great laughter and talking.

Annalisa was surprised at the high quantity of soldiers, which seemed more than usual. Being nosy, she asked why there were so many. Jack, who had introduced himself earlier, replied, "They are being shipped out to a big airbase near Munich. Myself, I will be in the next group. Why don't you girls go there as well? I can get you work at once."

"We would love to. It is so tempting but we have to go back home first."

"I will never forget you." And he pretended to cry.

Annalisa asked him, "Can you give us your full name and address so that we might take you up at a later date on your offer?"

However, Hannelore wanted to go there immediately, but really did not have the courage to do it by herself. "Annalisa, will you promise to come with me once we have taken all the stuff back to your mum?"

Annalisa had to think for a while. What was there for her at home? A settee to sleep on in the kitchen in the middle of the countryside with nowhere to go. No job, no money and so on. There was no contest and so she promised that they would be at the airbase within three weeks. He was over the moon and was such a lively fellow. They wondered if he was for real or just hot air. The girls went back to their dormitory after thinking about what a fun evening they had. Hannelore was so eager that she suggested they go home the very next day. After all, by now they were rested and able to start again.

The next day they ate a hearty breakfast and loaded up their bath, then said their goodbyes. They were also given some food for the journey. The lift to the station, they declined as Annalisa was not happy to go so close to the Russian front and wanted to put some distance between them and the Russians before finding a train station. As usual, Hannelore agreed, as thinking was not one of her strong points.

The roads were still full of people trying to get back home. They did not look out of place carrying the baby bath. However, if they thought that this journey would be easier, they were wrong.

The bath, with every mile got heavier, and the weather was unkind, with rain and wind. But at last they reached the next railway station and the next train to arrive was in the morning. But even that was not a certainty as it depended how long the Russians would hold it up to inspect it. Eventually it did arrive and by now it was filled to the extreme. But the girls got on and found a corner to relax. As the hours passed they felt happier and safe. The last station was Duisburg and another 50km before they reached Xanten. So, between hitch-hiking and walking, they managed. It had taken them over four days for the return journey, however, this was still great improvement on the four weeks it had taken before.

Mutti cried in relief when she saw them safely returned. She knew that they would do it and was now in her element as she had something to boast about to her friends. All her precious miniatures and figurines were unwrapped and hugged. Annalisa whispered to Hannelore that they must be worth some money, and indeed they were as they were all Meissen. Klara was deliriously happy, not particularly interested in their hardships on the journey. Hannelore then felt she should go home to her own family, so they embraced each other, thinking back over the hardship and danger thy had endured for these lousy few trinkets. Hannelore reminded Annalisa of her promise before she left.

When Emil came home from work she had never seen him happier. To him, the ornaments meant nothing, but his daughter coming home did.

For the next few days Annalisa slept on and off, shattered by the ordeal mentally and physically. However, as time passed she started to get very bored. Being stuck in the house day in and out with just the cows to keep her company did not provide any outlet for her energy. She started to play with Ingrid, who finally had started to put on some weight and was some fun to be around.

It was a very long walk into town, so that happened only when they needed something. Occasionally English lorries would rumble by as the English army camp was at the back of their woods, about ten minutes away. If they ever came into contact, they were always polite and friendly. This was in total contrast to the American soldiers who were big, brash and uncouth. They acted like they came from the Land of Plenty and could arrogantly buy or get whatever they wanted. Then the Russians were in between – clean, but wearing whatever they could find, making do with half uniforms and newspaper cigarettes. Then lastly, the German army were spick and span, with their heavy jack boots, intimidating in all aspects. Annalisa wished they could have adopted the English attitude of being friendly; things could have been much better. But their monstrous hatred of Jewish people had made horrific events unfold and brought misery to millions of people.

Everybody was too busy trying to survive and rebuild their shattered past. Food-wise, nothing had changed, and the black market became a currency. Precious articles were exchanged for everyday food. In so far as her family was concerned, they were not bad off. Emil was still working for the farmer for food only. But once or twice, Mutti let it slip that Annalisa, being grown up, should do the same. Mutti and Annalise did not get on well. Mutti's obsession with tidiness drove her mad. Nothing could be done once the lounge was cleaned – it would make the room untidy in case of visitors.

Annalisa decided to see how her partner in crime was coping, maybe it would not be such a bad idea to go back to the American zone and see about work.

"God am I glad to see you!" Hannelore shouted as she saw her, "I am going stir crazy here. My family are driving me crazy with their constant arguments." And she babbled on for a good five minutes before finally asking how Annalisa was.

"More or less the same," she replied. "There are only small disagreements in our house but I am bored and unhappy. I love the hustle and bustle of people. After all, I am a city girl."

"Why don't we go back to Munich and find our fellow for work?" Hannelore suggested. For once Hannelore had made a decision. Even so, it was on

Annalisa's mind also. And as nothing was holding them, they agreed to leave in a few days.

Vati was not impressed at all with Annalisa. "You are far too young to be roaming around in the country," he said.

But Mutti, whose will was always adhered to, would only say, "She's a big girl, she will look after herself."

The few bits of clothing she had, were washed and pressed ready to leave.

"When will we see you again?" Emil wanted to know, and gave her as much money as he could scrape together for the journey.

"I'll let you know as soon as I am settled," Annalisa replied as she hugged him.

Between hitch-hiking, sleeping rough and train journeys, they arrived in München (Munich). Munich was all Annalisa was looking for, vibrant, with people and not too much destruction from the war. The Americans were very much noticeable and wasted no time to wolf-whistle our two. The first thought was to clean themselves up and look more presentable. Munich railway station was already working fully and their toilets and washing facilities were in perfect order. They were not on their own, using them for their daily routine – lots of refugees were doing the same.

"Let's see if we can find work here," Annalisa suggested. "I like it here and would not mind staying."

Sleeping was the next problem to be sorted. They looked for empty railway carriages stored in sidings away from the station. After a while they found several looking as if they had not been used for a while. "Life is looking up," Hannelore said. So they sneaked in and settled for the night, barricading themselves in so no one else could get in during the night. A couple of heavy sticks were kept handy for an emergency.

After a good night's sleep, in the morning they inspected their refuge. Yes, these carriages had been moved here for further use and around them were broken rails. "This will do us for a while," Annalisa said. "Let's hide our blankets and bits and pieces and hopefully everything will be here tonight." Carefully, they crept out, trying not to be seen. First port of call were the wash rooms and toilet. Feeling a lot better now, being clean, food was the next issue.

Mutti's supply of sandwiches had run out and both were feeling hunger pangs. The station was very busy with people and refugees trying to get to their chosen destination. Quite a few had also spent the night in the station with nowhere to go. Some were eating. Hannelore and Annalisa looked longingly at one family; the woman saw their look and offered a thick slice to each one. Nothing had ever tasted so good than this slightly dry bread, and both girls thanked her with all their heart. Feeling a bit more nourished, it was time to explore the city.

As the day went by they were chatted up by a group of GIs, laughing and joking, and were invited to go with them to one of the many bierkellers to have a good time. If you had money you could always buy everything and have a good time, and after all the fighting and all the hardship on all sides, everybody enjoyed some fun, if only just to celebrate being alive.

And these young men, clean, well fed, the only thing missing on their three-day passes were women.

Annalisa and Hannelore were also up for some merrymaking. Their time was their oyster and they accepted. And it was a good time; they ate, danced, drank the day and part of the night away. Time stood still for the pair of them. Afterwards they crept back to their hideaway. Sometimes they would be invited to their billing to stay with some of them. If anyone said the swinging sixties were great, it started in 1947, with free love and enjoying life. And so, a routine started; sleeping in their hideout, washing in the station, looking for work, and by afternoon more merrymaking.

Food was no longer a problem. Both girls smoked a little, although Annalisa never learnt how to inhale, however, they accepted every cigarette they were offered. Cigarettes were a great form of currency. Two cigarettes bought one egg and on a good day even some bread. Any queue was to be joined as you never knew what might be offered.

They wondered if their friend would be coming to the Munich airbase soon. They kept an eye out for him as that would mean they could get a job, whereas at the moment, because they didn't have a permanent address they couldn't get any proper work. They became one of many sleeping in the abandoned carriages in the station. They provided at least basic shelter, however, the officials did not want squatters, so early one morning they heard loud barks from dogs and voices shouting harshly, "Raus, raus (out, out)!"

Peeking out of their window, they saw the massive Alsatian dogs and knew not to argue with them. They quickly gathered up their belongings and ran away as quickly as they could. The guards shouted after them, saying that if they returned it would mean prison.

After a good wash and some food, they were ready to review the situation. Hannelore was really in the dumps and kept saying, "I think I want to go home, at least I have got a bed there."

"Come on, Hannelore. Let's try once more to get work."

This time they made their way to the airbase as originally planned. Erding was about 40km away from Munich, no problem at all. Traffic was brisk, with American jeeps and lorries going their way. Very quickly they got a lift to Erding.

Erding is a small town outside Munich which had suffered too much damage from the war.

"Well, here we are."

They were dropped in the centre of town. What next, was again the question. A bed for the night was priority. Annalisa suggested, "Let's see if there is the Red Cross or some organisation for refugees. Our story will be that we are refugees from the Russian sector. And one thing more, I am going to say that I am eighteen years old, as there is a better chance of finding work."

Yes, after a lot of asking there was a church hall run by Catholic nuns for all sorts of needy people. They were made very welcome and told that this was a temporary shelter for seven days maximum. A remuneration was expected by way of work or money. Hannelore said, "We go for work, as money is getting very short. It was heaven to have a clean bed;

even so, it was only a camp bed in a big dormitory. They stowed their few belongings away. Evening meal was a thick soup with lot of praying.

Of course, both were Catholics to the nuns. But it felt safe that way and a very good night's sleep was had. In the morning, they reported to a very stern-looking older nun in charge of the kitchen. "You can peel potatoes," she told Annalisa, "and Hannelore can clean pots and pans."

The church hall held about sixty people to stay, and of course more for just a meal. But the amount of potatoes she had to peel looked more like feeding the starving five thousand. This was definitely the opposite to having a good time.

Having done their compulsory three hours, at last their time was theirs again. Hannelore complained about her hands and hard work. Hard work was not her number one priority. Yes, her hands were red and raw from the harsh cleaning stuff.

"It can only get better," Annalisa assured her.

They went into town to work out the next plan. As usual there were queues for this and that, and they joined one. As they were waiting, a fellow started chatting to Annalisa and invited them for a coffee afterwards. Some cafés had opened again, with imitation coffee and a few bits to eat. "We'd love to," Annalisa replied. He introduced himself as David, a bit on the scrawny side. He had been ill, he explained. The conversation flowed freely, all being young. It turned out that he was Jewish and had survived the horrors of Auschwitz. By now the girls had heard about the camps, but still not in detail what went on in there. David wanted to know what they were up to.

They explained their new story, that their parents were left in the Russian zone and they had been told that there was work in the airbase. "Our problem is, we need a permanent address before we can get work. This is what we are doing now."

"I might be able to help you with that. You see about work, and we'll meet up tomorrow in here and talk."

After he left, Hannelore was feeling a bit happier and off they went to the airbase. "What do you think about David?" asked Hannelore. "And how old do you think he is?"

"I think about twenty-five. Dreadful to think what he has been through," Annalisa replied. "That is why he is so thin, appearing even more so with his six-foot tallness. Nice to talk to, not the best-looking fellow," Annalisa commented.

The airbase was about half an hour away from the town. On the gate they were given forms to fill in, and told to come back the next day with them after doing their allocated work – Annalisa potatoes, and Hannelore pots and pans. The nuns had everyone working, even the smaller children. Annalisa felt sorry for them; never a kind word, and all were terrified of them.

David was on time at their meeting place and as chatty as the day before. "Well, how did it go?" he wanted to know.

"All right," they replied. "We got the forms but, again, the address. And what about your thoughts, have you got any more news?"

"Yes I have," he replied. "Here it is. My sister, aunt and uncle also survived in the camp need a housekeeper. All of them are not in good health and require some cleaning and general housework for a few hours a day in exchange for a bed and address. There is only a single bed so one of you has to make do with the floor. It would be all right for a couple of weeks until the second one sorted out a better way for herself. Of course, my sister would like to see you first."

So far so good, Annalisa thought.

The apartment was close to the centre of town and looked quite respectable. Making their way up to the second floor, no problem for the girls, but David needed to rest twice, he really was not well. As he tried to open the door, what greeted them, both girls were not prepared for. The floors were littered with boxes, ornaments, clothes and whatever one could think of. As they climbed over the obstacles towards the kitchen, it got worse. David's sister sat on the kitchen table amongst unwashed dishes, full rubbish bins, and again, more boxes and possessions. She looked like an old lady, grey hair before her time, dark eyes in sunken sockets eyeing the girls with suspicion. Annalisa tried her best to put a friendly face onto the situation. Her friendly 'good morning' was greeted with a grunt. She wanted to know why the pair were in Erding, and once more the yarn was spun that their parents were in the Russian zone. This raised a spark of acknowledgement from this lady.

"At least your parents are alive. Ours perished in Auschwitz, but David, myself, my aunt and uncle, survived, and here we are."

After some more probing, especially into Annalisa

having grown up in a Jewish household, she seemed satisfied. She laid out her conditions; four hours' work for bed and some food. "Let me show you the apartment," she said. If one ignored the state of it, the apartment was quite roomy, with three bedrooms and a broom cupboard with a small single bed. The room was so small, if one were to fall out of bed, it was not possible to turn. If all this was a shock to especially Annalisa and her house-proud mother, there was one nightmare still to come. The last bedroom was in semi-darkness with a small light shining. All windows were blacked out.

Two people, or more to the point, two skeletons, were sitting in bed with dark eyes burning into the visitors. Again, more rubbish around, which made both girls sick to this misery. David explained that his uncle and aunt had been treated very badly in the camp, hence the dark windows. After that, David said he'd see them in the café to talk. For a while both girls were unable to speak after the shock.

Hannelore was the first to say something. "I am sorry, Annalisa. I could not live there if you paid me, this has made up my mind to go home. I am not sure how you feel about it, but I could not do it." Hannelore had not seen much in her life, which had been quite spoilt, and Annalisa was not surprised by her attitude.

Annalisa, on the other hand, having been brought up with a disabled half-brother, many times washing soiled clothes, felt totally different. She was very disturbed by what she had seen and heard, and she was slowly coming down from cloud nine; how apparently wonderfully Germany had treated non-

German people. And of course, there had been Opa as well. She felt if only she could make a small contribution to make amends, she would try, even if it was maybe not appreciated. Of course, being able to work as well would be a bonus.

"I will give it a try, I have got nothing to go back for." A one-bedroom place for four people and a mother she could not please, unless she could boast about her daughter. "I am going for it," she replied to Hannelore.

No talking at this point could have made Hannelore change her mind.

David already waited in the café. He explained that his sister was satisfied with Annalisa and would give her a try. She thanked him, saying that Hannelore would not be coming, she has an aunt in the west and would go there.

"Give me one more day, and then I'll move in," Annalisa said.

He gave her the precious address and kissed both girls in gratitude. He said, "You don't know how hard it is to get anyone to look after sick people, and being the man of the house."

Now, as all was sorted, they made their way to the camp to hand in Annalisa's form with her fresh address and new age. She was told to come back the next day for an interview. The rest of the time was spent with Hannelore and Annalisa packing. All that done, they went once more in search of a bierkeller for some dancing and merrymaking. Both were exited and sad. They had been through a lot together and had a great bond, only to now part and try to make it alone.

On her own she went to the airbase at the allotted time. About twenty-five more men and women were waiting. A lorry arrived to take them to the mess hall to be interviewed. Annalisa was one of the last to be interviewed by a lady sergeant who seemed to be impressed that she lived with a Jewish family, but in a hurry to get this over with, asking not too many questions. Looking once more at the form, she told her, "Yes, you can have a job in our Wimpy Bar as a waitress."

Annalisa wanted to jump for joy to have something solid to look forward to. She hurried back to Hannelore to tell her the good news, only to find she had gone. She had left a letter to say she hated goodbyes and did not want to change her mind. Annalisa sat down and cried, sadness and joy mingled together. She spent the last night alone in the refuge. It was a troubled night; so many things were happening at the same time.

Morning finally arrived and she did her last lot of potato peeling, thanking the nuns for their kindness, saying she was nearby and glad to help if needed. For the first she saw a smile on the nun's face.

David helped her to move into her cubbyhole – it was her cubbyhole. He then disappeared and left her alone. The sister was also nowhere to be seen. For a while she sat in this dirty kitchen, not really sure where to start. She searched for the coffee, which she appreciated, and decided to make a start. It took a long time just to wash the dirty dishes. Next was her bedroom, another challenge.

No clean bedding to be seen anywhere, she decided she had to sleep in her sleeping bag. As evening drew near, David and his sister returned. The sister busied herself in the kitchen, only David came to ask if she was all right. By now her tummy started rumbling as the smell of food wafted through the apartment. She went to ask the sister if she could help, but a firm, "No," implied 'stay out of the kitchen when I am here'. Returning to her bedroom, she assumed she would be called for dinner, but she assumed wrong. She still had some bread and things left and ate this in her bedroom, feeling a bit depressed, and wondered if she should have gone with Hannelore. There was nothing other than to go to sleep. She was so exhausted that sleep came soon.

Being an early riser, at six-thirty she ventured into the kitchen. "Oh my god," she said. "How can anyone make such a mess cooking a meal?" After a nice cup of coffee she started to clean up this new mess. She worked quietly, when finally, the sister appeared. Any communication was cut short by another hostile, "No," when Annalisa asked what she would like her to clean. Very near to tears, she went back to her bedroom. Only when David appeared did she feel slightly better. He realised she was not happy and tried his best to console her.

"I don't know what your sister would like me to do, could you ask her to leave me a note so I can get on with it?" she asked David. "She apparently does not like to talk to me."

David explained, she lost her husband and child, and other relatives in the camp, and still carried a lot of hatred in her.

"I don't even know how to address her."

"Frau Schumann will do, otherwise just do your own thing."

"All right, if this is how you'd like me to proceed to live here, that is all right with me." And a pattern was established; Frau Schumann and David would disappear around eleven o'clock and would not return until the evening. Annalisa would work for a further two hours and then get herself ready to go to her other job. The hours she had to work were 2pm to 10pm. As she approached the gate, quite a few others were already waiting. First they were taken to the office to get their pass, to enter by themselves in the future. Work clothes were also handed out for the various jobs. Hers was a white overall with a small red apron on top. After all this was done, a lorry delivered them to their allotted places. With her, another girl and a nice fellow were also dropped in front of a long one-storey building. A soldier then took them inside to the office.

From the outside the building looked grey and not very impressive, but once inside it was very nice. There was seating with nice colourful tables for about 150 people. A lovely dance floor and big stage, more a nightclub setting than a Wimpy bar. Annalisa was very impressed. Her thoughts were, *I have fallen on my feet here.* She and the other girl were introduced to a girl in charge to explain the ins and outs of the running of the place. After that, they were introduced to the two managers in charge. One was the thinnest man with a face like an ape. He stooped as if he wanted to hide his six-foot height; not the friendly type, and said his name was Captain Jimmy Fitzgerald. His second-in-command introduced himself as

Freddie Courier. He was the exact opposite to Fitzgerald, on the short side, about five feet nine inches, dark curly hair and the nicest smile to make them feel welcomed. Later on, Annalisa found out that he was of American-Italian stock from Chicago, hence the schmaltz. With that smile he could undress you in two seconds flat. Even before she was told by the other girls that he was quite a ladies' man, Annalisa thought, *I have to watch out for that one.*

Then the manageress told them that they must keep their uniform clean at all times, so they would not be reprimanded. Her name was Elisabeth, and a friendly girl as well, however, some of the soldiers occasionally might struggle to keep their cool and Annalisa was to report this to her to deal with it. Next she was given her orders, clearly written.

To Annalisa's surprise all the Wimpy buns were baked on the premises in an adjoining room. The nice fellow who came with them on the lorry introduced himself as Bruno. A lovely fellow, not tall, about five feet eight, very muscular, with blond hair. Elisabeth explained that in their break they could eat anything, but were not allowed to take anything out of the camp unless they asked. If they arrived early they were allowed to go to the big mess hall, after the soldiers had finished, and eat what was left over.

It all sounded perfect to Annalisa, and for the first time she relaxed, not having to worry about food any more. Getting changed into her white overall dress and red apron, she looked a very pretty, wholesome young girl. The doors were opened and the first customers arrived. She was lucky, her allocated tables only filled slowly; this was giving her a break to get

179

the orders right. Armed with a notepad and a big smile, she took her first order. It was not quite as easy as she had first thought, with four solders on each table and everyone wanting something different, not to mix up the order. *Unbelievable,* she thought, *how many variations there are for a simple hamburger or hot dog and chips.* She could feel Elisabeth keeping a sharp eye on her, which was reassuring, and as the first couple of hours went by, to have her first break, a sigh of relief came over her. Elisabeth and Bruno came outside to congratulate her for doing well.

Annalisa adored her work in the Wimpy bar; she got on well with all the other people working there. As for the customers, they were mostly good-mannered nice Americans from all sorts of lives, conscripted into the army. She very quickly learned, the bigger the smile the better the tip. Tips could be anything from a couple of cigarettes to a pair of nylons, or perfume by the regulars. Sunday was her worst day for working, as there was a dance band on in the afternoon. Most of the soldiers would go to the bigger cities, or countryside, with their beautiful, famous Bavarian lakes, on their furlough. After all, Erding was not far away from the playgrounds of the rich, with all facilities from boating to swimming and skiing. And there were many rich people already using these relaxing pastimes.

The war as such had not done much damage and all was very much preserved. But the Wimpy bar was not busy and the band was playing to a handful of customers. The girls had to stand around and watch these few people enjoying themselves. Annalisa's feet were tapping away to this lovely dance music. But it was far better than being at home. The word 'home' was a joke as she started to dislike the place. Her working days were on a rota of five and a half days, which included working every second Sunday, whereby her arrangements with Frau Schumann were Monday to Friday. It was a very good arrangement, if only she could get on better with Frau Schumann. Her really badly upsetting days were when she had to clean the uncle and aunt's bedroom. On those days she had to enlist the help of David to remove them from their bedroom. The first time she cleaned she felt physically ill afterwards. There had not been any cleaning done for a very long time, or never.

It was a wonder that there had not been a serious pest problem with leftover food, dirty washing and hygiene problems of the aunt and uncle. But she persevered and finally got the room and bed more respectable. Both thanked her very much, which made it all worthwhile. But the more she was appreciated by them, and David, Frau Schumann grew more anti-Annalisa. On her days off from the Americans, there were many invites to take her somewhere nice, Freddie, of course, first in line. She would tease him that he would be the last person. Only if Niagara Falls would stop flowing would she go with him. His reputation for how many girls he had bedded was so bad. She eventually accepted an invite from a good-looking, suntanned soldier. He was very polite and told her that her he was Mexican. It meant nothing to Annalisa, a part of America, or so she thought.

Freddie was not impressed with her. "Of all the people, you go out with a Mexican."

Annalisa could not understand what was wrong with

Mexicans. As she asked around she realised, here was the prejudice again. Mexicans were considered second-class citizens, good enough to fight for America but not to mix with. Had the world still not learned after all the fighting? People were people. Of course, the red rag was waved at her, which made her more determined to go out with him. His name was Fernando and he was the most divine dancer, and most of their time was spent in the dance halls. They were good friends having a good time. As Annalisa was now more settled, she decided to ask for time off to visit the family. Still not smoking, she had hoarded 400 cigarettes, chocolate, and other luxuries to take with her.

Freddie gave her more cigarettes and other foodstuff, and a further three days of on top of her free weekend for the visit.

Another one of her admirers was Bruno the baker. They had become friends as they started on the same day. He told her that he would save a lot of burger buns for her, for the journey. Bruno was not the tallest man, about five feet eight in height, but was very muscular, with a great sense of humour. A real Steve McQueen sporty person. He was allowed to use the gym and other facilities on the base in his free time. His ambition was to become a famous boxer like Max Schmeling, Germany's famous heavyweight. Annalisa knew very little about boxing and he would tell her of his wins and losses as a welterweight. He asked what she would like in her buns. "A little bit of everything, but mostly butter, peanut butter and jam in the same roll," she replied. She still had her sweet tooth. About thirty of these rolls, he got ready; enough for a year, she joked.

Freddie had given her a very large, soft duffel bag as a present. First, in went the cigarettes in a tin box with all the other items. In theory, she was smuggling, going through the American sector to the British sector. The clothing was next and on top, all these burger rolls. Freddie then took her to Munich railway station. He sneaked a quick kiss from her as they said goodbye.

"Now behave yourself," Annalisa joked.

He replied to her, "I want a lot more of these kisses when you return."

Her reply was, "You would be so lucky." Inwardly she liked him more and more as time went by. She knew she could not easily handle rejection. She had at first hand seen the girls cry.

This time it was heaven to be on the train. All her problems had been sorted; she had a job, a place to live and good friends. The train was packed to capacity, nothing there had changed; people were still moving around Germany from A to B like bees trying to find the honey. But it all did not matter – any inconvenience was worthwhile. She settled down for a while, admiring the lovely countryside and enjoying her peanut butter sandwiches. As far as food was concerned, times were still hard with rationing. Anyone caught dealing in the black market was put into prison. What was more dreadful, you had to eat all that you tried to sell. To think, if you were smuggling salt herrings, a good item to barter with, the thought of having to eat them every day made her shudder. She thought about her cigarettes and became a little bit worried.

After a couple of hours, the train stopped on the

American border sector, before entering the British sector. Looking out of the window she saw the platform lined with coloured MP – military police. In their white helmets they looked very foreboding. Panic set in. All were shaken and frightened. Annalisa was also shaking like mad; she been there before and her memory was still so vivid. Some people were running about, trying to escape to the other side of the platform. But they were promptly caught by the MP. Her mind was working overtime; running was not an option, should she hide the cigarettes beneath her in the carriage? She decided to bluff it out.

The largest, at least six foot three, coloured MP, came to check her identity card and asked her, not a friendly way, if she was smuggling anything. She looked up to him with the biggest smile she could force herself to make, and replied, "No, nothing." He then asked her to open her duffel bag. On putting his immaculate white gloves into it, some of the rolls had come undone. His white gloves were covered in peanut butter and jam. If he had been shot the reaction could have been more dramatic. He threw the bag at her and shouted a lot of abuse at her. The air was blue with the language and disgusted with her, he left her with her Wimpy buns. Due to this incident he did not bother the other passengers. In the other carriages, some were arrested and taken away. When at last, the train started off again, when the all-clear was given, the whole carriage burst out in loud laughter. A few thanked her; because of her they also got away. Annalisa thanked her lucky stars for being so lucky.

The very last part of the journey, she had to hitch-hike. It had become a way of life as trains were still not running in some parts of the countryside. The few who had any transport, cars, vans, carts, gladly gave a lift. And of course, more so if it was a lovely young girl. There was never any question of her coming to any harm. Even with all that had happened, the feeling of safety remained.

As she arrived home, Mother and Ingrid were so happy to see her, and a lot of kissing and cuddling was done. Emil, when he came back from work in the evening, seeing his Shatzi again, sighed with great relief.

Annalisa unpack all her goodies and presents. She had also managed to buy a small doll for Ingrid. Ingrid being the opposite to Annalisa, loved dolls and especially this little one. Emil went out once more and exchanged some of the cigarettes for coffee beans. Two cigarettes bought you a thimble of real coffee beans. Klara was in heaven; it had been a long time since she had a real cup of coffee. For Emil, Annalisa had also brought a couple of cigars. Mutti then made a meal for all the family to sit down to. They all wanted to hear everything that had happened to Annalisa. She told them where she lived and her lovely job. Klara, of course, was very interested in where she lived. When she told her of her discord with Frau Schumann, she said, "Greet her from me," and told Annalisa to try to get on better with her. Klara was not impressed with her being a waitress after all the money that had been spent on her. But as Emil said, "She is working and happy."

With the three of them, not a lot had changed. Emil still worked for the farmer for the milk, potatoes, vegetables and some eggs. The meat rations were still very poor and far between. But as Emil also ate at the farm, there was enough for Ingrid and Klara. Emil had a talk with Frau Janson to build a shed at the back of the house. This was for chickens and a pig to rear. She would also benefit from this and gave her permission. Little did she realise at the time, that beauty did not come into this project.

Emil had never wanted to do DIY, but he felt this to be a sensible solution to increase their food supply even more.

After spending a very uncomfortable night on the settee in the kitchen, or the only room, she went to see Hannelore, her partner in crime. Hannelore was over the moon to see her and wanted to hear all about her latest adventures. Love life, of course, was the most interesting to hear, especially Fernando, Freddie and Bruno. Her comment was, "You never had a problem surviving or finding a man, in this case three." Annalisa asked her to come back with her, but she declined; she had settled down. Her parents were hairdressers and had managed to build out of the ruins of the ground floor above the basement. Part of it became the hairdressing salon. She and her brother both helped in the salon. But as it was Sunday she asked Annalisa to come dancing.

First, of course, to keep up appearances there was church, and afterwards all other enjoyments. There was always something going on in one of the surrounding villages – a fête or a church homage, an excuse for drinking and dancing. Drinking consisted of homemade potato schnapps, a vile concoction, but after the second drink it was not noticed anymore. It was a way to let loose and forget the past, all the suffering, and still now, the hardship everyone had been enduring. And how they danced, there was never a shortage of boys their age or younger available. Men were in short supply, most of them killed in the war.

There was a frenzy to rebuild the ruins and clear the roads. In the town the roads were still full of gaping craters, but slowly the picture was improving. Hannelore had lent Annalisa her push bike as she lived a fair way out of town. A push bike was already another rare possession, a step up again.

She pedalled home on a near-empty road. The occasional mostly English lorry would rattle by. It was freedom to have your own transport, even if it was only a push bike. The surrounding countryside was very quiet, as all the animals were still under lock and key – the most priceless possession to have. For a bull, his life was a life of plenty.

The remaining days went by very quickly, and once more she went out the following Saturday, dancing. She got herself all spruced up, as Hannelore and her brother were also going. His name was Gerhard and he fancied her a bit. They were already waiting when she got there plus a further six, all seventeen-year-old, lanky fellows. Those who had no bike had to ride side-saddle in search of fun. The occasional swig out of the bottle was taken and a bunch of merry, boisterous teenagers arrived. This village was about eight miles away, with the fun of the fair already in full swing, the usual Humpty band to be heard from the dance tent. Heaven for Annalisa – she had six fellows to drag around the dance floor.

As the evening went by everybody became more noisy. As expected, when some of the local lads asked the girls to dance, Gerhard was not having it. The boys were young and wanted to flex their muscles. A fight broke out with the whole dance hall involved and the police were called. Annalisa was terrified to be locked up as she had to get back to work. She pleaded with Gerhard to sneak away. The others did the same and left the police to sort out this fight. But it still had been a fun evening. Gerhard took Annalisa home, not too pleased as he got only a peck on the cheek for all his efforts.

The remaining days went by far too quickly, as she got ready to go back to Erding. She was happy that all were well and she could go back with a peaceful mind. This time she did not have to worry about the borders, as all she had were Mutti's sandwiches. Her three men were very happy to see her back. The only hostility was from Frau Schumann. She gave her the greetings from her mother, but only received a grunt in return. Annalisa was upset; what she done to this woman? She would have to look around for somewhere else to live. It was of course, easier said than done. The town was saturated with refugees, a large quantity of them Jewish. They were on their way to Austria. This was one way to leave Germany. The ultimate goal for them was Palestine, now Israel. The British and French sector did their best not to let these refugees through. Still. no one wanted them. They had survived the Holocausts, but their future was not promising.

The plan was to get to the Arnal Pass in Südtirol over the Krimmler Tauern Mountain, over 1,000 metres high. Most were from the Eastern countries, undernourished and without proper clothing. Those who made it ended up in the Italian harbour of Genoa en route to the promised land. How many died on this trek, is not known, but it is thought to be in the thousands. Apparently, no grass has grown back in one spot since then. So the route into Austria and Germany became one stretch of refugees. The hospitals were filled to capacity. What chance did Annalisa have to find somewhere to live?

Chapter 12

Christmas was a very quiet affair. Freddie gave her a most beautiful cardigan. His parents had asked what shoe size she was, to send her a pair of boots.

Fernando got his present in so far as he was going home straight after Christmas. He had been a very kind, lovely friend to Annalisa. It never went any further. He used to tell her how poor his village and the people were. Mostly without work and no prospects. To Annalisa, this was hard to understand. Yes, Germany was in trouble, but only temporarily. With hard work Germany would soon be on its feet again. She wished him well for the future as they said their goodbye. Of course, Freddie was over the moon; here was his chance, but she was determined not to let this happen.

New Year celebrations were taken very seriously. All day they were busy decorating the walls and tables with streamers, balloons and trumpets for the party ahead. By the time they had finished the hall looked great. Also, the biggest band arrived, about twenty-five strong. Most of the stage was taken up with all kinds of drums. Their practising noise was unreal, with the drummer making the loudest noise. Drums never been Annalisa's favourite instrument and her ears were throbbing from his practising. For once she should have kept her mouth shut about the racket, but she joked that she had to put earplugs in so she couldn't hear him. All the Americans who were about were in awe of him. It turned out he was the world-famous Gene Krupa, who had played with all the famous bands – Benny Goodman, Jimmy Dorsey, Glenn Miller and Satchmo. He had heard her remark and was not particularly pleased with her, and pulled her up on it. She did a lot of grovelling, saying it was the practising, and he accepted her apology. His pride was restored; after all, he was the star.

At last, all was ready and they were awaiting their customers. The rules had been relaxed to allow them to bring their own alcohol. It was very hard work to keep on top of it all as the club was full to capacity, everyone wanting to hear Gene Krupa. It left no time to wish to be amongst the merrymakers. As the hours ticked away with the music blaring, Freddie told her he wanted to see her in his office at eleven fifty-five no matter what she was doing. Well, she could not argue with the boss. He was waiting for her with a glass of champagne and a little box tied onto a balloon, to be opened after 12am.

They heard the countdown to zero and he gave her the nicest kiss and embrace. *Oh, what the...* she thought. *It is New Year!* And she responded. In the box was a little charm bracelet with her name on it. What could she say? He was such a charmer. In the morning, she would tell him no way would this go any further. The kitchen had closed and all the staff were allowed to join in the fun. The band played as they had never played before to keep everyone in high spirits. Finally, at 3am it was all over – 1947 was here to stay. What it would bring for Annalisa was hard to say.

They still had to clear some of the mess, but at 4am she was ready to go home. Bruno offered to walk her home, but Freddie's offer to take her by jeep was accepted. Her feet and body were killing her; after all, she had been working since 8am. A thank you and peck on the cheek for Freddie as he dropped her off. She collapsed into bed knowing she had to start again at 8am. Always, she had been a good timekeeper, but this morning she overslept and woke up at 9am. Her head and body were still throbbing as she dressed in a hurry. Frau Schumann sat in the kitchen very stern-faced. Annalisa wished her a happy new year which was ignored. Instead, out came a lot of verbal insults, especially about her coming home after 4am. On any normal day Annalisa would have shrugged it off, but this was not one of them. She had done everything to please this lady without luck. She replied that she was lucky to find someone to clear up her mess, she being the biggest culprit. As the argument grew louder David appeared to stop it, but he only fuelled it more. She accused her also of hankering after David. So at last, Annalisa knew what was eating up this lady.

She also accused David of lusting after this good-for-nothing girl, and a non-believer. Annalisa was shaking all over; she heard enough insults to last her a lifetime. Nobody called her unrepeatable names, and she told Frau Schumann she was leaving at once. She rushed to her room, uncontrollably crying, packing her few belongings. David came and tried his best to calm her and get her to think it over, but to no avail.

What a start to a new year, as she stood in the street with her duffel bag; her mind went homeless again. As she made her way to the town centre debating with herself what to do next, a police car drew up and arrested her. All her protests that she was not loitering fell on deaf ears. Their instructions were to arrest any young girl for examination. Venereal disease had arrived at an alarming rate, amongst other diseases. She was taken to a large hall adjoining the hospital. To her amazement there were at least one hundred girls there, all worried sick over the outcome of this. All were told to have a bath and clean themselves, to be examined the next day. Most of the girls had been loitering and were in real need of a bath. It was probably the first real bed and bath they'd seen in months. Annalisa was terrified about not being able to go to work. That was all she needed, to lose her job as well After a lot of pleading she was allowed to see the lady in administration to explain her predicament. After patiently listening to Annalisa she promised her, she would try to have her examined as one of the first. She thanked her wholeheartedly and made her way back to the others.

She did not believe that there was something wrong with her, but there were still nagging doubts. How does it show itself? She had no clue, having never encountered it. She had a very restless night, got up early and had her expected shower. All the cleansing did not help; she felt dirty and humiliated to be associated with something like that. The examination started promptly at 9am by about five doctors and nurses. The lady had kept her word and she was one of the first to go into the room to be examined. She felt this to be one of the worst experiences to be endured. The check was from top to bottom, including the check for head lice. Once more, she pleaded the point that she had to get work to not lose her precious job. She was promised that the specimen would be rushed through in the laboratory, and with luck she could leave at lunchtime. Her gratitude was over the top, but what the hell? As usual, one party was complaining about everything, but she stayed out of this.

Only now was she able to eat something provided in the hospital canteen. The waiting hours crept by and finally her name was called. A very kind nurse told her that all the results were 100% all right and she was free to leave. Now she broke down and from sheer relief sobbed uncontrollably. Quickly, when she calmed down she gathered her few belongings and rushed to the old shelter, to try and find a bed for the next few nights. One of the nuns was friendly to her as she had been a good worker, and said she could stay for seven nights only. Well, she knew the drill. She literally dumped her belongings down and ran to work. To her relief, being late was treated as a big joke; she was not the only one suffering from New Year blues. Little did they know. Of course, Ape Face had to reprimand her – it was his duty.

Freddie was over the moon to see her; he had started to worry, as she always was a good timekeeper. Luck was on her side; the club had not opened on New Year's Day, and she only missed a few hours. Having been through two of her worst days, his kindness struck home. Here was a person who cared for her, and how long would it be before she became his girlfriend. No? However, she did not tell him that she was homeless. That, she had to sort out by herself.

There was very little time to look for a place to stay, as she had to do the customary hours in the morning, peeling potatoes, and then rush to work. As the days went by and luck was not on her side for finding somewhere, she started thinking of sleeping rough again. On her way to work she saw a sawmill with lots of outbuildings, maybe after work she could creep into one of those sheds. Freddie offered her to take her home at night but she insisted that she'd rather walk.

The seven nights went by quicker than expected and once more she sat in the nearest cafés with her belongings. She could not afford a repeat performance of being arrested for loitering. Priority was to find a place for her belongings. This was not a problem; she already had started the process of taking one piece to work each day and storing it in her locker. Only a blanket and comb was kept in her big duffel bag. There was one obstacle at the sawmill, a big German Shepard dog to keep guard. This, also, she had been working on. Each day when she passed she brought him some hamburgers which he devoured. This was Sunday dinner for him, as meat was short and the average person still hungry.

So in a couple of days they became good friends. How he would react at night, still remained to be seen. Equipped with a small flashlight, she squeezed herself through a side gate. A barking, snarling dog came racing towards her, and as if she had pulled a string, the dog came to sudden standstill when he recognised her. She called him Prince and he gratefully accepted the hamburgers. In the daytime he was on a long lead, but at night he had the run of the yard. Indirectly, it felt very secure, the dog following her. She made her way to the smallest shed. Her calculations were right, it looked more like storage than the main working area. She climbed onto several layers of boards and made the best sleeping quarters she could. Even though it was winter, it did not feel too cold between the wooden boards. Prince settled down on the ground and stayed with her all night. Her only worry was oversleeping.

The anxiety and hard work during the day had taken its toll on her and exhausted, she fell quickly asleep. It was still dark, but her watch told her that it was time to get up. Normally work would start at 8am, but if someone was to arrive early she had to be out of there by 7.30am.

She gave Prince her last hamburger and ate one herself. A tidy up of her hair, saying goodbye to Prince, with a big lick from him, she left. Her nearest port was the railway station, not as well sorted as Munich, but a warm waiting room for a couple of hours.

Of course, she could not do this every day; being a smaller station, someone would notice and report her. But for this first day it was fine. It was not heaven but she had survived another day. She made her way to work early to have a good clean up. Lunch time in the canteen never tasted so good. Even so, these were leftovers from the soldiers. It was impossible to imagine while Germany starved, good food in large quantities was wasted. Freddie, of course, was his cheerful bubbly self and asked her if she would like to come this coming weekend with him to Tegernsee. So this was the next ploy to win her over, her mind thought. "Only if we have separate rooms," was her reply.

"Of course. I never planned anything else," he said, looking very innocent.

Little did he realise how excited she was; to sleep in a hotel between clean sheets and amenities sounded like heaven. Tegernsee, one of the most beautiful lakes in Bavaria, playground of the rich. Itself, it had not been touched by the war and remained mostly intact.

On her last visit home she had acquired two American blankets and brought them with her. Klara, at once, set into action to have them dyed and made into a trouser suit and coat. Navy blue for the trouser suit and red for the coat. But my oh my, the lady got it wrong and did them in the reverse order. And so, she ended up with a red trouser suit and navy coat. Annalisa loved it, but when she wore the trouser suit in Xanten people frowned. *But what the hell?* she thought. There is enough drabness around, a little bit of colour was needed to cheer everyone up.

It was a lovely morning, the air crystal clear when they set off on their trip. She felt great, all the worry seemed to fall away from her. She felt great in her red trouser suit. The jeep conquered the mountain roads quite well – not Annalisa's idea of fun. She much preferred to be on level ground, and was relieved when they arrived at the hotel. The hotel looked lovely, better than she had anticipated, and she was so excited.

A very friendly worker showed them to their rooms, but Annalisa came crashing down from heaven. It was the most beautiful room, but with a double bed. She gave Freddie the key and left. He knew at once that all was not well; he had deceived her with the promise of two rooms. She told him in not so many words that she wanted to go back. Of course, he had a ready answer on hand that theirs was the last room. He was so good at persuading her to have at least a break of coffee and cake. Well, he said the magic word – 'cake'.

The dining room looked so inviting with a fire burning, a crisp white tablecloth and flowers everywhere. This what she had known in her growing up years, not all the hardship of now. She mellowed a bit after a while and agreed to see the proprietor with regards to the rooms. Freddie had not lied in so far as there was no more room at the inn and it was up them whether to stay. After some more discussions she finally agreed to stay with a divider down the middle of the bed.

It seemed so silly, what was she protecting. Her virginity had gone with Yurie and she had no regrets. It was just not the right time and place. But after a lengthy discussion an agreement was reached and they enjoyed this beautiful town. They were good together, liking the same things. Mealtime in the dining room was also terrific, as if there had not been a war. All too quickly, the vacation ended and they had to return to everyday reality. Annalisa's thoughts were, *Will this be the end to this friendship?*

Of course, the other girls had heard about their holiday, and were either envious or sorry for her. She managed to laugh it off. It did not matter either way and deep down she felt the same. But Freddie never changed, he said he had a wonderful time and would like to do it again. She did notice that he stopped flirting with the other girls when she was around.

What a comedown when she had to go back to her shed at night. Prince ran to her, so happy to see her. But the weather was changing and getting colder, with snow forecast. All she needed was to get ill and then what? She saw David several times in town and he told her that his sister was sorry and she would like her to come back. Should she swallow her pride for the time being? But fate took this decision out of her hands. One of the workmen came in very early one morning for an urgent job. On not seeing the dog, he started to look for him. There he was, guarding his sleeping princess. He gently shook her and asked why she was sleeping rough.

He felt pity for her and said he would speak to his wife to see if she had some room for her. Annalisa thanked him very much and they arranged to meet after work. His name was Heinrich Muller and he kept his promise to meet her. He had spoken to his wife and the only room available was under the stairwell, and if she would accept he expected her to help with a little housework. At least it was indoors, and she accepted gladly. She spent one more night in the shed and he collected her early in the morning, before he started work.

Annalisa was overwhelmed with emotion, arriving at his apartment. Being refugees themselves, they had been allocated this apartment. A semi-maisonette greeted her with the lounge on the first floor and a couple of rooms under a sloping roof. His wife greeted her very warmly, as a long-lost friend, and told her to call her Ushi, short for Ursula. She noticed that she was in the later stages of pregnancy. Two smaller children hung on her skirt while she tried to prepare food for them. *Oh God,* Annalisa thought. Where, where in heaven's name was there room for her? A cat would have problems finding some room.

After feeding the two little boys, Ernst and Johann, and a cup of imitation coffee gladly accepted, Ushi showed Annalisa where she thought she could sleep. They went downstairs and showed her where she could sleep, under the stairs. She had already put down a mattress and Annalisa gladly accepted. A sort of arrangement was made for helping with the work and also in lieu of pay, sixty cigarettes. This was no hardship for Annalisa, especially with Freddie around.

Both of them smoked. Heinrich sometimes got some cigarettes when he did some work for the Americans. When she settled for the first night into her bed under the stairs, never had it felt so good – not even a bed in a palace. Such lovely people to share the little they had. A routine was soon established, with Annalisa helping with the housework and the boys. The boys were lovely, aged two and a half years and fifteen months. When she was home, babysitting became a pleasure. Freddie also started taking her home at night and befriended the family as well.

There was only one thing Annalisa could not come to terms with. Ushi would take in washing for the American soldiers in payment for cigarettes. In her condition, to do this, especially the ironing... But she kept her thoughts to herself. She also went to see Frau Schumann as David asked her to. Both apologised to each other, and for the first time the two women talked properly and respected each other. As she had not found another domestic, Annalisa told her she could come and clean once a week. It was not from the kindness of her heart to do so, as she had very few hours left to herself. But with a baby soon arriving, would there still be room for her at Ushi's?

What had started as a very bad beginning to the new year, had turned out all right. Life was good and every hour she did not work was spent with Freddie. As time passed they became lovers. She could not understand why such a big deal was made of this thing called sex. Freddie did not set her house on fire. Maybe she was frigid, she wondered, when she endured the lovemaking. He was happy, but she had no one to talk to about this, least of all the other girls.

In February Ushi gave birth to another boy called Hans.

They were a little disappointed, they would have preferred for it to have been a girl. Ushi was a lovely person but somewhat untidy; it was difficult to keep on top of all these people in this small two-roomed flat. But she took it all in her stride, and she always amazed Annalisa, not only looking after everyone, but also being a terrific cook. She would stand for hours rolling out pastry to make small pastries and the traditional Knödel (potato dish). But somehow, as she watched her, Annalisa knew she wanted more from life than being a mother and housewife.

Her spare time was terrific. Any minute she and Freddie had, they would go away in his jeep. It was nearly back to her early years with the motorbike. More uncomfortable, as the wind blows in everywhere with the open sides. Freddie's parents wanted to hear all about this steady girlfriend. After all, they were of Italian stock, and Freddie, at twenty-eight, had not yet produced a grandchild. They started sending small presents like clothes for Annalisa, which were much appreciated. There was, of course, a fly in the ointment. Freddie started telling her that his mother was a devout Catholic and ran her household in very strict Catholic tradition. As far as Annalisa was concerned this was no problem to her, or so she thought. After all, they were a long way away in Chicago. But as long as he kept his religion to himself, all was well.

It was early spring and the countryside and hills were looking terrific. Close to her birthday, he suggested spending a whole week in Tegernsee as he was due some furlough. He, of course, would square with Ape Face that Annalisa would have the same time off.

He said he would try to rent a small apartment for the week. Annalisa could not believe her ears, this was heaven on earth. A whole week away; no more customers, however good they were; no more Frau Schumann and no more crying babies, however good they were. And they started setting their plan in motion. On their next visit to Tegernsee they went in search of an apartment. Finally, they found one in one of the big Bavarian houses. Three storeys high with a large overhanging roof and flower boxes on each storey. They were offered the last one on the third floor under the sloping roof. A small lounge with adjoining bedroom, and the kitchen in an alcove. It was so pretty, with chintzy bedclothes and light wood furniture.

Freddie asked Annalisa if that was all right. What a stupid question, she was jumping for joy. So he paid the lady with some goodies, like real coffee, cigarettes, chocolate and some money.

The couple of weeks up to their holiday passed very slowly. Annalisa did double shifts for Frau Schumann, which made her happy. The aunt and uncle were still firmly lodged in their bedroom, but they appreciated their spring clean. Annalisa always came away from there very depressed. How could anyone in the name of religion, colour, or creed inflict pain on another person or creature?

At last the day arrived and having packed her few possessions, they set off to their holiday home. How can a person always be so cheerful, as if there was not a problem in the world? Annalisa had a few doubts over being together for a whole week.

But Freddie did not seem to suffer from these doubts He had scrounged together enough food for a year. "If we eat all that," Annalisa joked, "I'll come back a stone heavier."

"Well you'll be ready for work again," was his reply, "and I like my women nicely rounded."

To settle in, they felt like a couple of honeymooners. Days were spent on long walks in the beautiful countryside with gentle or steeper hills to climb. And if they had any energy left they went dancing. There was always somewhere to go, as the resort had gone back to pre-war entertainment. Maybe the people were not the same, but all were there to have a good time.

The day of Annalisa's birthday arrived, with

Freddie waking her with a lovely breakfast and a single rose. Oh, this man was romantic, declaring his undying love. She laughed it off, always teasing that the Italian was coming out of him. That evening, they planned to go to their favourite restaurant. Annalisa spruced herself up with her long blonde hair curled up, feeling pretty good with herself. Freddie managed to order a bottle of champagne to celebrate. As they clinked glasses he gave her his present. A tiny box with an even tinier ring and stone was in it. Not exactly to her liking, she liked bolder things, but she pretended that she was in love with his present. He had watched her carefully to see her reaction, and realised that she was not impressed. For once he did not look his cheerful self. Eventually she asked, "What is wrong?" He said, "Don't you realise what this ring means?"

She did not have a clue what it could mean.

He then said, "It is an engagement ring. I'd like to marry you."

It is not customary – or she did not know about it – in Germany to give engagement rings, hence her not knowing what the ring represented. A few moments ago, before this, she had been slightly tipsy from the champagne, but was now stone-cold sober. Marriage. She was seventeen years old, not nineteen as he knew. Marriage had never entered her head. To settle down, have kids and be a good hausfrau...

He saw the horror in her face, feeling totally rejected. She had explained that it was not him, but the surprise of the proposal. Her next explanation also had to be that she needed to think about taking this big step. And also, did she love him? Yes, he was fun to be with, but all her life? The age difference did not bother her, as her father was twelve years older than her mother, and theirs was a very good marriage. Father doted on Mother; whatever her wish was, he tried to please her. She could see with Freddie it would be similar. They decided to leave it alone for the time being, but the spell of the evening had gone for them.

"Please keep the ring, look after it well as the minute sparkle is a diamond," Freddie told her.

Next morning, while Annalisa had a very restless night, Freddie was his usual cheerful self again, as if nothing had happened. She played along with it; maybe it all had been a joke. But then there was the ring. On her return she would have a jeweller look at it.

He left it alone for the next week, but when she felt safe he had forgotten, he asked again. She had been thinking a lot, at first angry with herself. How did she get herself into a mess again? And then maybe it was not such a bad idea. And on one of their next outings he asked again and she agreed to become his wife. He jumped up and down like a puppy being given a toy. His excitement rubbed off on her and she also felt very happy.

It was sad to leave Tegernsee; it had been a lovely, wonderful vacation. Annalisa wanted to keep the engagement quiet, but Freddie, in full swing, managed to tell the whole world in a few seconds. Ushi thought, when she told her, that she had done well to nail this lovely man down and she told her so. "You will be going to a great country with a husband who adores you, and a ready-made business. Annalisa had not even gone so far in her mind as leaving Germany and everyone behind. She needed time to think. But

Freddie did not give her that time. The very next day he went to see his superior, the camp commandant, and a time was set to go with Freddie, together, to see the commandant. He asked a lot of questions but then agreed to put the request forward. To Annalisa, he said, if this was to go ahead she needed her parents' permission. *Little did he know,* she thought. *One step at the time.*

Freddie asked how long they had to wait and was told about six weeks. She still had not told anyone about the paperwork, as to her date of birth being wrong. She just had to swim with it and deal with it on the day. For the next problem, she was not prepared. Freddie told her that next, they had to see the priest.

"Which one?" she asked, she being Protestant and him being a Catholic.

"Catholic, of course," was his reply.

The priest was not so obliging as the commandant, explaining the sanctity of marriage for what seemed hours. But at last, he also agreed to give his recommendation.

He asked Freddie to bring Annalisa twice a week to instruct her in the Catholic religion. She could not believe what she was hearing, and as soon as they had left the priest she tackled him about it.

"What does it mean?"

His reply was, "When the permit comes through you change and become a Catholic to get married."

Never in her mind had she considered, that he had no doubt she would oblige.

"But why can I not stay as I am, being a Protestant?" she wanted to know.

"Oh, that is not possible. Mother would not allow that."

Her teeth went on edge. Was she marrying his mother? Her head was hurting too much to take in at the time; she needed to think. Mother and the whole clan were over the moon that Freddie was to be married. Her being German did not seem to bother them and they all sent their greetings. How many were there of them? Brothers, sisters, aunts, uncles, it sounded like the whole of Chicago. Her mind went back to their Italian lodgers in the war and she tried to picture this nationality. Even Hitler had been persuaded to become their bedfellow, but that turned out badly for him.

Next morning, she decided for the time being to go along and see how things would develop. Once more, the decision was taken out of her hands. Freddie got his demob papers and was being shipped back to the States. What a coincidence, so quickly after he applied to get married, he was being shipped out.

Well, Freddie did not seem too perturbed about it, telling Annalisa that he would get their new home ready, and when the licence came through he would be back for them to get married. Strangely, she was not too upset about him leaving; she felt so much had happened in a short while.

"You will keep up your religious studies," he asked her, "when I am away?"

She promised to be a good girl. And then he was gone. Of course, she missed him, but she also appreciated he freedom to make her own decisions again.

A new second manager arrived in the form of a lady captain. A lovely blonde person who tried very hard to appear young, but would never see at least forty again. Ape Face was all over her, but he did not stand a chance in hell. Annalisa admired her, she represented glamour – not a natural blonde but glamorous with the help of Max Factor. She interfered very little with the staff, as long as they were a happy bunch. But to everyone's dismay, after a short while she obtained a licence to sell alcohol. Beer at first, and hard liquor later on. She advertised in the camp magazine that on the day of opening there would be free beer, but the customers had to bring their own mugs.

Ready for their new era, Annalisa and all the other girls awaited with apprehension for the customers. A queue had formed outside and on opening the doors, a horde of men came crashing in. Chaos was the wrong word to describe the scene. All the girls tried their best to cope, but soon mugs were mixed up, barrels ran dry and discontentment swept through the club. And then of course fights started and the MP were called in to restore order. After achieving some order and making sure they were seated, the biggest problem was to find the right person for each mug. The MP stayed for the rest of the evening to keep an eye on things.

A sigh of relief came over all of them, when eventually the last customer had left and the doors were closed. They all crashed out and were totally exhausted. Rita Holmes, the captain, thanked them for coping so well. As of tomorrow, no more free beer. It should improve and she had taken precautions. Annalisa thought to herself, if this was the scenario of things to come, all was not well.

Bruno offered to walk Annalisa home, as there were still a few soldiers stumbling about. She welcomed this wholeheartedly to have his protection. Not the tallest of men, about five foot nine, but being an amateur wrestler (welterweight) and very fit, he could take care of her.

The next day before the opening, precautions came in the form of three heavy, big, coloured MP standing by the doors. Yes, the customers were more orderly, but they drank as much as the first day. Behaviour towards the waitresses was very coarse and they all had to bite their tongues to avoid starting another fight.

After a couple of weeks, by now the club had their own glasses; the atmosphere should have improved. But instead of improving, it got worse. Customers were fewer; the nice customers stayed away and they were left with the hardened drinkers. Bruno would carry on taking her home and they became good friends.

"Would you like to come to one of my fights with me?" he wanted to know.

"Yes," was her immediate answer. Anything was to her was enjoyment.

His opponent was a big coloured fellow and on the train home she praised Bruno. Being still excited, she talked louder than normally and mentioned the word 'negro' – in German, 'Neger'. This was the only word in German she knew with no stigma attached, praising him for the brilliant fight even though he lost.

On the other side sat another coloured man and he also took offence at what she had said. All her explanation and saying sorry did not help. Bruno got involved and of course a fight started. The whole carriage joined in until one frightened passenger pulled the stop cord. The train came to an abrupt stop with the guards running towards their compartment. Peace was restored in so far as Annalisa, Bruno and the Neger were arrested and taken to the nearest police station. By now Bruno had explained to her that 'negros' as she knew them, were called coloured people in the English language. The word 'negro' was an insult in the English language. It was a hard lesson for her to learn, but in the morning, she said sorry over and over; after all, she had been praising the guy, and the apology was accepted.

Later on, they were released and no charges were being pressed. Bruno also explained that in America in the big cities, whole districts were populated by either coloured, Jewish, Irish and Italians. Yes, America was the land of freedom as long as they knew which box they fitted in. Annalisa was very distressed with the issue. She had grown up with prejudice and assumed it was all over.

The following week she was called into the commandant's office. He was delighted and pleased to tell her that the permission had come through for her to marry Freddie. She feigned jubilation but deep down she had hoped that the decision about the marriage would be taken out of her hands. With her mind not fully on her work, the inevitable happened in the afternoon.

Carrying half a dozen mugs full of beer, she slipped on some spilled beer. Crashing down onto the floor, she landed badly on her back. The nearest soldiers rushed to her, trying to get her up, but she was unable to stand. An ambulance was called and she was taken to the camp hospital. On examination by a nice doctor (not Hawkeye) he said that she had bruised her back, but it would be all right in a week or so. However, her x-ray revealed that she had torn her ligament in her ankle and with rest would take about six weeks to heal. Then an ambulance took her home.

Ushi fussed over her like a mother hen, one more for the fold. The next day Rita came to assess the situation. Annalisa told her she would be back to work in three days' time; she knew there were scores of people waiting for her job. The next day things looked bad, her right foot had swollen to twice the normal size. Ushi brought buckets of ice-cold water to get the swelling down. After feverishly working on her foot, the swelling, after three days, subsided a little bit and she was able to put a slipper on. Bruno came and helped her to hobble to work in a slipper and a shoe. The pain was excruciating but with the help of the other girls – they knew what was at stake – and strong painkillers, she managed to do her shift. On the way home Bruno practically carried her. He joked to her, "Tomorrow I'll bring a cart and wheel you to work." The pain was so bad she could not even force a smile.

Luck was on her side – one more day and it was her free weekend. It was impossible to do Frau Schumann's work and Bruno went to tell her what had happened. She sent back her best wishes. Strange, how she had changed and was now her best friend. Feeling very sorry for herself during the weekend in Ushi's shoebox flat with crying kids, she made her decision. She would try for a few more days, but if her ankle was not any better, she would go home to her parents.

Freddie had been in touch before to say that he would like to meet her parents. Perhaps she could persuade him to collect her for the wedding. Monday came and she hobbled with one shoe and one slipper to work. But halfway through the afternoon she found it was impossible for her to carry on. She went to see Rita and explained that she wanted to go and see her parents and get better. She was promised by Rita that her job would be held open. As it happened during working hours, indirectly Rita was responsible for this accident, and was glad not to be blamed. Ape Face also showed his concern.

Last but not least, she went to see the priest. This, she did joyfully as she was not happy with the situation anyway. "You will keep up your instructions with the local priest in Xanten?" he wanted to know, and her reply was that she would try her best with her foot. That was definitely not happening. Somehow she thought she might not come back at all. As to the future, who knows? Life on the outside of the camp, as she thought of Germany, was as bleak as ever. Her birthplace and home town, Essen, especially the district she grew up in, the Segerott, was in the newspaper as far as Berlin. The article reported that due to the shortage of food children were starving, and many husbandless women took to prostitution and drugs to feed their children. While she been working, in her free time she had sewn concealed pockets into her jacket in preparation to go home one day. They were filled with the most precious commodity – cigarettes. She had hoarded them with vigour. The rest – chocolate, nylons, perfume and anything she had been given as tips by the customers – had to go to the bottom of the duffel bag. Bruno had also looked after her, with thirty or more filled Wimpy buns. As he always had a sweet tooth he filled most of them with peanut butter and jam. She put these on top of all other items.

Ape Face had become very friendly of late, as she had found him a girlfriend, and he took her to the station. Bruno was very sad to see her go; he really liked her and would have liked her to have been more than a friend.

Chapter 13

The train rattled along and this time she was not searched on crossing into the English sector. Relief came over her and she spent the next few hours shutting her eyes for a little rest. But this was not easy, with too many problems still in front of her. She knew deep down she was not going back, being very disillusioned with the work, since the change to selling alcohol and the type of people it attracted. The nicest people, when drunk become different people – most of them in the club wanted to be nasty. She even started to question going to America. This feeling had been there from day one when Freddie asked her to marry him. There was no one to talk to about this.

Mother would say, "What a great opportunity, him being so well off, even his own restaurant." She would not have needed to scrimp to make ends meet.

Well, Vati would say, "You must follow your heart as this will be forever." She could hear it now and as before, it was her decision to make. But first she had to get home and settle back into the humdrum routine.

The last kilometres from Duisburg to Xanten were easily achieved. Never had her hobbling and thumb worked so well. Also, being by herself and not as before, hitch-hiking with Hannelore.

They last couple of miles were harder from town; by now she was hurting all over. She spotted her mother and Ingrid in the distance, also walking towards home. Eventually she caught up with them; both were over the moon to see her. But Mother could not hug her, she had her arm in a sling, all bandaged up. "What is wrong with your arm?" she asked Klara.

She burst into tears and between the sobbing, replied, "I have been shot."

"What do you mean you have been shot?" Annalisa wanted to know.

She started telling her that a week earlier, as they were walking home, the same as today, a bullet had ricocheted off a tree and gone straight through her upper arm. The soldiers in the camp had been on manoeuvres and used some live ammunition. But luck was on her side. They were also using the road and found her quickly, to take her immediately to the hospital. The bullet had gone straight through her upper arm and other than pain, had done no real damage.

For once, she was really happy to see her daughter. Of course, the English captain launched an enquiry, but nothing ever came of it. However, he had been and offered an apology. To think what the whole family had gone through the war unhurt, for this to happen. If it was not so serious, Annalisa felt like laughing. She said to her mother, "Good luck was on your side. At least you are alive, and the arm will heal." Call it intuition or telepathy for Annalisa to come home to look after Klara once more. "Well, we are a right old pair. You with your arm and me with my foot and back. How will we manage to look after each other?" And this time they all laughed.

Emil, when he came home from work, was over the moon to see his daughter, and of course wanted to know all the ins and outs of her forthcoming wedding. They knew each other too well and by her tone he knew that all was not well. He did not probe any deeper, he knew she would tell him in good time.

Frau Janson was also relieved to see Annalisa. Indirectly, it had put a strain on her to make sure that Klara and Ingrid were all right. With all the excitement and what had happened, Klara had one of her stomach turns and stayed in bed the next day.

But as the next day turned into two and three, they all started to worry. This was not like Mother. Usually she managed to get better within a day. Annalisa hobbled to town to see the doctor. "I will come by later on to see Klara, and what is wrong with you?" he wanted to know. She explained her predicament, and after looking at it, he was satisfied with her progress.

She also went to see Hannelore. Not a great deal had changed since her last visit. She was settled into working with her brother in their parents' hairdressing salon. Of course, if everything was all right she would attempt to go dancing with them on Sunday.

The doctor came in the afternoon and other then telling Klara to have complete rest, he could find nothing seriously wrong. Once more, Annalisa had to walk into town to get the medicine. The walk, normally thirty minutes, seemed to get longer each time. But at least with all this going on she was too busy to think.

Erding and the camp seemed such a long way away, as if in another chapter or world. But even after another couple of days of rest and medicine, Klara did not improve. All she would say was, "I am not feeling well. Nothing hurts." She also spent the nights downstairs on the sofa, as the stairs became too much for her. This, of course, created a problem for Annalisa, as upstairs there was only room for a small double bed and a small mattress on the floor for Ingrid. So Ingrid had to sleep with father and Annalisa had to make do with the mini mattress. Well, not a lot had changed as she tried her best to cope.

Emil was the first to wake up, as he had to be at work by 8am. He had his breakfast at the farm of bacon, egg, black pudding and fried potatoes. He went downstairs and there came a loud shout from him. "Annalisa, come down quickly!"

She nearly fell down the stairs, something bad must have happened in the night. Frau Janson also heard Emil and came rushing across.

The only one still asleep was Ingrid, which was good. The sight that greeted them was something out of a horror movie. Emil had managed to sit Mutti up; she looked as if she had a glass eye and one side of her jaw had dropped. Frau Janson took one look and said, "She's had a stroke, Emil. Take my push bike and get an ambulance."

Never had Emil pedalled so hard to get to the hospital. They loaded the bike in, and in no time he was back. In the meantime, Klara tried to talk, but she was not able to, her whole left side was affected. Frau Janson and Annalisa cleaned her and made her look presentable. Emil then went with Mother to the hospital. *Whatever next?* he thought.

There was one blessing – Annalisa being back to look after Ingrid and Mother. After a thorough examination Emil was told, yes, she had suffered a stroke, being the bad news, but in time she would regain all her functions. Emil asked, "How long?"

"This is hard to tell. Every patient is different. Her speech should come back within a week. As to the rest, it could take up to a year or more."

He went back to see her, forcing a smile. "Shatzi, you have done it in style this time," he joked, "but everything will be all right." And he told her to rest. She would be in good hands and he would be back in the evening. As he walked home, dropping by to tell the farmer why he had not come to work, he tried his best to hide his emotions. He could not hide anything from Annalisa, they knew each other too well, and he broke down and cried.

After a while, when he had calmed down he explained to her the truth about the illness. He had already worked out how much it would affect her.

"Look, all is not bad. Mutti is alive and will get better, that is the only thing that is important." Her positive outlook cheered him up and they were able to start organising the future. They then hugged each other and wiped the tears away.

While Klara was in hospital Annalisa had her sofa back to sleep on. It was not so much how to sleep, but the few hours of privacy when the two of them went to sleep.

Sleep did not come easy that night; so many things were going through her mind. Fate had again taken a hand in her future. No way could she leave Mother in her condition for a couple of years. That left only one thing she had to do – call the wedding off. Indirectly, she was relieved. What had made her turn against the marriage, was the insistence from Freddie and his clan for her to change her religion. Deep down, she felt hurt that she was not good enough as she was. So, her decision was made to write a 'dear John' letter the next day.

She spoke to Father about it the next day. He said he was not surprised. "I noticed your heart is not in tune with this wedding. And also, you are still so young, the world is your oyster and things will improve."

Strange to talk about the world, as most of the time was still taken up with survival. Food was still number one priority. As Emil worked for the farmer they were much better off than others. By now they had about twelve chickens, a pig and one sheep. The sheep was allowed to graze during the day on the opposite side of the road. The chickens were on three ledges above the pig in the pig shed. Each evening, Emil would bring home two litres of milk.

The milk was poured into flat dishes on the window sill. In the morning, the cream was skimmed off to make butter. This was Emil's job on Sunday morning. The cream was shaken until it separated into butter and buttermilk. It was Mother's favourite drink and was reserved for her. As for bread, they also baked with the flour from the farmer. Anything that was harvested, Emil was given a share. All in all, hungry they were not, and were lucky to be in Xanten.

Annalisa met Hannelore the next day and told her

everything that had happened. She was very sorry to hear about her mother, but horrified that she was thinking of calling the wedding off. "Surely you can appease the mother-in-law," Hannelore commented. "Think of all the good things waiting for you. Car, business, no more food or money worries and a doting husband. Here in Germany, for our age group there are no men – they are either dead, damaged or mentally or physically disabled."

But Annalisa's mind was made up. The letter was one of the hardest things she had to do, trying her best to blame circumstances rather than the real reason – her love was not strong enough to overcome the obstacle of the religion. The strangest thing was, she was not very religiously inclined. It was against her beliefs to impose any sort of brainwashing on another person. It probably was the red rag in front of the bull. Her motto by which she tried to live was 'live and let live'. This done, she posted the letter at once so she would not be able to change her mind.

Frau Janson looked after Ingrid for a while; it was hard for her to look at Mother. But as the song goes, what a difference a day makes. Klara was sitting up, nice and clean, trying her best to smile when she saw Annalisa walk in.

Klara tried to smile and joke with Annalisa and even asked after Ingrid. Annalisa promised that on her next visit she would bring Ingrid too.

On leaving, she felt a lot better; Mother was in good hands and was being looked after well. She was looking forward to going dancing with Hannelore, her brother and friends.

Sunday arrived and after making dinner and cleaning up, it was her turn to get ready. Emil had been to see Klara and he was satisfied with her progress. Putting on her best dress, she set off to town. She had also put some make-up on, something she learned to do well from her last boss, the American captain. It was still frowned upon in this backward town. But the rebel in her said, *This is me, like it or not.* It made her feel good. She was not a natural beauty, but in later life appreciated the pale blank canvas her face was. So, some nice foundation and the rest made her look very presentable. Her biggest asset was, of course, her long blonde hair.

The others were already waiting for her. She had brought along a sort of wrap for over her dress, so as not to get it dirty. Both girls had to ride side-saddle but the boys did not mind doing their bit in turn. This time they went to a small village about 10km away. From afar they could hear the fair already in full swing. On the way, of course, they had managed to get through a bottle of potato schnapps.

Homemade potato schnapps was one of the foulest things one could drink. However, after a slug or two it grew on you. All were in the most boisterous mood when they arrived. As usual the girls were appreciated by the farmer's boys, but not so much the boys – they were competition as there were two boys to every one girl. But the evening went by with good merrymaking. As the hours went by, Annalisa's feet were hurting, especially her bad one. She could not walk or dance another step. Most of these fairs last into the early hours and three days, but as they all had commitments they called it quits at 3am. They said their goodbyes in town but not one offered to take her home, which was just as well, at least there was no commitment.

It was not easy to walk the dark road. Every sound made her hair prickle. She had long since taken her shoes off and was walking barefoot. Every bone in her body was hurting. Had it all been worthwhile? Yes, it had had, only the thought of having to do it all again in the morning to see Mutti put a shadow on it. She grabbed a few hours' sleep and then went back to the old routine of being Mother. The first needing her attention were the animals. Feeding the chickens and pig took some time, and taking the sheep across the road to graze.

"I am off to work!" Emil shouted. "Kiss Mother for me."

Only she and Ingrid were at the breakfast table, and afterwards she made Ingrid look very pretty to see Mother. Annalisa knew if both girls were not spick and span she would get a telling off, or at present, bad looks from Mother.

Klara looked so happy to see her two daughters, one so grown up and the other still very small for her five years.

Klara's face had improved some more and Ingrid did not seem too upset by this. On leaving, she wanted to stay with Mother and it took the nurse a lot of effort to persuade her to go home. "She is coming home soon," she kept saying. "You have to help Annalisa to get the home ready."

And the good news came at the end of the week; she was able to come home, being well enough to do so. Emil had asked the farmer to borrow a buggy and horse to bring Klara home from the hospital. Klara was over the moon, him standing there with a pretty buggy pulled by a gleaming black horse. He had worked very hard in the evening to clean the buggy and horse. The horse's tail was nicely plaited and he had a large flower in his mane. Anything for Mother, to make her happy. The nuns were very impressed and Klara enjoyed the limelight. For him, it brought back memories of the time with his father and the coal business. He asked her how she was feeling as he had another surprise for her. "I am very happy," was her reply.

Trotting along a near-empty road with the sun shining through the trees on either side, he went past the house.

"Where are you going?" Klara wanted to know.

"It is a surprise, enjoy the ride."

After about half an hour of trotting along, he stopped by a roadside pub/restaurant. It had survived the war and was again in business. Of course, the menu was very limited but to Klara it was caviar and champagne.

All the memories came flooding back of their times as a family with Moses and his boys. How she missed them. Moses had been the father she had never known, and the boys treated her like their mother. The only consolation in her mind was that Jacob was all right in America and Moses and Sal did not suffer too much. She shed a few tears of happiness for Emil being so thoughtful and was grateful for having her girls. Emil saw to the horse, to feed and rest, as everyone admired the buggy and horse. But all good things have to come to an end. Mother started feeling a bit worn out, and they trotted home.

Annalisa made Mother comfortable on the couch. Emil had nailed together a sort of bed to sleep in the cowshed.

"Are you sure you are all right?" Klara wanted to know.

"Of course I am, it is nice and warm in there."

Annalisa, for the time being slept upstairs in the double bed with Ingrid. It was nice to have Mother back. In the following weeks Klara's willpower made her take big strides to get better. To her, this was only a short setback. The women managed together to feed the animals, clean out the pens and bring Rosie the sheep across the road, while Ingrid had to collect the eggs. It really did not need three people, but Mother insisted on helping and Annalisa let her as much as she could.

Klara's face and speech returned to normal in a very short while, but her left arm and side did not improve much. She also vacated the couch and went back to her bed in the attic. Once more, Annalisa was happy to have her own space back.

A letter arrived from Freddie, asking Annalisa to reconsider. He wanted to come and see her if there was a chance of her changing her mind. She never had thought he would take it so hard, as he told her how heartbroken he was.

Looking around her, it would be the easy option and she was sorely tempted. What was there for her here? No job, only a mother and sister to look after.

For a few days, she fought with herself. No, she had made a decision and she did not want to change that. She had a feeling it was not right, and another letter was written, telling him of everything that was happening of late. With Mother, it was impossible for her to leave.

He did reply. Being half Italian and half French, he understood were her duty lay. However, he asked to keep in touch, but Annalisa knew this was the end. The only excitement left was for the Sunday dances, but they were also losing their appeal. Somehow, wherever the boys went the boys wanted to fight, and quite often the police were called. Annalisa realised that it was only a matter of time before she would end up in prison. Mother had also heard rumours from friends about this band of hooligans.

"I am not happy you going around with Hannelore," she remarked to her.

"Don't worry, Mutti. I am already distancing myself from them," was her reply.

On a recent visit to town she had bumped into an old school friend. Reiner was a couple of years older, but their connection was the church, he also being a Protestant, a rare breed in Xanten. He was a lovely fellow and had a very kind nature. Good looking but not her type. What was her type? More the Clark Gable look. But as a friend, he was great. At least someone to talk to. He also had a bicycle and the transport situation was solved.

Mother approved of him wholeheartedly as he was always polite to her, this smart young man. He also worked in a solicitor's office, which Klara thought was great. To Annalisa, he was a friend and no more.

She also met two more of her old school friends, another Annalisa, Anne for short, and Maria. As much as Klara approved of Reiner, she disapproved of Anne. To her, that family reminded her of the Segerott, where the poor lived, and had no ambitions in life to improve themselves. As for Maria, she was indifferent, she came from a fairly normal family. Klara did not realise how hard it was for Annalisa to make friends; she was treated by the locals as an outcast, foremost because of her being a Protestant and coming from the big city.

How many times Annalisa told her father of the unfriendly people not talking to her. Emil asked her, "Did you try to talk.?"

"Yes," she answered, "but they don't want to know."

Anne was working in a newly opened factory (the old Krupp), which changed from guns to making all sort of pots and pans. Klara, of late, had been pushing for her to get a job as she was much better. Anne told her that they were still interviewing new people and Annalisa went along. Anne had put in a good word for her and she was taken on. Not that money mattered, you could hardly buy anything with it. But it was a status symbol to have a job. The location of the factory was only five minutes' walk away on the main road, a blessing to Annalisa. And to work she went the following Monday, first making sure that all the animals, Mother and Ingrid were all right.

She was happy to go to work. Of late, Mother had started criticising her for everything. If she wanted to sew she would not let her – it would make the room untidy. Or if she read – Frau Janson lent her books from the library – she would say, "You are not paying attention to me."

Most of the time this created an atmosphere in the house. The only one who could do no wrong was Ingrid. And how Ingrid played on this, being spoiled was putting it mildly.

Arriving at work, she was taken onto a big factory floor which she could only describe as having big sinks all around. In front of these sinks, as big as a third of a bath, would stand a boy and a girl swirling something grey, looking like mud. One end was taken up with big racks where grey items were stored on boards. The foreman stopped by one of these basins where a fellow was waiting. "Hi Karl," he said. "Here is your new helper, she looks strong enough to turn out a decent day's work, not like the last one!" he shouted to him, and left Annalisa there.

Karl was pleasant enough, as he asked her name and whether she done something like this before.

"I have not got a clue," she replied, laughing.

He tried his best to explain the procedure. "We make all sort of household items from cups to big bowls. You hand me the metal items behind you, I dip it into this brown mud liquid to cover it, then it goes onto a board, and this is where you come in. You take the board to the big racks and push the board in."

All day they tried, even Anne came over to show her the trick to keep these boards steady. Yes, she improved, but by the end of the evening she felt like crying. It was not so much the work, but her pride was

227

hurt; her snobbishness came out. There was Anne without any decent school reports, who could do it, and she was not able to learn such a simple thing. There was one good thing, though; Karl was a very patient man and by the end of the shift she liked him.

She knew that everyone was on piecework with a small allowance for teaching. He must have lost money the first day, having her with him. She literally crawled home, totally demoralised and hurting all over. As usual, Father was the only one showing some sympathy and was able to console her. Mother said she was making a big thing out of nothing. She did not want to but she started crying and again Vati took her in his arms. "Look, Shatzi, there will be better jobs one day," he told her.

When they went to bed, she made herself semolina with treacle, comfort eating. Her downfall was her sweet tooth and this was the only thing available. Tomorrow was another day to worry about. The next morning, the same routine. First Mother and Ingrid and then the animals. She arrived at 8am hoping she would do better. But it was not happening, they were still tumbling down. When evening came she wanted to give the job up, but Karl told her not to be silly. For a whole week this fight lasted, and when on Saturday the last pot stayed on the board, she wept for joy.

Karl was also pleased with his protégé and he asked to go for a drink to celebrate. Side-saddle, of course, into town. She was happy not being branded stupid. Even Mutti said well done.

Sunday was spent going dancing with Anne. The following week also went by successfully and she started relaxing. Maybe it was not the most glamorous job, but for every one job ten people were waiting. Again, Karl asked her out for drinks and she accepted.

On Monday morning when she got to work Karl's attitude had changed, he seemed very grumpy. She asked him if anything was wrong but got no reply. In her lunch hour, she asked Anne if she knew what was wrong with him. Quietly, she said the jungle drums been working and he had been told by his family and aunt and uncle not to start a friendship with this Protestant girl. Annalisa could not believe what she heard. Surely not. There had just been a war fought over prejudice. If that was true she might as well stitch yellow patches on her clothes, instead of Jew, non-believer. At first it hit her hard but she decided there and then, if that was the case, and they did not want her, she did not want them either. And so, in weeks to follow any invite from the local boys was firmly refused. She had Reiner, Anne and Maria. But with all this, she still settled into the factory routine.

Fate, again, took over. Emil came home one evening very excited. Klara wanted to know what this great news was. "It concerns Annalisa," he commented. "You know that young boy I work with? His father is a tailor."

Annalisa and Mother could not see the connection, where this was leading to, but he rattled on.

"The tailor is looking for an apprentice, as one of his girls has finished her apprenticeship and is moving on to greener pastures. But he is a male tailor."

Klara could not understand. "Why Annalisa?" she asked.

"It does not matter, girl or boy, when it comes to sewing. Maybe in later life, if she wanted to become a master, it would matter."

Klara and Annalisa looked at each other, trying to understand.

"She has always been good at sewing and at least she has a trade, a good trade," Emil said.

Klara agreed. "Yes, she is very good at sewing and hairdressing."

It would be a three-year apprenticeship with very little money earned. Apprenticeships were very important; even shop girls had go through one, otherwise farm or factory work were the only options. Annalisa had only just settled into factory work. To change again, was a lot to ask. But when Emil was excited about something, he would keep going until he had achieved it. So, she promised to go with him after work, to meet the tailor. It was one of those grey, dreary, wet, late autumn days, when they arrived at the smallholding tucked behind the factory where she worked. She could not believe her eyes as they entered the yard. A variety of animals were strutting about, with half-naked kids playing in a sea of mess. This could not possibly be the right place. But the tailor, Herr Molders, came out of the house with a chicken leg in his hand, chewing away, greeting them.

Surely, Annalisa thought, when they entered the house, things would improve. His wife passed them – pregnant again, in desperate need of a bath. He then took them into the workroom. A very obese girl was sitting on top of the big cutting worktable, hand-sewing. The tailor was waving his chicken leg about as he explained all the details to Emil. He underlined that he would be doing him a big favour, to take on such an old girl. Annalisa's ears pricked up. Old? What was he talking about? He explained as a rule, apprentices come to him at the age of fifteen, and complete after three years at eighteen. He argued that he could only pay her the rate of a fifteen-year-old. The princely sum would be six marks for a six-day week. Pay in England for trainees was about fifteen shillings a week in comparison. He then turned his attention to Annalisa, asking a few questions. He was a man of about five foot eleven, bald-headed, but with a twinkle in his eyes. Quite friendly, or was this a smoke screen? Annalisa was never quick on the uptake when she was being teased, and as he tried she gave him one of her looks. Oh, if looks could kill, he was doomed. He must have realised that this girl was no pushover.

Emil thanked him and said they had to speak to Mother. On walking home, he asked Annalisa about her thoughts. Well, first and foremost she could not get over the dirt, a repetition of Thüringen. And also, three years of nearly no money. She would be nearly twenty-one years old. "Would it all be worthwhile?" was her reply.

Emil told her that Herr Molders had a first-class reputation for being a tailor, and customers seemed to ignore the dirt around. When he told Klara of the outcome, she was all for it. At least her daughter would be out of the factory, and once more she could show off her daughter being a trainee tailor, a trade held in high respect. And it was decided that Annalisa would take the apprenticeship. Annalisa was not too unhappy to leave the factory; she had given it her best shot. She gave in her notice. The foreman was unhappy to see her leave. After the first disastrous week, he had been impressed by their output. Karl also was sad to lose her and asked her out for a drink.

She said yes because his family could take a running jump, she did not want or need their precious son.

December first, 1947, she set off with her box of sandwiches to her next adventure. Had she done right to agree? Time would tell. The weather had turned cold, the workroom was freezing. Maybe he had not paid the fuel bill. He introduced her to her workmate, Hildegart Bruckmann. To him, Bruckmann and Hohmann, never first names.

Annalisa asked her when the heating would go on.

"When he comes to work, which is seldom," was her reply.

How can one sew in this icebox? Her hands were feeling very cold.

Hildegart gave her a broom to clear up the previous day's rubbish. She, by all means was her superior, having completed her first year of training; even so, she was nearly two years younger than Annalisa. At last, after 10am Herr Molders made his appearance and lit the stove. He told Bruckmann the work of the day and threw her an old suit. God, did he look rough. He had the look of someone with a big hangover. Washing had not been on the agenda either. The oldest pair of trousers adorned his thin frame. She had not noticed before, but he had a nose like an eagle, underneath his watery blue eyes. Again, her thoughts were, had she done right? He then fiddled around for a while and disappeared. "Is this the usual way?" Annalisa wanted to know from Hildegart.

It was quite an eye-opener when Hildegart said, "Let's start work."

What work? Both girls then sat themselves on the table. Annalisa was given the old trousers from the suit. "What am I to do with these?" she queried.

"The whole suit has to be unpicked, and clean the edges with a razor blade. It is then ready to be turned to the left side and stitched up again. You see, as there is no material to be bought, this is the next best thing to a new suit."

It made sense as her father's suit was only allowed to come out on special occasions, and always looked like new. Especially when farmers had bought their suits in the best materials in the past. After all, it probably was meant to last a lifetime. And so, the girls set to work to take this suit to pieces. They had to be very careful not to rip or make holes – that would defeat the object of the enterprise.

Sitting eight hours on top of the table, except for lunchtime, Annalisa's back was hurting. But she enjoyed the day. The work had come easily to her, as if she had done it before. Even Eagle Face, the name she called Herr Molders in thought, did not put her off. During the day, he had poked his head in several times, always with something to eat in his hand, to check progress. When evening arrived, Annalisa was glad to go home. It had been a good day, but was she tired. Maybe it was the concentration, so as not to make a mistake.

They all wanted to hear of her new job, especially Emil. Had he done right, to pull her out of one job to this new one? His face lit up when he listened to his daughter; he knew her well, she was so like him. Either yes or no with very little in-between. Mother, of course, was more interested in the family. Annalisa had to be very careful, as all would be gossiped to her friends, and then would come back in a different version to her employer. Oh, how she hated these women and their gossiping. Maybe this was the only excitement they had in life, to take other people apart with their criticising. The only one she would speak her thoughts to was Reiner. He was a soothing influence to her as a mate, not a lover. Good-looking, dependable, but the spark was not there.

After a couple of days, the suit was ready to be put back together again, inside out. A nice young man came to be measured up.

*

The suit had been his father's, who had been killed in the war, and Eagle Face set work for the redesign. For the next few days they all worked on this suit. A first fitting went by and now the final stage was attempted. Such care Eagle Face took to insert the sleeves as they went in and out. In a good suit the sleeves dictate the hang of the jacket. Hildegart busied herself with the trousers, and Annalisa learnt how to hand-stitch the edges. Eagle Face treated Hildegart with contempt as she was a little bit dim. She should have been further in after the one year she been with him. But she just was unable to grasp more knowledge. So far, he had been all right with Annalisa.

Friday came and the client tried on his new blue suit. The smile which came over him made all three of them very happy. No one could have known that this old suit in mothballs would turn him into a prince. It was then that Annalisa realised that Herr Molders was a genius in his field, forgetting all his other failings.

She made her mind up to learn all she could, a decision which set her up for all her later life. She still looked forward to her Sunday dancing, her love in life, and she kept moving between Hannelore, Maria, Anne, and Reiner. The one she felt guilty about was Reiner. Many times she went to a dance with him, and then danced all night with others.

Mother was improving all the time, her face nearly back to normal. Only her arm and hand still had trouble. She learned to cope with it; at least it was her left side. The distance that had to be walked to town, was more a blessing than a burden. It kept her busy and active as Emil and Annalisa were at work all day.

*

One big excitement also occurred. Both girls had to attend college one day a week for further training in their field. This was a day Annalisa looked forward to very much. The college had been able to reopen after enormous repairs to the building. As it was fifteen kilometres away, they had to go there by train. All this was great fun; at last she was a student again. Mother was proud of her once more. Studies came easily to her, it seemed she had found her vocation.

On Christmas Eve, Eagle Face finally let the girls go home at eight thirty. Hildegart came for a sleepover to help Annalisa with baking, and preparing the Christmas Day dinner. Christmas Eve in Germany is not celebrated outside the house, other than going to midnight mass – a must for a Catholic. They stoked the stove up and started on their tasks. Mother, Father, and Ingrid had gone to bed. The girls giggled and had fun for the next few hours, whilst cooking and baking.

Hildegart was very happy to be allowed to this sleepover. Her mother was very strict, never allowing her to go to dances or sleepovers. So, this was freedom for her. Her father had been killed in the war. The pair found some of Emil's homemade wine, which helped with the tasks.

At last, the final present was wrapped, and the last cake baked. Both girls crashed out in the kitchen. They had been working for twenty hours. Of course, everything had to be tidy by 9am, when the others came down.

A lot of kissing and hugging went on as they wished each other Merry Christmas, and sat down for breakfast. By now Reiner had also arrived with presents for all. By presents, this meant even a new pair of socks was gratefully accepted. Annalisa only got a few little things and felt disappointed. Emil was not able to look at her disappointed face. With a twinkle in his eyes, he asked them all to come to the cowshed. *Whatever is he up to now?* Annalisa thought. As they went through the inner hall, a big parcel stood there in the most hideous brown paper next to the cows. All of them looked perplexed as he said it was Annalisa's present, and they had to guess what it was. He had made such an effort to hide the shape that they were not able to. He told Annalisa to start unwrapping. As she was ripping the paper off and had the first glance of a gleaming wheel, she started shrieking. It could not be. The others started helping, and finally a pushbike appeared. Not new, but it was great. She was laughing and crying at the same time. There was no better present Mother and Father could have given her. To her, it meant freedom. And so, all six of them crammed back into the small kitchen, to celebrate Christmas.

Reiner and Annalisa took Hildegart back to her mother, and wished her a happy Christmas.

*

Annalisa would have liked to have ridden around on her new bike all morning, but she had to help Mother with dinner. Dinner in Germany is eaten around 1-3pm. One of Mother's chickens had been sacrificed. Klara was not a good cook, but between her and Annalisa they produced a great meal. The rest of the afternoon was spent riding around with Reiner.

When, later on, she asked Father where the bike came from, he said, "Come with me." He took her to their shed and pointed at the pig. Emil had managed to strike a deal with a family, where food was more important than the bike. Money still meant nothing. Besides the one third of the pig, he also had to part with vegetables and potatoes. Feed it well and earn the one third. Yes, the pig was nearing its time to provide food for the family.

The week between Christmas and New Year, Annalisa and Emil were having a well-earned rest. Annalisa started to relax. Mother was getting slowly better, and Father and Ingrid were also all right. It was time to celebrate with the New Year around the corner. She decided to celebrate it with Hannelore and her gang. She had ready-made dancing partners who were fun to be with.

It was a very cold night as the bunch set off to the dance hall. How she appreciated her new gleaming bike. No more walking home alone, or with a friend who wanted more. The pub with dance hall was opposite the old Rhine. A while ago the old Rhine had been separated from the mighty river, the Rhine. During the summer this became a tourist attraction, for sailing and leisurely picnics by the banks. Annalisa remembered, a few years ago, again with her gang, they hired a boat. Werner, Hannelore's brother, always up to mischief, had rocked the boat so hard that she went overboard. To teach him a lesson, as she was a good swimmer, she stayed down as long as she was able to. When she finally emerged, he sighed in loud relief. For once he learned his lesson and thought twice before teasing her again.

The gang decided to hide their bikes a bit further away, under some bushes on the steep bank of the Rhine, and walk the rest of the way. Bikes were a commodity well exchanged for other goods. By now all eight of them were in good spirits, as they managed to get through two bottles of potato schnapps. It had to be done as they were not allowed to take drinks into the dance hall. They were not the only ones; every farm boy had done the same, now feeling like superstuds. The landlord had recognised their little gang and took Werner to one side. Being six foot something and towering over Werner, he told him, any trouble, he would break his arms to put an end to his hairdressing. For once Werner lost his bravado and decided to play ball. There would be other times to pay muscleman back. They drank, sang, and danced. In all, a brilliant start to the New Year.

What would it be? Annalisa thought. *Better than the years before?* Everybody kissed and wished each other a happy New Year. But as one by one, they could dance no more, it was time to go home. In their inebriated state they walked back to their bikes. It was a full moon, freezing cold, and the Rhine looked like a milk pond. Was it their imagination or was it for real? The water seemed to be very near the road. They looked at each other, having sobered with a jolt. *Oh my god.*

The Rhine had risen during the night and was nearly level with the road. They ran to where they thought their bikes were, but they could see nothing. Well, there was no other option. They formed a line, took off their shoes, turned up their trousers and waded into this freezing water, to feel for their bikes.

The water reached Annalisa, to about her knickers. It felt warm, peeing into the water. After a lot of probing she felt something, and so did all the others. One by one, muddy bikes were pulled out of the water. With their teeth chattering, they pedalled home as if possessed. All eight of them had raging colds the week after. Even as exhausted she was, and needed sleep badly, she still cleaned the bike a little bit. Emil would not be impressed to see it in its present state. But as if he knew he got up early, and caught her cleaning. He did see the funny side of it. After all, he could have biked all the way to the North Sea on his own with a bit of wind.

So, this was the start of 1948. Work was good for Annalisa; she quickly learned whatever Herr Molders gave to her to do. But Hildegart was not doing well. She still needed help with a better pair of trousers. So, the roles started reversing, Annalisa would help Eagle Face with sewing jackets and coats. As he disliked work with a vengeance, this was his way of doing as little as possible. But also, another picture was emerging. If he could get away with it, he would not pay their wages, always pleading poverty. When a garment was finished, most of the time he would deliver to the client direct. Afterwards, he found the nearest pub to spend the money.

There had also been a devaluation of the German mark. Emil and Klara's savings had been declared null and void, which left them penniless. Both took this very hard, being reduced to paupers. The only money coming in was a few pennies from Emil, as his earnings were mostly paid in food. Mother soon started complaining that Annalisa was bringing in very little from the tailor. Annalisa started defending herself, saying that she wanted her to work for the tailor, but she was unable to win this argument. She got very depressed with this situation, and broke her head to improve matters. Any word to Emil also fell on stony ground. All he would say was, "You have to learn to get along with Mother."

It got so bad, her biggest passion, she could also not manage. She simply did not have the one mark to go dancing. Reiner lent her the money many times, something she also did not cherish. One of the first steps she took to resolve this problem, was after work, if Eagle Face had not returned from a delivery, to find him.

And now it was the pig's turn. They heard one very loud squeal from the yard, and then it was all over. The real work started now in earnest. Clara had rustled up some friends to help with the sausage making and frying of the meat. It was laughable – two women in the house, Clara not able to use her left arm and hand due to the stroke, and Annalisa's right hand because of the nail-less finger.

The butcher had already separated the meat and taken his cut. Of course, one third went away for the bike, and the helpers were also waiting for their cut. For a while Annalisa managed to keep her finger dry, but when they made the liver sausage, the bandage got wet, and she had to work with the hand where the nail was off. In the weeks to follow every time they opened a jar of liver sausage she declined to eat, remembering her bad finger had been in it. The only good thing was, that it had not done her finger any harm, and a strong nail soon appeared. It felt sad in the next couple of weeks to see the pen empty, but Emil soon brought home another little piglet. Work at the tailor was still very enjoyable; it was a pleasure to see a finished suit appearing from the oddest material, or making old for new. Eagle Face had long given up on teaching Hildegard her new skills. It suited him to use Annalisa for the complicated items, leaving him with very little to do.

To the outside world Annalisa appeared a very strong and capable girl, very well built and slowly putting on a few extra pounds. She knew why this was; it was due to her making semolina pudding in the evenings, to ease her craving for something sweet – the only thing available. Even this did not help as she thought about the poor pig being killed. She also remembered the time when Mother said to her that one of her hens was missing. At first she laughed; surely she had miscounted. All the ledges were checked, but no missing hen could be found. The mystery lasted for a couple of weeks, when one day they were sitting in the kitchen and heard the most horrendous noise from the shed. Both rushed out and found the pig trying to eat one of the chickens. As the chickens flew up to their place to sleep or lay their eggs, they would first fly onto the ledge of the pigsty, and then fly to their ledges. While they were resting for a second, the pig would jump up and try to catch one. So now it had number two in its mouth. Both pulled hard to get the chicken away from it and after a while succeeded. The chicken had only suffered a bite on its backside and lost a few feathers. Klara took it into the kitchen for a few days to recover. Of course, when Emil came home and was told this story, he had to make a few alterations to the ledge to prevent it happening again.

And now it was the pig's turn. They heard one very loud squeal from the yard, and then it was all over. The real work now started in earnest, Klara had rustled up some friends to help with the sausage making and frying of the meat. It was laughable, two women in the house, Klara unable to use her left arm and hand due to the stroke, and Annalisa's right hand because of a nail-less finger.

The butcher had already separated the meat and taken his cut. Of course, one third went away for the bike, and the helpers were also waiting for their cut. For a while Annalisa managed to keep her finger dry, but when they made the liver sausage, the bandage got wet, and she had to work with the hand where the nail was off. In the weeks to follow every time they opened a jar of liver sausage she declined to eat, remembering her bad finger had been in it. The only good thing was, that it had not done her finger any harm, and a strong nail soon appeared. It felt sad in the next couple of weeks to see the pen empty, but Emil soon brought home another little piglet.

Chapter 14

Working for Herr Molders (Eagle Face), the tailor, was very enjoyable; it was a pleasure to see a finished suit appearing from the oddest material, or making old for new. Eagle Face had long given up on teaching Hildegard new skills. It suited him to use Annalisa for the complicated items, leaving him with very little to do.

It also suited her, she loved creating nice things and was a very quick learner. As always, the money situation did not improve. Annalisa would still follow him to price a few marks out of him. Eagle Face treated this as a game; instead of being ashamed, he thought it to be funny. She did not tell her father as Emil would not have her waiting outside pubs. To make a few more marks she started knitting for a shop in town. Again, she loved doing this, to see little tiny boots and jackets appear made her happy. She was not too keen when she was asked to knit a cardigan for an obese farmer's wife. As this cardigan grew, the weight bent the knitting needles. Also, to her horror it had one-inch stripes in grey and blue running across. But when this monstrosity was finished she was well paid. The lady must have realised she spent a lot of time on it. To make time, she would knit in the evening after work till about eleven o'clock, after helping Mother with dinner and washing up. She would get up at 4am to knit some more, feed the animals and, was off to the tailor for 8am. It was not easy but she enjoyed listening to the small radio and knitting.

One day a week she and Hildegard had to attend college; this was the happiest day of the week, to be carefree and enjoy life as a teenager.

Yes, she did at times question herself: where to or what next? But she soon would snap out of these negative thoughts. She knew she would not spend the rest of her life in this little town, which she loathed, with their prejudice and small talk. She would find a way somehow. For the time being, there was the Sunday excitement to go dancing and take her mind off her problems. She was seeing less of Hannelore and her gang; they were quickly acquiring a bad reputation for fighting. Wherever they went, a brawl would start. And as Mother did not approve of Anne, she would go most Sundays with Maria.

Maria came from a nice background; a very pretty girl with brown hair and blue eyes. Very easy to get on with and polite, and Klara approved. All she wanted out of life was to have a steady boyfriend and settle down, how boring. But it was a body to run around with. For a while it was a mystery to Annalisa why she could not hold a fellow.

"He has not turned up again," Maria complained when they arrived at this week's dance. "You know, the boy we meet last week."

"He seemed very nice," Annalisa replied. "What happened?" Annalisa started probing deeper.

To her horror, sweet innocent-looking Maria was a pushover for a one-night stand.

"I cannot help myself when the kissing starts, I never want it to stop," she said.

"But that is where the problem lies. Boys enjoy one-night stands, but don't want to carry on seeing you," Annalisa told her. "You have to make them wait if you want a steady boyfriend. I will keep an eye on you in the future."

To Annalisa, sex was never on the agenda. Maybe she was frigid? Well, at least Maria did not do it on the doorstep. Pedalling to dances about twelve to fifteen miles away, and not returning for a few months, her reputation had not suffered. Poor Mother; if she only knew.

There was one fellow Maria really liked and had seen him often. He managed to chat her up and she was in seventh heaven. Annalisa stuck to her like glue, not giving her a chance to disappear to have another one-night stand. After the dance, they all pedalled home together. Hers was the first stop and they said goodbye to meet again. He then asked Annalisa to take her home; she said there was no need but he insisted. She appreciated the company, as it was not fun to do it alone, but fun with a friend for company. The next couple of weeks this pattern was repeated, with Maria behaving.

"I have only given him friendly kisses," Maria told her. "He has also not tried to seduce me."

Uwe was a nice gentle fellow, not bad looking and

Annalisa was happy for Maria to have a steady boyfriend. Annalisa had no inkling that he had a yearning for her. When they said goodbye at the next dance, he became very amorous, telling her that he wanted her all the time, not Maria. She could not believe her ears and told him rule one. A rule she lived by, never do to others what you don't want done to yourself. Also, married men were taboo for her. He accepted the refusal and they parted company. The following Sunday when they met, he was all into Maria; not a word was mentioned, as if last Sunday never happened. However, Annalisa left before the dance had ended, with the excuse that she needed to work early, and for him to only take Maria home. Uwe and Annalisa both knew the reason, but Maria accepted it without a thought. Still, for the time being this threesome went everywhere together.

Her eighteenth birthday was a bit of a low-key affair. The whole household seemed to suffer with a cold. Mother took promptly to bed to be looked after. Annalisa sneezed and sniffled all day as she tried to concentrate on her sewing, until Eagle Face had enough and sent her home. Little Ingrid also laid about, the only strong one, as usual, being Father.

Reiner came visiting as usual, giving her a precious present. Two pairs of ten-gauge nylons. Where he had acquired them, he would not say. He seemed of late not himself. From one moment being very excitable, to extreme bouts of depression. When she was feeling better she needed to find out the reason why.

Klara had managed to have a new dress made for her. It was a beautiful deep lilac organza creation.

It must have cost Klara dearly, and when later she

fed the chickens, yes, one was missing and some of the jars of liver sausage were also gone. The black market was still as strong as ever – anything could be acquired. The currency was food. "Thank you, Mutti," she kept saying over and over. It was a great eighteenth birthday.

There was great excitement in town. The annual circus and fair had arrived. As Annalisa had a few days off because of her cold, she pedalled into town. She watched in amazement these circus people getting ready to perform. Like a swarm of ants, they pulled and pushed to get the canvas up. Each one of these nice muscular man had their specific place to pull and push. Finally, the middle mast was covered to display a lovely arena. She was glued to the spot when one of these good-looking fellows came over and started chatting her up. He asked her if she was coming to the evening performance. "I would love to," she replied, but the tickets she wanted were all sold out. This was not the case, a white lie on her part, the real reason was she, as usual, was stone broke. "And it is also my eighteenth birthday, so I am even more disappointed."

He asked her if she would like to come. What a question. Of course she would love to come, and so would her little sister of five, she replied.

"Be here at 7pm and ask for Antonio at the entrance cash till, and they will give you two complementary tickets." He then had to leave, as there was still a lot for him to do before tonight's performance.

Annalisa could not believe her luck. She pedalled home as if there was a house on fire. Ingrid was so excited to go to the circus, the cold was forgotten. Annalisa had to keep telling her, maybe this fellow would forget and she had no money to buy the tickets.

The afternoon seemed to drag on forever. Annalisa still had to see to Klara, the animals and cooking. But at long last they put on their best clothes and off they went. Annalisa was wearing her red trouser suit and brown boots. Even though she had a red nose, she managed to hide it under make-up. Another thing frowned on in this little town, but she wore make-up to feel good, and in defiance, not to be dictated to. She was satisfied with how she looked and Klara also said, she looked nice. With her heart in her hand she went to the cash till and asked for the tickets, referring to Antonio. Oh yes, not only had he left the tickets, they were the best ringside seats, reserved for the dignitaries in town.

She had managed to buy a few sweets for the two of them before they sat down. By now the tent was full to capacity and the atmosphere electrifying. The band started playing and the troupe and the animals paraded around the ring with Antonio in the lead. He was the main star, and looked every inch of it. His sequin leotard showed off every muscle in his body. As he walked by them he winked at Annalisa. Ingrid had seen it and said loudly, "That man winked at you!" Her face turned the colour of beetroot, as other people around her were looking at her and her heart was beating loudly for others to hear. The clowns came in and being ringside, made a big fuss of the two girls, especially Ingrid. She was giggling away, nearly choking. Most beautiful were the girls on three beautiful horses, doing handstands and other aerobics. They did feel sorry for the bears, made do all sorts of tricks. And then it was Antonio's turn to dazzle the people. Dazzle, he did all right, especially the women straining themselves not to miss one inch of him. He made his way to the centre of the arena where a rope was lowered for him. He wrapped it around himself and foot by foot, he got nearer to the top.

The trapeze took up the whole of the arena with a safety net underneath. With each daring stunt flying back and forth people cheered him, and were exited. When he finally came down, the people would not stop cheering. God, how Annalisa envied him. She would have given anything to be up there with him. But that was a dream too big even for her. Or was it?

Ingrid wanted to rush home to tell Mother and Father all about the evening when it was finished. But Annalisa said no, even if she sulked to get her way. "We have to stay and say thank you to Antonio for our free tickets," she told her. Annalisa waited until nearly all the people had gone, and then made her way to the exit with Ingrid. He had already changed and was waiting there for them to talk. But Ingrid, being spoiled Ingrid, made it difficult for them to speak, other than thanking him for the tickets, and the lovely show. He asked Annalisa if she would like to meet him the next day in town for a coffee. He said the magic word and she was besotted with this gorgeous man. A time and place was arranged for them to meet. When they got home the first thing Ingrid did was tell Klara about this man chatting up Annalisa.

Klara was horrified that her daughter would consider meeting with a circus fellow. Even though she might be poorer, her entrenched belief that all circus people were gipsies who would steal, and lowlife vermin, came through. Suddenly, a perfect day turned into the opposite as a massive argument started. Her poor father did not know what to do; he wanted to support his wife but he couldn't in his heart agree with her extreme views. He asked her to think back to Moses and his boys and the terrible prejudice they have suffered and probably died from. This made Klara think and even though she wasn't happy, she agreed to let Annalisa go. However, when he had a quiet moment alone with Annalisa, he tried to tread lightly, but get her to understand that people do have opinions and when you live in a small town, people can be quite nasty and gossip. Her reply was, "Well, they don't like me already so I might as well go my own way. Let them talk!"

As she made her way into town to meet him, her heart gave an extra beat. She liked this guy so much. Annalisa felt that a fellow should not just be good looking, but they had to dress smartly too. In a casual way he came towards her, the essence of Steve McQueen. Not the tallest man at 5ft 10ins but with a beautiful muscular body that demonstrated strength and security. Her feelings for Yurie had been lustful whereas now they were more about wanting to know the whole person.

Strange, she had imagined him to be very forward, but she was surprised that he was quite shy and very absorbed in his work. Annalisa was telling him how she admired the whole showbiz thrill and her ambition had always been to be part of it. But as life never offered an opportunity, she had to be satisfied with her life at present. He was easy to talk to and the couple of hours he had free, were soon over. He asked if she wanted to come again in the evening. What a silly question, of course she wanted to. For the rest of the week a ticket was always there for her to watch the show. They only managed coffee and cake once more as Annalisa had to go back to work. Klara was pleased; the jungle drums had been busy and she had heard about their meetings.

Sunday was the last day for the circus, with no performance. There was only one big thrill being performed by Antonio. This special event was, a thick wire was to be attached to the steeple of the church and would run down to the market square. Antonio would slide down on it. It seemed unreal; during the war everything around it was flattened but the cathedral remained standing, with only one steeple damaged.

The couple of hours they spent together after the show, never progressed beyond the friendship stage. When Sunday came he asked her to come early, as he wanted to show her something. She was very intrigued as to what it was he wanted to show her, and she could not wait for Sunday to arrive. He did ask her not to put her best clothes on, as they might get dirty. She decided to take her one and only dress with her to change into.

Sunday tradition was still the day when almost everybody spruced themselves up and went to church in their Sunday best. As always, he was already waiting for her in jeans and tee-shirt. Her dress was put into his caravan which he shared with several other fellows. They were all very friendly to her and made her very welcome. He still had not told her of the secret surprise. They started walking and ended up in front of the cathedral. "Now I'll tell you the big secret," he said. "I'd like you to come and inspect the cable with me, where I am sliding down on this afternoon. But only if you have no fear of heights."

Here was the red rag again. Afraid? Not her, she answered. They made their way to the back door and started climbing. The staircase was narrow and dark, winding its way upwards.

It seemed like hours they were climbing, but finally she saw a glimpse of daylight. The last couple of stairs had been the hardest, but then they arrived on a small platform to look outside. Annalisa nearly died; she had lied that she was not afraid of heights. Looking down onto the market place, the people looked like ants. She felt faint, but hid it with lots of bravado. Antonio busied himself with checking the cable was securely fastened. Why in heaven's name would anyone want to slide down this thick wire? It seemed irresponsible to her, to say the least. But she admired him for his courage.

All checked, they made their way down again, much easier than up. She had to sit down in the caravan to get her breath back and change into her Sunday dress. Afterwards when she had her coffee and cake, she felt her usual self again.

Antonio asked her, "What are your thoughts with regards to the wire?"

Her reply was, "I think you are very brave."

"I really don't do it to show I am brave, it is more the money I am interested in," he uttered. "Anything like this is very well paid. People come to see me fall, but I won't give them the pleasure. Would you want to do something like this yourself?" was the next question.

"Yes," she replied, "especially if there is money involved." But how could she? It would take years of training.

She was bedazzled by all the razzmatazz, the applause of the people and seeing different places. Yes, she would like to do the same. The hard work was never a problem to her.

"Well, come with me when we pack up tonight," he suggested. "I am lonely, and it is far better to be a two-person act on the trapeze."

Her heart said yes, but her head had to say no. It was hard to explain about Mother. Even though she was getting better with each day, it would take some more time for her to recover. At this moment, she had about seventy-five percent of her faculties back, a remarkable achievement. She felt like crying. Every time she was dealt a good hand, it was at once taken away from her. Lady Luck definitely did not like her.

Antonio comforted her by saying, "I'll be back here in one year. Wait for me and I will write as often as I can." This seemed a good arrangement, and time would tell of the outcome. All there was left to say goodbye; the others had packed while he performed his stunt and were ready to move. The market place was by now filling to capacity, and great excitement was in the air for the main event. the oompah band also played their best tunes, as everyone waited for the thrill of a lifetime. It is strange how people through the ages liked to see blood and gore, a little bit like the present bullfighting in Spain. She had a place next to the rope where he would land.

There was no more room on the square, when Antonio appeared on the platform of the cathedral. A big almighty roar went up from the people to this mad fellow. And then it was all over, taking just a few minutes. Annalisa hugged him and gave him a big kiss. Well, he did not fall down, he was sound and well.

People were now pushing and shoving her out of the way to speak to him. She blew him a big kiss and waved goodbye. Will she ever see him again? Sadly, she pedalled home. It had been a very exciting week for her, but she had no illusions as to the future – a year is a very long time. Mother, of course said that it was a good thing the gipsies were gone. If only she knew the sacrifice she made. She kept this as her own little secret.

As the month went by Herr Molders, or Eagle Face, changed his tactics; he went later and later to deliver the finished suits to his clients. That meant Annalisa could not wait outside the pub, for him to come out to pay her. Mother was pressing all the time for the money she had to give to her, and arguments would start. She kept saying what a lousy job it was, all the other girls of her age were bringing money home; she had forgotten that it was her who wanted Annalisa to take the job. Eventually she told her father of her predicament. Emil was furious when he heard she had been loitering outside pubs for him. He went to see him to tackle him for the outstanding money. It was a very heated argument and Eagle Face promised to do better in the future. He did say that the next time he had to come again, his hands would not be fit to work. Never before had she seen her father so angry. Well, his birth-sign is the bull and he pushed him a step too far. But as time went on he went back to his ways.

As Sunday arrived, Annalisa did not have the one mark to go dancing, Mother refusing to help, or did not have it herself. Maria said she would lend it to her, but she would like to go further away. The girls pedalled their hearts out to a slightly larger town for their Sunday dance, where Annalisa met Stefan. She had not seen him when they came in, but when she looked up, she saw this handsome blond vision in front of her, asking her to dance.

Six feet tall, in the most immaculate blue suit, shirt and tie. Always a pushover for Annalisa to see a nicely dressed man. He had come from the next bigger town, about 20km away. They danced their hearts out, and in the course of the evening he told her, that he was a refugee from East Prussia and worked in the coal mine. She was pretty smitten with this handsome fellow by the end of the evening.

The next Sundays to follow, were taken up to meet in the various dancehalls en route for both of them, with Maria in tow. He also came a couple of times to visit Annalisa at home. Klara was also impressed by this handsome fellow. Most of all that he was working. But easy-going Father did not take to him.

"Why don't you like him, Vati?" she asked after one of these visits.

"I have worked with these fellows from East Prussia, you can eat a sack of salt with them, and still won't know them," he replied. "Just keep your eyes open with him." For Father to have this prejudice was strange; he always wanted a peaceful life.

*

Spring turned into summer and it was time for little Ingrid to start school. She looked so little amongst the other children. Klara had nearly recovered from her stroke and was able to take her to school and back; it was a good thing for her, the daily walks. Annalisa thought back to her school days, especially her first day. But Ingrid, because she was so little, was always made a fuss of, and settled in quite well.

In the weeks that followed it became apparent that Ingrid was very lazy with schoolwork and tried her best not to do it. The hours spent at school were nine to one o'clock, with a lot of homework in the afternoon. Where Mother and Father had been tough on Annalisa with learning, the exact opposite happened with Ingrid. She ruled the roost and did whatever she wanted. Annalisa tried her best to encourage her, but was rejected most of the time. This created another atmosphere in the house, with Annalisa being the big bad wolf. To escape this unhappy atmosphere, she started leaving very early on Sunday mornings to pedal the thirty-three kilometres to Stefan, to spend the day and evening together. Occasionally he would take her to the cinema, another passion of hers. But there were little things starting to annoy her. As she never had any money, he had to pay for everything. He did this with a big grudge, always telling her how lucky she was to have found him. When he bought sweets, he held onto the bag, sharing the sweets out. The same thing happened when they went for coffee; he told her how much she was costing him. And as time went by, Annalisa started to realise what Father had tried to warn her against. This fellow was mean, something Annalisa was not used to. In her family they always shared everything gladly.

Chapter 15

Christmas was on the horizon when something dreadful happened. As she was working away on the top of the table, she experienced the most excruciating pain.

In the weeks before she had experienced small bouts of pain, but had ignored it. This was different, she was not even able to stand up. Hildegarde rushed to Eagle Face to tell him; he took one look and called the ambulance. After a quick examination, it turned out she had acute appendicitis and needed an immediate operation. Herr Molders then went to tell Klara and Emil. By the time they got to the hospital it was all over. Annalisa had her operation. It was the quick action of Herr Molders which had saved her life.

They all came to visit, and Mother shed a few tears. After the first day, Annalisa started to enjoy the fuss they were making over her. The hospital was run very efficiently by nuns. Even though Germany was still on food rationing, the food in the hospital was very good.

It was a week before Christmas when she had her operation and left Eagle Face with a lot of work.

Father went to see him and thanked him for his swift action. However, as usual the talk turned to money, to what was owed to Annalisa. Emil then told him unless he paid up to date, a princely sum of over 100 marks, he would not allow his daughter come back to work.

Emil of course thought that it would not come to this. Little did he know that the arrogant ex-SS officer would rather not do the work and let his family starve than give in to Emil's demands. Equally so, he actually did not have the money. So Annalisa became the pawn in the middle. When she came out of hospital before Christmas Eve, Emil told her. So once again the New Year arrived with Annalisa without a job.

New Year was a washout. Stefan came to see her at home and her mother even laid on a spread. However, the more Stefan talked the less Emil liked him. But there was a glimmer of hope on the horizon. On the grapevine, they heard that a tailor in the next village was looking for an apprentice. So, making sure she looked presentable and with a big smile on her face, she went to see this tailor. What a difference greeted her. Where Herr Molders' place was the dirtiest place you could imagine, these work rooms gleamed with cleanliness. It was like a small factory with five people sewing away happily. Annalisa was offered the position with an extra two marks as she was a second-year apprentice now. She would now earn ten marks a week.

Ten marks a week felt like a fortune. However, as it was in another village her first option was a thirteen-kilometre bike ride in each direction. Annalisa looked forward to starting as she loved sewing and enjoyed he prospect of being taught again.

When she arrived on her first day she was given an overall to keep her own clothes clean. Then the tailor gave her a pair of expensive half-lined trousers to make up. Annalisa was horrified as she was only used to making up the everyday items, as Hildegard always made up the expensive clothes. Well, there was nothing for it, she would just give it a go. She looked around for someone to ask for help but everyone had their heads down, working silently and intently. At lunchtime she tried flashing her eye at a young fellow but he ignored her too. Eventually, at four o'clock she had managed to complete the task. The tailor ushered her into his office with the trousers. What came next, she did not expect.

He explained that she had taken more than double the time allowed for making up a pair of trousers; simply put, she was far too slow. Annalisa tried pleading with him, saying that she would work through her lunch breaks in order to get up to speed. But the tailor was adamant he needed a qualified seamstress who could work at the required standard straightaway. And so, by the end of her first day at work she was jobless again. For most of the way home she cried her eyes out and her pride had been knocked as well. Hoping for some sympathy when she got home, that didn't happen either. Her mother just said, "You had better find another job quickly as you cannot sit around here all day not earning any money." There was no such thing as social security in those days; if you didn't work you didn't eat, it was that simple.

Annalisa became depressed; she felt useless, feeling that nothing went well for her. Emil tried his best to cheer her up but nothing helped and Annalisa even started to lose weight as her depression set in. Annalisa wondered what there was to look forward to. Germany had started to improve after the war, however, in this dreadful little town there were no industries to speak of and hardly any jobs were available. She could find a job as a maid but that went totally against the grain.

All her life she been told that she was destined for better things, and now to end up like this did not make sense, having studied and worked hard. Being a maid belonged to another area. She was on the point of saying, "What is the use?" All her fighting power had left her. Even her love life started going wrong. Stefan was getting meaner with each visit. Yes, he paid the one mark to get into the dance, but told her she better make do all evening with the one drink of lemonade. He himself would put no limit on his beer drinking. The lovemaking was still good, but sex was never her main priority.

Reiner was still visiting once a week, but something was wrong there as well. From a kind patient friend, he had become a very moody person, with constant mood swings. Trying to deal with her own problems, she left him alone for the time being. She was at a crossroad, with Klara nearly back to normal. Should she go back to the camp to work? Maybe Bruno was still there. But fate showed her another way. She saw an advertisement in the local newspaper for a waitress in a wine bar with accommodation. This would solve both her problems, she would still be close to the family, but would not live at home. Geldern was about fifty kilometres away from Xanten and it was a heck of a long way to pedal. But she made her mind up to have a go.

She explained that most of the girls were not locals, hence the sleeping arrangements because of the late opening hours. One of the girls was leaving, due to being pregnant, hence there was the vacancy. The wage was small but tips were generous as these were wealthy clients visiting the wine bar. It all sounded good when the lady boss explained the work. With her past experience, she was satisfied and offered her the job. Annalisa was feeling good to at least have something to look forward to. She was not too happy to pedal in the dark all this way home, and it took her until the early hours of the morning.

Mother was pleased that she had found work, but Emil had some reservations, which he was not explaining to her. He knew his girl could take care of herself; he was not able to offer a better solution for work. In the meantime, Emil tried his best to prise some money out of Herr Molders, but he just ignored him. Emil always went for a quiet life, but this rattled his cage. It was his little girl who was cheated out of her hard-earned wages.

When all the asking went ignored, he went to the tailors' union. After hearing this pitiful story, they promised to look into this. But after a week a letter arrived saying that they were also unsuccessful and would finance him, to take the tailor to court. The outcome of this was that he owed even more, because he had underpaid her all this time – a princely sum of 145 marks. But it did not help. The man had nothing, the house was riddled with debts and with seven kids the order was not enforced to pay.

Annalisa could not wait for the week to pass, to start her new job, and at last loaded up her bike with her few belongings to leave. Once more she said her goodbyes; she had no guilt over leaving Mother, her conscience was clear. Klara had recovered about ninety percent of her faculties, and she was only going a short distance away. She hated this town with a vengeance, especially after the disaster with Herr Molders.

It was a very crisp morning as she rode along a near-empty road. On arrival, she was allocated her bed and a small wardrobe by one of the girls. A couple of the girls were still sleeping, others were sitting about in curlers, chatting. The atmosphere was friendly and they showed her a small gas stove where she could make herself a drink or a small meal. She made herself a cup of imitation coffee and ate some of her sandwiches she had brought along.

After some time, Lady Boss arrived. "My name is Lara and I'd like to welcome you to our little group," she purred.

"I am Annalisa, and thank you for the welcome," Annalisa replied.

"There is no need for you to start at once," Lara told her. "After that long journey you must be tired and want to rest. When you are ready come down and join us."

There was something disturbing Annalisa; first, Lara's voice, neither high nor low, more like a rasping purring sound. She was a tall girl, on the wrong side of forty in a very slinky evening dress with a fabulous figure. Her make-up was also immaculate. Long blonde hair surrounded a nice full face.

"Yes, I will have a short rest," was her answer to Lara. After the last week of ups and downs she was ready for a rest, and only woke up around midnight. Very nice, romantic music came wafting through from downstairs. Too nosy not to go down, she put on her one and only organza dress and make-up. The lights were very low with a jukebox playing soft, sensual music. Some of the girls were swaying to this music or sitting with various men. All of the girls were very scantily dressed; her dress looked very much out of place. But something she had not seen before – two men dancing in deep embrace. She had heard of these relationships, Father sometimes spoke to Mother about this, when he worked in the coal mines. Lara was behind the bar chatting to several customers. She introduced her as her new hostess. Annalisa felt herself being undressed several times over by these men and blushed a deep crimson.

These customers were all very well dressed, most of them on the wrong side of fifty-plus. The only younger men were the gay men, usually together with these older men. She helped Lara prepare the drinks.

She realised this was far from what she had expected and also figured out what was causing her to be disturbed by Lara. She was also a man; her movements behind the bar and her hands gave her away. She was truly beautiful and Annalisa admired her/him. She explained quietly that the girls only drank champagne, a special bottle being kept under the bar. This apparent champagne had the lowest alcohol contest, more like coloured fizzy water. Lara also explained to her, "Never sit with any customer unless he offers to buy you a drink. In one hour I expect you to have encouraged him to have bought at least three or four drinks. Remember, your wages are the tips and a percentage of what they spend. With regards to the amour, I will explain tomorrow. But for the next few days I'd like you to help me behind the bar. I might keep you for myself," she joked.

What did she mean? Annalisa worried. By four o'clock most of the people were leaving, or encouraged by Lara to do so. Annalisa helped with the clearing and tidying up and finally at about 5am went upstairs to bed.

Lara herself retired to the second floor, where she had her office. It had been an eye opener for Annalisa; she was not happy, this was not what she had expected. But she was far too tired to worry about it as she hit the pillow. She would worry about it tomorrow.

As she opened her eyes in the morning, she observed the other girls. Some were already dressed to go to town and others in the process of making breakfast. She could feel her tummy rumbling, telling her that breakfast would be a good idea. One of the girls offered her some bacon and bread and said she could return it when she had been shopping. Greedily, she ate her bacon sandwich. The girls were talking about the previous night's customers, their good and bad manners. Annalisa was told to watch out for the priers wanting to touch for nothing. They also talked about one girl not being there. She had gone with one of the customers to a hotel for the night. This was allowed as long as Lara agreed. Annalisa nearly choked on her bacon sandwich. So that was what Lara wanted to talk to her about. What the hell had she got herself involved in?

It dawned on her what was happening here. This was a glorified knocking shop with Love for sale. Torn between leaving at once or observing for another night how things would develop, she decided to stay. During the day, Lara handed her a nice pair of black trousers with a glitzy waistcoat and white flimsy blouse. She was still decent and looked very nice, and extremely sexy. "As you are helping me behind the bar," Lara murmured, "you might as well look like a barman."

Like a man she definitely did not look, she was far too pretty for that. "Thank you for looking after me," she replied. But she was not alone in evening trousers; some of the gay couples were in evening suits.

The evening developed quite pleasurably with everyone enjoying themselves. Lara taught her how to make cocktails and mix all the other drinks, always in favour of the house. She was quite a shrewd businesswoman. She referred to her as a woman because that was how she came across and Annalisa admired her. The hours went by and Annalisa was beginning to relax. After all, she did not need to drink with the customers, only supply them with the drinks. She was safe behind the bar, in her opinion. The odd customer would by a drink for her, and she dutifully drank her imitation champagne.

She knew that every glass earned a tip. It was nearly morning when all the doors were closed and the last customer had gone. Annalisa was so tired, but her last thought, as she drifted off to sleep, was, *This is not too bad.* All she asked was that it would carry on like this. Late morning, she went into town to look around, with a few marks in her purse. The world was her oyster; she was working, and she had money to spend. Yes, she also liked this town and she would stay a while.

For the next few nights nothing changed, the usual music, chatting, mixing drinks and creating a warm atmosphere. The other girls were still friendly, but there was a feeling of suspicion towards her being teacher's pet. Did they know something which in her innocence she had not noticed? She had to find out if there was more to what was going on. The girl who had given her the bacon and bread the first day, had stayed friendly with her. Her name was Imogen and she was very beautiful, but at least thirty-five years old. A bit old for this kind of work, but with good make-up and low lights she was a favourite with the punters.

"Tell me, Imogen, is there something I have done? The other girls are a bit distant with me," she asked her.

"All I can say is, they are worried that you might tell Lara things about them. And while we are on the subject, I have to warn you about Lara. She has big mood swings and can be very fickle with her likes and dislikes."

"Thanks for telling me this," Annalisa replied. "I will take it all on board." She realised with this on board not to give Lara any reason for complaining. She concentrated on her work and was getting good at mixing cocktails. She never realised how many things would go into one. Saturday nights were always the busiest and the club was packed with customers.

They all worked very hard to keep everyone happy. However, a very butch, muscular fellow made a play for Lara. At first he asked her nicely to dance. When she declined, saying that she had to look after the bar, he became more insistent. He would not take no for an answer and started making trouble. Friday and Saturday nights, she did employ a bouncer in case of trouble. He started calling her a pervert; he had heard about her bondage preference, amongst other things. As it was getting out of hand, the bouncer threw this nasty fellow out of the premises. Annalisa's ears pricked up when she listened to this slanging match. Maybe this was what Imogen tried to tell her, to be wary of her? Him. She actually had not noticed any preference of Lara towards male or female. But that was her business, nothing to do with her.

After this encounter Lara excused herself with a headache and went to her apartment. She took some of the takings with her but told Annalisa to bring the rest up after closing. As Annalisa made her way up to Lara's apartment all she could think of was how tired she was. She had never been in her apartment and what greeted her came as a big shock. If the club was glitzy this apartment was a setting out of a Hollywood movie, the whole floor being covered with a white fur carpet. A beautiful red chaise lounge standing in the centre of the room.

The other pieces of furniture were all French, adorned with gold beading, King Louis the sun god style. A large white marble statue of two women embracing filled a corner. Annalisa just stood there for a moment taking in this scene. Lara herself was semi-laying on the red chaise lounge, draped in the most beautiful negligee. In front of her on a white marble coffee table were two champagne glasses, and a bottle of champagne in a cooler. Suddenly Annalisa was wide awake, alarm bells starting to ring in her head. She could not figure out this woman. The guy had called her a lesbian, but that could not be. However, she had heard about operations gone wrong.

Lara beckoned her to sit next to her and offered her a glass of champagne. To lighten the atmosphere Annalisa joked, was it the real thing or the fizzy water from downstairs?

"I only drink the best up here," she answered. "I want us to become real friends," she said, the emphasis on the 'real'. By now, Annalisa realised all was not kosher and she was in trouble. She was breaking her head trying to handle this situation. Shattering how beautiful everything was, Lara took her by the hand and showed her the bedroom. If all so far had been unbelievable, the bedroom was out of this world. An enormous bed, big enough for four people, in a matt silver frame, took up most of the room, the ceiling being one big mirror, looking down onto the bed and more mirrored furniture. *How could anyone acquire such beautiful things in these hard times?* went through her head. Maybe she was ex-SS and had plundered some poor unfortunate people. What better disguise than to parade as a woman?

She realised that she had to get out of there, and told her she was very tired and also had a splitting headache. But Lara insisted on having some champagne with her. "Just a very small glass," she told her, "and then I go down." But what she had dreaded happened, Lara started making advances to her. As much as she admired her as a businesswoman, she was repelled by this – 'it'. To her, white is white and she was not able to cope with any other relationship. There was one thing Annalisa was clear on, she was definitely heterosexual, pushing her away when she tried to embrace her.

She got up with a jolt, excusing herself, saying she was not feeling well. She nearly fell down the stairs to her bed and flung herself on it, not sure if she should laugh or cry. Too exhausted to think, she decided to look at this situation in the morning.

Waking up, her whole body and head was throbbing. Imogen realised something was wrong and came over. "I realised when you were late coming down that something had occurred."

Annalisa confided in her and told her the whole pitiful story.

"There is very little I can help you with, but this is what I know. If Lara feels rejected, she will become very nasty, I have seen it all before. She will push all the undesirable men at you, and compromise you in any way. Myself, I am planning to leave soon. I have saved enough to start a small business. If possible, you could come and work for me. I am so glad that I was never her type."

With this advice, Annalisa had already decided she would leave. She would not give Lara the satisfaction of taking her scorn out on her. She went to see Lara to tell her about leaving; her excuse was that she was homesick. They both knew this was a lie, but she accepted it gracefully and let her go. Packing her few things, she could not believe this latest development. Out of a job again, what would Mother say? She would not be pleased, but surely she would understand.

At least she had a few marks to tide her over, until she found another job. She also could give Mother a few marks to keep her happy. As she cycled home, she felt very despondent; surely her luck had to change soon. It seemed to take forever, but at long last she arrived home. Mother's face said it all, "Oh no, the cuckoo has come home again." In her own way she tried to tell her what had gone wrong, but she was not having it. Annalisa was deeply hurt, a hurt which stayed with her all her life. Did she not realise that her daughter had been only a very short step away from a life of drugs and prostitution? Or she could have come home pregnant, another stigma. Was she really so innocent to the way of the world, or did she shut out anything unpleasant?

When Emil came home from work, he was the total opposite and very happy to see his daughter back. He was far more understanding, it had been his worry from the moment she left home, but he dared not tell her. "You have done the right thing," he kept saying in front of Mother over and over again. "Something will turn up, you'll see," he said as he hugged her. "Are you also happy, Klara, that our girl has returned unharmed?"

"Of course I am, but—" she wanted to say.

He cut her off. "There is no 'but'. We have survived as a family through all our problems and Annalisa will get sorted."

There was nothing else, but for Klara to agree reluctantly.

Reiner came visiting as usual on Sunday to take her dancing. But again, she noticed that he had these up and down moods within minutes. He would also disappear often. She assumed he had gone to have a cigarette. At the dance hall, Annalisa was happy to hear music and laughter when they arrived.

For once she stayed with Reiner all evening. She was too worn out to flirt or dance with any other boy. Reiner appreciated this very much as he whirled her around the dancefloor. But he did disappear a couple of times and left her alone. When he came back he seemed very flushed and not his usual self. Eventually she tackled him as to this unusual behaviour. After a lot of probing he admitted he was on drugs. Drugs? She thought she did not hear right, and he confessed he was taking coke. What was happening? Had she not just run away from this alien world? Her knowledge of drugs was limited. To her, all drugs are bad. So this was the reason for his mood swings.

"Why are you doing this?" she asked. She wanted to know, he always seemed so stable.

"I simply cannot cope with the pressures of life," he told her. "The work is very demanding and at home, also, things are very precarious."

Annalisa told him she had noticed his mood swings for a while and pleaded him to give up this terrible habit. In the first instance she wanted to say, 'Don't come and see me anymore,' but he was her best friend. "Is there anything we can do together to stop this?" she wanted to know.

"Not really," was his reply. "It is up to me to conquer this. We could find a flat and live together, then it might be easier for me to give up."

She had not expected this. He had often hinted of

marriage but neither living together nor getting married to him appealed to her. To her it would definitely be a solution; she would be away from this town and could probably find work in another town. "I'll give it some thought and let you know, this has come to me as a total surprise."

Living together would make her parents unhappy and marrying him was not for her.

He said his only happy times were when he came visiting.

He had to promise her, she would only give his proposal serious thoughts, if he tried to start giving up the drugs. Also, never take them when visiting, or tell her parents. With this promise he took her home and left her.

Annalisa sat on her sofa, munching away on some cakes Mother had made and left for her on her return. She could not understand him; he was settled in a job and seemed happy. Why the drug-taking? With all the problems she had been through, she never considered turning to smoking, drink, drugs, sex or religion. Maybe being a bull, she had been able to withstand these temptations. In the next few days, to earn a few marks, she applied to the local newspaper for a paper round. She must have been the oldest girl amongst the others, but they took her on. At least she was out of the house for a few hours, and still had time to look for other work. Some of the farms were a fair way away, to get to, but she loved being out in the fresh air on her bike. However, there was one place she dreaded to deliver to. They were Mother's friends and close by the house. Postman and dog, comes straight to mind. This smallholding had about thirty geese. Geese are better than any guard dog to protect the property. She had to come in from the top field track, and had to pedal though the farm to the house and leave by a locked gate on the bottom.

These geese hated her with a vengeance, and looked forward to their daily entertainment. First she was wearing her red trouser suit; in theory red should only make a bull angry, but they spotted and heard her coming. And as soon as one would see or hear, they ran towards her, biting her feet and legs. She even walked the bike on tiptoe to avoid them, but never succeeded in fooling them. This one particular day, they were more vicious than on other days. After delivering the newspaper she found it impossible to even get back on her bike. As she struggled to get on, the biggest of the lot bit her hard on her leg and would not let go of her red trousers. At last, she got on her bike, but he would not give up, pecking away, and she gave him the hardest kick she could manage. She still had to open the gate with the others chasing her. Not big boy, he seemed to be a bit dazed. At last she managed, with a tear in her trousers. She cried over her trousers; her best possession. The farmers were Mother's friends and come visiting often.

The next day when Annalisa came home, the farmer's wife was sitting down having coffee with Klara. Frau Hovel Mann was crying and sobbing her heart out. After a while she was able to speak. "Oh, Klara," she said. "Just guess what has happened. This morning I found my biggest gander dead, and I cannot understand what happened to him. He was all right when I last saw him at night. It is a total mystery." Even her husband could not understand why. "He will not even eat him, worried about what might have been wrong with him."

Annalisa listened to this, staying very quiet; she knew it was that hard kick she gave him, but she could not feel sorry for him.

"Klara, would you like to have him? I don't know what to do with him."

Of course, Klara was over the moon and accepted gracefully.

In the evening when Emil came home from work, Klara was busy plucking this enormous goose. She told him the story she was told by Frau Hovel Mann, and he also was a bit worried as to the cause of death. Annalisa winked at him, to say she needed to speak to him. They went to their secret office, the cowshed. She explained the whole laughable saga to him. He could not believe it at first, but then he burst out laughing. "Bad luck on the goose's side and good luck to us," he said, between laughing. "But we keep this our secret, Mother might tell her friends and you will be in the doghouse." Both went back to help with the plucking.

The next day they had Christmas in the spring, not in December, tasting every bit as good or better. This gander must have been the ringleader. When Annalisa delivered the next day's papers, the others were still vicious but not as bad.

Chapter 16

As she had not seen Stefan for a while, she decided to visit him. She dared not tell him why she was again out of work, and decided to tell him that she did not like her (ha ha). On arrival at his lodgings the landlady opened the door to her. "He is working late, about another two hours, before he'll be home," she said. "You are welcome to wait." And she asked her to come in. Annalisa accepted this gladly, it had been a long journey and she was also a bit tired. His landlady seemed a nice kind person, as she made a cup of imitation coffee for her. Perhaps it was a change for her to have someone to talk to, and talk she did.

The talking of course led to Stefan. Annalisa asked her what it was like living with him. At first she was a bit reluctant to talk about him, she wanted to know how serious she was regarding him. But put two women together, it did not matter, young or old, talking about men, they spoke the same language. She came straight out with it, what Annalisa already had suspected, saying, "If you marry this man you will have a very hard life. He is extremely demanding as to having his meals on time and his clothes always looking pristine." There had been times when she wanted to tell him to leave. Only relying on his money, which she depended on, being a war widow, stopped her doing so. "If I was your mother I would try my best to stop this romance."

She herself already knew it would not be a bed of roses. When he arrived home, he was not pleased to see her. He had made arrangements with his friends for the evening out and needed a rest before doing so.

"Can I come along?" Annalisa asked him.

"No, that is not possible," he answered. "Pubs, men and women don't mix very well, and I need time by myself with my friends."

"So that is just for tonight, or always?" she insisted on an answer. "I won't be with you in the pub." She wanted to know.

"I told you," he said, "and there is nothing more to talk about."

He then turned to his landlady, asking for his dinner and telling her he will see her on Sunday. Annalisa just stood there, not believing she had been dismissed, like a servant. She could not believe what had happened to her just now. She had biked thirty kilometres to see him, and he could not be bothered to spend one hour with her. She said goodbye to his landlady outside, bursting out in tears; she started sobbing her eyes out.

The landlady tried to comfort her, saying, "This is what I tried to tell you. He will do when and what he wants to do with no regards for your feelings."

Annalisa thanked her for being so kind to her, and started biking back home. Anger started setting in now. How dare he treat her like this? She will put him straight when she sees him on Sunday. To her, this was a world she was not used to; even Mother's nagging was never mean. Maybe Father was right once more – they were a breed to themselves where he came from, where men were men and women there for their pleasure and to look after them. *Well not this girl, he better look somewhere else.*

He arrived promptly for afternoon coffee and cake, all spruced up. God, was he handsome with his blond hair and blue eyes, a true German specimen. Klara of course could not do enough for him, but Father as usual only spoke a few words to be polite. Stefan knew he was in trouble with Annalisa; she greeted him with a stony look. They set off to go dancing as usual. He asked her why the bad looks.

"How dare you ask me why the evil eye?" she spat out. "It was your behaviour when I visited you in the week."

"Let's find a place to stop and talk this through," he asked.

It was a beautiful spring day with the sun shining and nature waking up to bloom and love. Maybe not the best setting, as they found a place amongst the trees by themselves to have this discussion. He listened to her intently, as she told him, that in all these years Father never once went out by himself. Their whole life was being together. This was not what she was looking for, there had to be give and take, but not one-sided. Yes, he could have friends and spend time with them, but so should she. She would rather finish their relationship now than carry on, if he felt she was asking too much. For a while he just sat there; no-one had spoken to him like this before. At last he answered her that he admired her parents for their lovely relationship, something he also wanted. His parents were the total opposite; his father ruled with an iron fist and discipline. If not obeyed there was the belt for the kids. His mother never disagreed with him, she was too frightened to do so. They never went anywhere together, and Mother only cleaned and looked after the children. "My feelings for you are very deep. That is why I come all this way to see you. I will try my best to please you more in the future," were his last words.

How could she still be angry with him after that? A sort of truce was established. But somehow, deep down something was nagging her, as he caressed her and made love to her. How gentle he was with his lovemaking, the opposite of the problem they had just discussed. He had to leave early as he had a very early shift.

When Annalisa arrived back home, Emil had noticed that all was not well in Loveland and asked her. She told him about her visit with his landlady and his behaviour, and the talk they just had. All he would say when she finished was, "You know, Shatzi, I only want you to be happy, but I still don't think he is the right man for you."

Mother, of course, thought he was lovely and could see nothing wrong. all she would say was, "After all, you are not perfect either."

The weeks that followed were becoming more and more difficult, especially with her not having a full-time job. Ingrid also became a constant argument between these two women. Her reports from school were dismal; she was lazy and simply did not want to learn. When she came home from school just after one o'clock, she would have her dinner and a rest period. After that she needed to do her homework, but all persuading on Annalisa's part, fell on stony ground.

All Mother would say was, "Let her play, she is only little, and all the studying you did has not helped you to get a decent job."

Annalisa felt very hurt by these words; she only wanted the best for her sister. She also let slip that it probably would be better if she looked further afield. On one of those disagreeable days, Emil came home from work with news of a job for her. Annalisa cringed, the last one did not work out too well.

He was saying that his farmer had a visit from their friends. They had come to show off their new baby. The lady was a distant relative of theirs, and on one of her visits she had fallen in love with one of the farm hands. Her rich parents were outraged that she might marry beneath her, but in due course she did. The parents did not want to associate with the pair and bought them a small nursery garden centre, about ten kilometres away in the next village. In their employ was one farmhand and a maid. After the maid had been with them several years, she left to get married, hence the opening for a job.

"So this is what I have finally come down to, being a maid." The word servant, maid, Knecht, had nasty rings to it. She was nobody's servant, this was a thing from the dark ages, and not the modern times she grew up in. Klara was all for it; she had been a maid for several years and it had done her no harm. She simply could not understand why her daughter made such a fuss over it. What happened to her snobbery, only to be used when it suited her? And so, Annalisa set off with a heavy heart the next morning to see the lady for the job.

The time was 10am when she arrived and was shown into the kitchen to wait. After about one hour of waiting the lady of the house finally came. She was dressed in a very nice dress, as if she was going out. Her hair, also, was well groomed. She introduced herself as Frau Jagermann in such a way that you knew immediately she was the boss. Not the prettiest of women, about thirty-something. Annalisa at once realised that she had passed the sell-by date in her grandeur circles and would be lucky to still find love. She asked Annalisa a lot of questions and seemed to be satisfied with the answers.

Her descriptions of what she expected of her regarding the work, were long and varied. With regards to the wages, it was a pittance, but she told her that every Christmas they give their maid a new dress for a present. Annalisa had to bite her tongue, thinking, *The first chance I get, I am out of here,* even if she did not get a new dress (HA HA). And so Frau Jagermann said she would give her a try and dismissed her.

Pedalling home, if she had been the crying type, now was the time. Oh, how down she felt. She had tried so hard to please her parents with studying, now it came to this. "Well, maybe," she said to herself, "I cannot go any further down the next phase. I have to get a break." It was not the work, that never bothered her before, it was that the attitude of Frau Jagermann made her feel like a servant. She swore to herself that if ever she became an employer, she would treat each one of her employees as equals. She also had no regrets of not getting married as a way out. This, to her, was another form of bondage. She was a free spirit and she let nobody take that away from her.

On arriving home, Klara was happy that Annalisa got the job. To her, it was one less mouth to feed, and no more friction for her being there. Father knew what was going on in Annalisa's head, they were soulmates. He tried his hardest to cheer her up, saying, "You have to understand Mother, she also lost everything. She loved her beautiful home and her boys, and also to came to this existence. All she has now are a few lousy china plates you saved for her. She cannot accept that there are millions of people worse off, without even their loved ones. As one example just look next door, Frau Janson lost a child and husband in the war. Myself, I don't say anything, but I am not over the moon either, over the present state of the work I am doing and the whole situation. Things will improve, I have been there before. You are young, give it a chance."

Annalisa felt better after the pep talk. She and her father were soulmates who understood each other. And once more, after a couple of days she set off to start another job. She was shown to her room by Herr Jagermann. It was in the loft, two storeys high, away from the main living quarters. She thought, *This is not too bad, a room for myself with a bed in it.* But this happiness was short lived. He then showed her a small adjoining room, a pretty room, all painted blue with animal murals on the wall. He explained to her that due to the difficult birth by his wife, she needed a lot of rest, and the baby sleeps at night in this nursery.

Frau Jagermann never mentioned to her that she was to be nanny as well; she knew exactly what was in store for her having brought up Ingrid. Not that she minded children, she loved them, especially babies, and he was adorable. She was going up in the world; she was the nanny, not the maid. How snobbish can she get? She laughed to herself.

Putting her few belongings away and changing into her work clothes, she made her way to the kitchen. Frau Jagermann was nowhere to be seen and the two men were busy working in the nursery. She started clearing away the breakfast dishes and tidying up. Close to lunchtime, Frau Jagermann appeared, dressed to take Baby for a walk.

"Make sandwiches and soup for the two men and yourself," she told Annalisa, not showing her where anything was. For a while she stood in the kitchen, not sure where to start, and then realised that the only way was to get on with it. After searching the fridge and cupboards, she got lunch together. She went into the nursery and called the men. Herr Jagermann was a pleasant enough man when his wife was not around, definitely with little schooling and unable to give orders. The other man, his name was Johann, friendly towards her. Not the best-looking fellow, a short five feet six inches with red hair. The trio hit it off. And lunch was appreciated, which made her happy.

The fly in the ointment was Frau Jagermann, as soon as she appeared the atmosphere changed. To her, all three, even her husband, were servants below her. After lunch she had to clean their apartment and the house. Thinking there might be a little rest period for her, how wrong could she be? The next few hours she had to help in the nursery, weeding the plants. Then it was time to prepare the vegetables for the evening meal, with Frau Jagermann doing the cooking. Herr and Frau Jagermann retired to the house to have their meal and left Annalisa and Johann to eat in the kitchen. By now it was roughly seven thirty and Annalisa still had to clean the dishes and kitchen. At last she was finish at eight thirty, to go her room. She collapsed onto the bed – it had been a hard day. Maybe when she had settled into the routine things would work out all right. But oh no, promptly at 10pm, Herr Jagermann knocked on the door and handed her Baby Anton. During the afternoon Frau Jagermann had shown Annalisa the prepared bottles for him. His next feed was to be at five-thirty in the morning. There are three sets of parents in this world. The first category: live and let live, baby knows when he is hungry. The second parents read every book and swore by them. Everything went by the clock and never varied.

Frau Jagermann definitely belonged to the second group. She could not understand how any mother could give a helpless little life to a total stranger like her. But then Frau Jagermann maybe knew better, being brought up by nannies. Annalisa rocked Anton back and forth and eventually he was ready for sleep. She too, was totally exhausted. But as she knew from experience, no baby of that age sleeps through the night. Sheer wishful thinking. And at two o'clock prompt, first a little gristle developing into full-blown screaming. Half asleep, she picked him up, trying to calm him, but nothing helped. He was hungry. She had been told to let him scream, but this was against her inner instinct, and eventually she went down to the kitchen to collect a warm bottle.

Within seconds he stopped crying as she put the bottle into his mouth. As he suckled, she dozed and then made sure to burp him, before putting him down to sleep again. She looked at him, all contented, such a lovely chappie. When her alarm clock went for a repeat performance she could hardly open her eyes. Anton was stirring for the first feed of the day. The next hour was taken up with cleaning and feeding him. This done, she made the fire in the stove to have porridge and egg and bacon ready, for the men to start work. This done, she spent the next couple of hours in her room with Anton to rest and play. Ten o'clock, prompt Herr Jagermann collected Anton, and told her to prepare breakfast for his wife and coffee for the men. Between all this she managed to eat a bite. And lunch again, was there to be made – soup and thick sausages. And as the day before, Frau Jagermann appeared after bathing the baby to go for a walk.

She was not too pleased when she discovered the missing bottle, and told Annalisa so in no uncertain terms. But Annalisa told her, in her home it was thought of as cruel to let any child cry, and she had no intention of starting now. She backed down, muttering that she was spoiling him, and left. The rest of the day continued as the day before, with cleaning and later on helping in the nursery or the fields. She counted the hours she worked, amounting to fifteen hours, not taking in the nights. Call it slavery or a labour of love.

During the weeks that followed, Stefan came to visit her once. Frau Jagermann was not pleased, and finally after clearing up the dinner plates and kitchen, let her go at 8.30pm. Other than that, she saw him every other weekend, her time off. This started at 8.30pm Friday evening until 6.30am Monday morning. It was sheer bliss to pedal home in the dark and back again, whatever the weather. Nothing was keep her there, in her prison, any longer than necessary.

Stefan had become more considerate but however much longer this affair was lasting, she knew he was not to be her life partner. On her weekends off she would also go to the labour exchange, to look for anything better. Germany was improving, but not her town. Most people travelled out of the town for work. At last, even Mother was sympathetic to her plight.

The work in the nursery was getting harder with each day. Her most hated job was the roses. However much she covered her arms, after a few days they looked as if a dozen cats been attacking her. Next in line were the tomatoes in the greenhouse. By the end of the evening after plucking them, she looked like a green-eyed monster. But last and not least, backbreaking work was the weeding in the fields. The two men took great delight in racing her, as she struggled to keep up. No, this gardening work was definitely not for her. She was a city girl born and bred.

A little relief came when Frau Jagermann went away for a whole month with Anton on holiday. And there, she thought she was on holiday all the time, as little as she did. At least after dinner she could do as she pleased. Not that there was anywhere to go, but the whole evening and night were her own. As much as she loved Anton, he was becoming a handful.

That month was a pleasure; the men were happy

with her cooking and not very demanding. Even Herr Jagermann seemed to enjoy the absence of his wife. But all good things have to end. Frau Jagermann returned with a vengeance. She saw dust where there was none, and picked on the smallest thing not one hundred percent correct. Even her husband was in the firing line. How could anybody treat a husband like that? It was degrading to watch, making sure he knew his place, as it was her money which gave him the status of a boss. Anton had grown but not forgotten Annalisa as he smiled when she cuddled him.

She wondered if Frau Jagermann had given in to the night feed, or let him cry. Well, she would soon know, as she put him down for the night. And two o'clock prompt, he started stirring, but Annalisa was ready with his bottle and clean nappy, and went peacefully back to sleep. Not a word was said over the missing bottle, and an extra one was prepared for her.

Autumn was setting in, with most of the flowers and vegetables being sold. The work was getting easier, however, Annalisa was deeply unhappy.

Autumn changed to winter with Christmas on the horizon, when the break came, she had prayed for. On one of her many visits to the labour exchange, she was told there was work in England. England? How could that be? But after a lengthy explanation, she was told with so many men killed in the war, there was a shortage of workers. For those with good education, they would be able to go into nursing, and all others into factories for a variety of jobs. Her head was spinning; to go to a foreign country, leave alone to work, was unheard of in her circles. She was given a variety of forms to fill in and pamphlets to read, biking as fast as she could to get home, to read all this information when she was alone in the evening. Yes, it was all true; her passage would be paid, with a guarantee of a job waiting. The wages quoted were unbelievable, after the pittance she was getting at the moment. There was not one moment of hesitation on her behalf.

Anything had to be better than her present condition. Her immediate thoughts were not to tell anyone about this. And so, she set to work to achieve her goal of leaving. The first hurdle appeared as she read through the application, that the form had to be signed by two people in government, or one could be the local priest. She could not think of one, let alone two. But as many times before, she would sleep on it and in the morning, think with a clear head. But however hard she tried to find the answer, all she was able to come up with, were the local doctor and her Protestant priest. The doctor might be all right, as she got on well with him. But the preacher, a different kettle of fish. Only a few years ago she had called him a liar. Her decision was to go and see Herr Waldmann, the doctor, on her next weekend off.

Stefan came promptly on Sunday to take her dancing. He looked so handsome in his blue suit and blond hair shining. How could she possibly leave him? During the evening, he had noticed her absentmindedness and asked her, "Is anything wrong?"

"No, it is work, I am so unhappy there," she replied.

The lovemaking did not help either; she was wrestling with a big decision in her life. This was not Munich. If all failed she could walk home, but

England, a foreign country, not so easy to return to Germany. But it was only for a couple of years, until Germany had recovered even more from the war. Never had a fortnight seemed so long, before she could put her plan into action.

Herr Waldmann was pleased to see her looking well; not so long ago he had operated on her. He was surprised to hear of her plans. "This is a very big step you are taking. Have you thought it through?" he inquired.

She told him a little about the last few years of hers.

"I gladly give you my reference and I am pleased you thought of me," he said. "I wish you all the luck in the world. You have not had a lot of it until now, and bon voyage."

Next, she put the preacher's name down; she decided to hope for the best. Maybe they would not check too carefully. Also, all the details about her education, last or present employer. All this done, on her next weekend off, she handed all the paperwork in to the labour exchange.

Well, it was now with the gods for the success of the application to be improved. She was told it would take at least a month for the approval.

Chapter 17

Christmas arrived and Frau Jagermann, true to her word, gave her a dress for a present. If she wanted to wear it she would truly look like a servant, with its white collar on a dark woolly material – drab, drab. It was a good thing she was not able to read her mind. *Little do you know.* Annalisa packed it away to give it back to her to give to the next slave.

She had an extra day off, which made it a nice Christmas. Father had managed to buy a bike for Ingrid. The weather was very pleasant, cold and crisp. The girls went out on their bikes; Ingrid was quite confident, she had been learning on her friend's bike. As they were riding along on a near-empty road, a fox shot out in front of Ingrid from the bushes. She put on the brakes and as Annalisa was behind her, they collided with each other. Ingrid's new bike was twisted badly; she started crying her eyes out. Annalisa also felt like crying; her best pair of nylons was ruined and she had a big bruise on her knee. They pushed the bikes home. Emil was not impressed, it had cost him dearly to buy her bike.

Of course, as usual, Ingrid managed to twist it in such a way that it all been Annalisa's fault. She must have been too close to her to bump into her. Mother promptly took her version and commented, "There is always something going wrong when you are around," to Annalisa. Nobody took any notice of the deep cut on her knee, bleeding away. All the fuss was being made over poor Ingrid. Annalisa then realised, she made the right decision to go to England, if they would have her.

New Year came and Frau Jagermann had invited her parents. This would be their first visit after burying the hatchets. She started cleaning the house, as if it had not been done for a couple of years. Each evening Annalisa ached from top to bottom, and then Anton still wanted to be played with. Poor husband, he also was told in no uncertain terms to get the place shipshape.

They arrived in a beautiful old Mercedes car, chauffeur and all. If Frau Jagermann was difficult, her mother was near enough impossible. She had all four of them running around to please her. Her interest in her grandson was non-existent. Annalisa was told, to take Anton into another room; she would get a migraine listening to him.

The grandfather was no better; all he was interested in was reading and having a drink. And as for their son-in-law, they treated him as if he was invisible. But after a week of this agony they departed. Everyone sighed with relief; even Frau Jagermann had a smile on her face. Annalisa could not wait to get home on her free weekend. Maybe a letter had arrived. No such luck, but as Mother and Annalisa sat in the kitchen, there was a knock on the front door. Annalisa had the shock of her life.

The preacher who she was not fond of stood there. For a moment she was speechless. Very friendly, he asked if Klara was in.

"Please come in," Annalisa offered.

Klara was also lost for words but recovered quickly and offered him a cup of coffee. Annalisa made the coffee in the best china cups they had.

"How have you been?" he asked Mother. "And how about Ingrid, Annalisa and Father?"

Mother launched into her long list of illnesses for the next half hour. Of course, all the other problems were mentioned. He then said, he fully understood their hard times but would be grateful to see them in church sometimes now she was better.

Klara promised with all her heart to try better in the future. Not once was the last argument mentioned.

"I do have a special reason why I came." And he dropped the bombshell. "As you know, Annalisa has applied to go to England to work." Did she know about it?

Mother's face was blank, but very quickly, she said, "Oh yes, she had mentioned in passing, but did not think any more of it."

He wanted to know how she felt about it, as she had put his name down for a reference.

Well Klara was in full swing now, saying, "Even though we have not been to church for a while, you of all people know that she can take care of herself. There is nothing here for her and if she can better herself we all should help to do so. In the past few years and all the years prior she supported the family to survive in the hard times. She is a hard worker and very caring."

Annalisa found it difficult to believe her determination to set him straight. But he still was not satisfied. He turned to Annalisa, wanting to know why she wanted to leave the country. Her reply was, "Mother has said it all," but she would be very disappointed if his reference about her was not favourable. The other one had come back with glowing colours, she bluffed.

At this moment, it would only be for two years, but time would tell. He seemed satisfied and after Mother once more promised to attend church, he departed. He was leaden with mother's goodies of homemade liver sausage, black pudding and other items. His bike squeaked under the load. He had promised to give a good reference.

When Annalisa returned to the kitchen, Mother's face was like thunder and lightning. "How dare you put me in such an awkward position?" she shouted.

"At this moment it is only a pipedream, I was not telling you until I knew more," she defended herself. But as always. it was not her leaving, only not knowing which hurt her pride.

When Father came home the first topic was her applying, not leaving, and not telling. Emil, as usual, calmed her. "Look, Klarchen, did she tell you about all the others she applied for? I am sure if this one is for real, she will tell you."

Father was impressed.

"So Schätzchen, what Hitler did not manage, you

might do and go to England." He said it with a twinkle in his eyes. But with a more serious look, he asked if she had thought this through carefully. After all, it is a foreign country with different ways and language.

She showed him all the government pamphlets and their involvement to satisfy his mind.

"Let's hope you get the work. Here, luck has not been on your side." Most of all he was happy that she was telling Stefan to sling his hook; he hated this fellow with a vengeance.

Monday morning, she made her way back to the nursery. What greeted her, she did not expect. Herr Jagermann greeted her to have a talk. They had also been approached for a reference. Herr Jagermann was very impressed by her going to England. He sighed. "This is something I wanted to do. I won't stand in your way and will give you a good reference."

One down, one more to go – this would be tough. At lunchtime Frau Jagermann appeared with little Anton. She greeted Annalisa, friendlier than all the other times before. Of course, she came straight to the point, saying she had been contacted by the labour exchange in connection with the British government. "Asking me for a reference as to your work and character. I am surprised you want to leave us, I thought you were happy here."

Annalisa's brain was working overtime; she knew everything hung on her reply. She replied, "Yes, I am happy here. Especially with little Anton, he is a treasure. But I am a city girl, I love being amongst a lot of people and the hustle and bustle of a big city.

Also, I felt the garden and field work, I am not doing my best."

"You underestimate yourself," she answered. "My husband and I are more than satisfied with your work. I see your mind is made up. I would like you to stay, but if not, I will give you a good reference."

Annalisa thanked her profusely, eating humble pie. "It will be some time before I leave, plenty of time for you to find a replacement." After that, Annalisa disappeared into her bedroom for a few minutes to recover. Her nerves always showed in her face and neck, which were now the colour of beetroot. Did she pull it off? She felt she did all right.

Life after that carried on as normal. Anton was becoming more and more of a handful. Frau Jagermann let him sleep a lot during the day, hence for him, playtime was at night with Annalisa. She felt sorry for the little chappie. Whatever else, she had bonded with him very much, and she loved him. Parting from him would be difficult.

How can you explain to a baby? Parting had to be done, if she did not want to end up like Herr Jagermann, grateful for being allowed to slave his life away. On her next visit home, still no letter had arrived. She felt down; even going dancing with Stefan did not cheer her up.

Tuesday evening, after that weekend, she was just washing up the dinner plates. Emil appeared. Shocked, seeing him she assumed something was wrong with Mother again.

"Calm," he told her. "All is fine. Your letter has arrived, and rather than have it lying about for twelve days, I brought it here to you."

He was a good dad to pedal all that way after work to bring her the letter. Her hands were shaking as she opened the large envelope. Full to the brim with pamphlets and information, and the news for her – she had a job. The date of departure, the 13th of March 1949. The thirteenth – a good or bad omen, once more time would tell. She jumped up for joy and hugged and kissed her dad.

"I knew you would do it, Shatzi," he said, laughing. "We'll talk more soon, but now I have to get back to Mother," and he biked off.

Herr and Frau Jagermann were very impressed that this mouse had achieved something like that. Annalisa ate more humble pie; in their own way they did help. They now went about in earnest to find a replacement for her. The next days and weeks, she did her work in a daze, thinking, *In a short while I be free again,* to do as she pleased.

Mother was very impressed with her daughter, something she could boast about, to anyone willing to listen. Reiner was waiting for her on her next visit with tears in his eyes. Sobbing, he said, "I am so sorry to see you leave, I always hoped one day we would be an item." He had been a very good friend to her in all these years.

If only she could have felt more for him, there would have been no need to go away to support herself. He was by now earning enough in his job to support a wife and family. But he still had not given up his drug habit, and however much he tried to hide it, she knew. The extremes of his behaviour and getting slimmer told the story. But it was his life and his own decisions.

On the last visit of Stefan, Annalisa had arranged to see him at his lodgings. Her thoughts were, better to see him on foreign ground about her news. As she waited for him to come home she chatted with his landlady about her forthcoming journey and leaving him. "I think you made a very wise decision and I am pleased for you," she said. Strange how both Father and her disliked him, surely two different people cannot be wrong.

He was pleased to see her and kissed and hugged her. Thoughts were tumbling through her head; was she right in what she was about to do? Still more caring towards her, it made her think, if he can change why not her? She steered him to the furthest corner of the coffee bar, trying very hard to break the news to him. But he dug his own grave with his words, as he mumbled, "I think you only come to see me to spend my money."

This gave her the courage to tell him. "This will probably be the last time we see each other, and then there will be no need to spend on me."

"What do you mean?" he asked after the shock sentence by her.

Annalisa tried to explain to him of her years in Xanten. She hated this small town, and her dislike for the people. The struggle for food and the struggle for a decent job. The only job she had enjoyed was with Herr Molders, the tailor. As for this last job; job description: slavery. "I have only signed up for two years, and who knows after that?"

After they left the café he burst out, "You strung me along all this time while you were looking for better pastures. And I thought at times about marriage. How could you have been so deceitful?" He rattled on and on.

Yes, she had to admit, that she did not feel proud of herself, not telling him. She was glad she had this conversation on neutral ground. For a while they walked back to his lodgings in silence, to collect her bike. As they were parting, he gave her a long, lingering kiss, saying, "You hurt me deeply, at least there is not another man. Promise you'll write to me, when you are settled. I will not promise to wait for you, but at least keep in touch, and after all, two years is not that long."

Annalisa did shed a tear as she biked the long way home. Emil knew by her expression what had happened, but kept silent. She will tell him in good time.

Frau Jagermann managed to find a replacement very quickly. Poor little Anton; there will be many changes in his lifetime. She was extremely happy to spend the last couple of weeks with the family. Mother was in her element to help her get clothes ready for the journey.

Mother managed to get material for a new dress, beautiful georgette. Annalisa had put weight on, because of her sweet tooth, and was now a size sixteen. She was still able to carry it with her height – five foot five.

Stefan came once more before she was leaving. Emil was civilised towards him, as he knew the romance was over, which pleased him. Mother still swooned over him, and she made a nice meal with fried potatoes. When he had gone, Annalisa washed up the dishes, a chore she did not like. Water had to be fetched from the pump, then boiled on the stove, and finally washed in a small bowl. But she was happy, it had been a lovely Sunday. After the three of them had gone to bed, she settled down on her sofa and did some knitting. A few hours had passed, and it was getting near midnight when Emil rushed down, saying Mother was in terrible pain, having one of her attacks. Annalisa knew at once the cause of it – fried potatoes were the culprit. Mother knew she should not eat them but carried on regardless. Emil brought her downstairs to keep her warm, and Annalisa stoked the fire up to make a warm drink for her. But however hard they tried to make her comfortable, the pains would not let up.

Emil was getting very worried, the pains were not subsiding. As a rule, in the past, after several hours she would be better. She even refused her favourite cup of coffee. He decided not to go to work, take Ingrid to school and get the doctor. Not very long had gone by, when he arrived back with the doctor in his car. The doctor was one of the few people to possess a car. He must have impressed the doctor with the urgency of the situation. One look at Klara and after a short examination, he announced, "She has to go to the hospital immediately."

"What is wrong with her?" Emil asked.

Herr Waldmann answered him, "She has gallstones and needs to be operated on at once."

"Is it life threatening?" Emil wanted to know.

"Yes, if we don't hurry up to get her to the hospital."

Annalisa gave Mother a quick spruce up and then they helped her into his car. Absolutely devastated after what she had just witnessed, Annalisa sat down and made herself a coffee. This was not happening to her, she thought. *I am to leave in the next couple of days.* How could she? She felt sorry for Mother, but not again. If it all went wrong, she would not be able to go to England.

Xanten, being a very religious town, had a very large Catholic convent. The nuns were running the hospital with an iron hand. She worried that Mother would not be so well looked after, because of her religion. But when Father came back, he told her, seeing how ill she was, they showed her a lot of compassion. "She is having her operation this afternoon because of the urgency, and we can go and see her tomorrow morning. There are a few things she needs and when you go, take them with you. I myself will go in the evening. Now I have to go and tell the farmer why I missed work and come back to have the afternoon off."

Annalisa dared not ask any more details, seeing how worried he was. She just carried on with cleaning and collecting Ingrid from school. There was one good thing – as Ingrid now had her own pushbike, it was far easier. She was taking the news with Mother badly – after all, she was her favourite – crying all the way home. Annalisa tried her best to console her, but when she tried to get out of doing her homework, her patience snapped. "You can wrap Mother around your finger, but while she is away I am in charge and you do homework first, and then play."

Father listened to this conversation and said, "I totally agree with your sister."

After some more moaning she sat down and did her homework. Most of the time, when the two of them were together, they got on all right. However, as soon as Mother was around, she gave Annalisa a hard time. Emil went to the cowshed for a wash, another big performance. Water had to be boiled on the stove for this to happen. Then he made himself look handsome and put on his best suit and shirt. He wanted to be there when Mother came out of the theatre. She would still notice if he did not try to look his best. The girls also had to have their bath, to look good and waste no water. He then set off to see Mother. His last words were, "I don't know how long I shall be, so don't worry."

It was late afternoon when he arrived at the hospital, and went in search of information. He was lucky, the surgeon was in attendance and explained the operation to him. It was a lady surgeon and she was very sympathetic to his worrying. "Gallstones is an often-performed operation with very little risk to it to it," she told him. She would operate in one hour and advised him to go home, as Klara would be happily sedated and probably would not come around till midnight. But he wanted to be there and asked if he could stay. Of course he could, and a room was provided for him. Emil was happy that the lady surgeon was performing this operation, not Herr Waldmann. He had been in the war, a field surgeon – his nickname in town was the butcher. He was never concerned how big the scar was, as long he had saved their life.

Annalisa herself had one of these enormous scars, when he did the appendix operation on her. Many doctors in later life would ask her what it had been for, and then shake their heads when she told them. Close to midnight, one of the nuns came to fetch Emil. Klara had her operation and was in the recovery room. "You are only able to say hello and then let her rest," he was told.

Not really sure if she heard him, he bent down and gave her a kiss. She did feel him and smiled. But she was very weak and he decided to go home. The nun told him all had gone very well and the surgeon would speak to him in the morning. He pedalled home as quick as he could to tell Annalisa the good news. She was relieved that everything had gone all right. For Emil, she had saved dinner, which he devoured – he had not eaten all day.

In the morning Emil told Ingrid that Mother was all right. For joy, she started crying again.

"Come, stop that nonsense. You are seeing her tonight. I am seeing the surgeon this morning, and tonight we will all go to see Mother." He took Ingrid to school and left Annalisa to her work. She kept herself busy with cleaning around the two small rooms. Emil went to work for a few hours afterwards.

As they sat down for their evening meal, the girls were eager to hear the news. Yes, he had spoken to the surgeon – the operation had been a hundred percent success, but Klara had been very lucky for the quick action by Herr Waldmann. The girls did a little victory dance. It was time to visit Mother, and all three biked to town. Expecting to see a very ill-looking mother, they were in for a big surprise. Klara's knack of making friends quickly worked again. She had befriended one of the nuns and another lady, who were only too happy to make her look pretty. They had washed her and combed her hair and put on her best nightdress. If you did not look at the pipes coming out from underneath the bed, one could wonder why she was there.

Relief came over them, as they kissed Mother. She proudly showed her gallstones, one as big as a pigeon egg. The lady surgeon came by, pleased with Klara's progress.

"How long will she be in here?" Emil asked.

"Your wife is a very strong and determined lady. About ten days, approximately, if there are no complications," she said.

Emil's ears pricked up. "Complications?"

"None are expected, it is only a figure of speech," were her final words.

He thanked her once more and returned to Klara's bedside.

The week went by as normal with Father working and Annalisa being Mother. Saturdays and Sundays had double and longer visiting hours. They arrived, all cleaned and spruced up in their Sunday clothes. As soon as they entered the hospital, a nun came rushing over to see them at reception and asked them to wait. Emil and the girls went white, expecting bad news.

The head nurse appeared and asked them to sit down. "Please don't be alarmed," she said to Emil.

"Your wife is back in the operation theatre."

"Whatever for?" he cried out, unable to control himself.

"The surgeon came by, not usual on a Sunday. Your wife was in some discomfort, when she noticed that one of the pipes was not draining and blocked. At present, she is sorting it out and it would be better if you came back for visiting this evening."

Emil got very angry, unusual for him, and shouted, "Someone slipped up, not checking enough." He would take this further; this was sheer negligence.

Annalisa calmed him down. "Look, Vati, Mother's nine lives are holding out. The surgeon is with her and will sort it out. Her luck was with her, for the surgeon to come around on the off chance.

Three very quieted people made their way home, saying a silent prayer. Evening could not come fast enough for them to return.

Klara, again, looked nice, as if nothing had happened. Emil kissed and teased her, saying, how could she give them all these shocks? "If it had not been a lady surgeon I would have started worrying. As for the attention, I am sure you'll get it from now on."

He wanted to complain and report the incident, but Mother stopped him. "I am alive and grateful," was her comment. "Please let it go."

She had to promise him, at the slightest pain, she would ring the bell.

"It is all this cleaning and rubbing they are occupied with, instead of looking after their patients."

But all four were relieved that all was well.

Annalisa was getting more and more frustrated as the day of her departure was fast approaching. She did not dare raise this subject to her father. All the paperwork had been delivered and was in place for her departure.

Monday, as usual, was washday, and she decided to wash her red trouser suit for the journey. It was a cool spring day when she hung out the washing. Some more chores and she was off to collect Ingrid. Late afternoon, she went out to collect the dry washing, but where was her trouser suit? She just stood there, had it blown off the line? No, the pegs were still there. It could not be; thieves had stolen her best possession and left all the other laundry.

Both she and Frau Janson had been in all day, with the exception of her collecting Ingrid. She burst out crying and ran into Frau Janson to tell her what has happened. The house was a distance away from other houses and town, for thieves to pass by to steal. "I'll have a look for you," Frau Janson said. "See if I have a spare pair of trousers which would fit you."

All Annalisa could think was, *What else could go wrong?*

Emil was also very upset, not so much for the pair of trousers but the broader picture emerging. Today it was trousers, what would it be next? "In future, you keep all doors locked at all times," he told Annalisa, "and I will warn Frau Janson, also, of the danger."

In the evening, going to see Mother they looked uptight. It was amazing to see the improvement in Mutti, looking very well. Emil went to see the lady surgeon for news.

"If all carries on at this rate, you can take your wife

home this weekend," were her words.

Emil and the girls were overjoyed with the news. After the slip-up, the nuns could not do enough for Mother, and she was in her element.

After arriving back home, Annalisa thought the time was right to approach her father. "Vati, what are we doing with me leaving?" she inquired.

"Look, Shatzi," he replied, "I have not forgotten, but needed to be certain with Mother. You know I want you to go, and I know there is nothing here for you in the foreseeable future. I have already put wheels into motion, and spoke to the farmer. He has given me fourteen days off to start with, when Mother comes home. He will also keep giving me all the extras, including milk. So if nothing else happens, you can go on your journey, not that I want you to go. I will miss you even when at times it does not seem so to you, but you know I don't like disagreements."

She hugged and kissed her dad and cried for joy.

"Let's see if any of my work trousers fit you for your journey."

They laughed as she put on a pair of his work trousers; they were too long, but otherwise they fitted. Her total wardrobe consisted of Dad's trousers and the georgette dress. Speaking to Frau Janson, she also promised to look after Klara and Ingrid.

A few days later, while Mother was making remarkable progress, Emil spoke to her about his plans when she comes home. He did not expect the outburst which she threw at him. All her life, towards Annalisa, she had been indifferent to her being around. She now strongly objected to her leaving. She was saying, she had brought up a child, and now she needed her help she was off to a foreign land. Annalisa felt very hurt by this, telling her that in her opinion she had done more than was expected of the average child. But Klara stubbornly refused to change her mind. This created a rift between the two women lasting several years. As predicted, Mother was brought home on Saturday by ambulance.

For the remaining week, Annalisa had been cleaning, so as not to leave a speck of dust anywhere for Mother's homecoming. The downstairs couch was also ready for her. But Klara kept sulking and spoke only a few words to her. She also made a special dinner for them. After clearing and washing up, she had made arrangements to go dancing for the last time with her friends. Hannelore and her clan were all up for it. Usually, most dances were on a Sunday, but this one was being held in a local pub for some commemoration.

Laughing and singing, they walked along, when doubts again started creeping into her head. Here, she had friends. Will she make them in a foreign land? But those thoughts were soon squashed, as the boys started getting restless and wanting to flex their arms. The landlord had forewarned the boys, any sign of trouble and he would phone the police. Annalisa was terrified; this was all she needed, being arrested, and at the earliest moment she sneaked out and went home. All right, they probably would not speak to her for a while, but she was leaving on Monday, and who knows when she would see them again.

Sunday was not a happy day. Mother was being

very demanding and not speaking to Dad very much. Emil had made arrangements for Frau Janson to take Ingrid to school, and make breakfast for Mother. Annalisa and Dad had to leave very early, to take the early morning train to Duisburg to the meeting point. Saying goodbye, she tried her hardest to make up with Mother, but she refused. She left with a heavy heart and cried.

It was not as if she was ill, she was already walking again. The surgeon told her on leaving to walk as much as possible. With Father at home for the next fourteen days or more, she was well looked after. As they got on the train she tried to forget the parting, and think of the future. After all, it was not easy for her either. Emil, as always – the two were soulmates – cheered her up as the train rattled along.

Duisburg is one of the large cities, similar to Essen. It had suffered as much as Essen during the war, with heavy industry and coal production. The journey lasted about an hour and half. Annalisa thought, whereas they rumbled first through green fields, when they got closer, devastation; the misery that was caused by every kilometre they went through. And here she was going where Hitler wanted to go and had fought over and did not manage with all his might. It is strange even now, knowing of all the bad things, and atrocities committed. She wondered what makes a person bad enough to let these things happen. That is one thing nobody will ever know, as you cannot look into the mind of another person. He destroyed Germany, her life, and as for the future, hard to predict.

It is March 1949 and in a few weeks' time she will

be nineteen years old.

And then they were in Duisburg. From a distance, as they walked along the platform they heard lots of loud laughter and chattering, as they headed towards this noise. It was still early but lots of other girls had arrived with relations. By lunchtime this group had swollen to about one hundred and fifty teenagers.

The leaders responsible for this group arrived and started checking, of course in triplicate forms, the assembly. Then the girls had to say goodbye to parents or friends. Annalisa hugged Emil and shed a few tears. Both knew this time she could not come back so easily. There was a channel between them. Both had been through a lot together and Emil knew, his darling, Shatzi, was flying away. There was one consolation; he knew she could look after herself.

"I hope you find what you are looking for." Mumbling these words to her, he walked away quickly, so as not to let her see his tears. One by one, all the other people left as well, with the one hundred fifty girls remaining. They were given a bag with food for the journey, and told which coaches to get on when the train arrived. Annalisa was not going hungry; she had brought along her own bag of food.

By now it was afternoon, when the train arrived at the station. In orderly fashion, they got into their allocated seats. So far, all looked good. Annalisa started feeling better, when the whistle blew, and the train started heaving away. Over the next couple of hours' travelling the girls got to know each other. After all, it was nearly the same as a school outing.

"Do any of you speak any English?" she asked

them. Their reply – no – she was the only one. If ever she had regrets, this was the time. She should have paid more attention in class. But soon she would see how much she remembered. After some time, the train stopped at the first border, Holland, and the Dutch border control police checked all passports. Of course, some of the girls were being cheeky, but Annalisa had learnt from the past to keep a low profile.

At long last the train rattled on again. The Belgian border went without a hitch, but no such luck for the French border. The French border guards were not impressed, to be teased by the German girls, and they dragged them out for a long time. Get a bunch of teenagers together, they feel big. No difference here; all of them, including Annalisa, were still very arrogant. They were Germans and all others were in a different class. After all, they had been brought up with this doctrine and knew no better. But once more, the train was allowed to carry on.

After what seemed forever they arrived at the end of their train journey, but not their destination. The countryside they passed through, to Annalisa seemed very much like Germany, some places showing heavy destruction, and others calm with animals grazing. Getting closer to Calais, she felt the villages which had survived were in desperate need of a paintbrush.

Now the change was into buses. The weather had been gradually getting worse and it was now starting to rain heavily. The dusk and then darkness made the last journey foreboding, the countryside being totally flat with the odd light shining. All the girls must have felt the same as her; the talking had stopped and all were quiet. Approaching the harbour, the sights did not improve. Yes, there were a few more lights, but the sea looked black. Large waves were pounding the harbour wall, wanting to get further. None of the girls wanted to leave the security of the bus, and if there was a choice, they probably would have wanted to go home. They all ran through the driving rain to the harbour hall. It was warmer than outside, but the most unfriendly dark hall greeted them.

Full to capacity with the new influx of German girls, room was hard to find. Because of the bad weather on the English side, ferries had been cancelled, and now the bad weather was here as well. All the people made themselves as comfortable as possible with the situation. Nothing had been cleaned up, with dustbins overflowing. The group leaders tried their best to find out the state of the present position, as to when the next ship might sail. The border control police were also not happy to control this large amount of travellers, and looked very stern. This was the first time Annalisa had seen a Frenchman. Even with their guns, helmets and uniforms they looked small compared with the butch German soldiers. Annalisa kept together with her train compartment friends, and they found a small bit of space on the floor to sit.

From the look of things, it was going to be a long night. By now the wind and rain were lashing against the windows. At least she still had food for some time. Munching away again, her mind wandered to the past; no wonder the invasion had not been expected in weather like this. She had a little wander around, now her place was secured, to look at the other people, what they were like, and why they wanted to go to England. She felt sorry for the children crying and went back to her stash of food, to give a little away to the neediest. Lots of different languages were spoken. To her it sounded Polish, or Russian, but surely not. A third language intrigued her, sounding like a baby language. She was told, being nosy, it was Latvian. "Do you mean Germany?" she asked in all her innocence. The Baltic States, she had learnt in school to be German, with their own language. This was the first rebuff she had, telling her that all three different countries had their own identity. But definitely not German. She apologised for her mistake.

The organisers tried again to find out more news.

Yes, the good news was, that a ferry was attempting to do the crossing from Dover. The Channel on the English side had improved. With a lot of luck, it would arrive in about two hours. The news perked everybody up, and the girls attempted to have a cat wash to look better.

Then the leaders called a roll call. "Can you form two separate lines, the first with surnames A to H, the other the rest of the alphabet?"

Doing as they were told, they did want to know.

"Line A to H, when we get to London is being shipped to the Midlands, and the other to Scotland," they explained to them.

Most of the girls did not know anything about England, but Annalisa knew. She sighed relief; the one place she did not want to go was Scotland. She knew that it was a harsh climate and cold most of the time. Also, she had met some of the Scottish solders, and not understood a word they were saying. She lost a couple of her friends to this new way.

The news came that the ferry had made it and docked. But surely they did not want the passengers boarding the ship.

Annalisa, with the rest, was terrified to climb on board. She had never been on a ship, let alone to start now with this monstrosity bouncing up and down. She gritted her teeth and went up the gangplank. Inside greeted her with warm decks, with sailors rushing around. They were clearing up from the passengers who had just left. *So this was a sailor's life,* she thought. *Glorified housemaids.* In disbelief, she saw all the various decks, filled with lorries, sleeping quarters, and recreation decks. To her, this ship was enormous. They had been given coupons to spend in the restaurants.

Annalisa decided to go first to the very top; the smell of sick from the crossing before made her gag. Some people attempted to get food but did not make it to a table. Starting off was not too bad, but on reaching the open sea the ferry heaved up and down. This definitely had to go down as one of her most frightening experiences. She went down to her friends and the comfort of the ship. Next, to spend her food coupons was a big decision. Nothing ever tasted so good as the first cup of coffee with croissants and a sandwich. To Annalisa this was all magic, forgetting the discomfort of the weather. The enormous sea with no land to be seen, and the occasional ship. She fell in love with ships, and when she had money she would like to do this again, only with better weather.

It seemed like an eternity, when at long last land

came into sight and then the white cliffs of Dover. Lots of exited people rushed up to the decks, to watch them getting closer and closer. The rain was forgotten as a surge of happiness filled the ship. The cliffs looked greyer than white, rising out of the sea, to a majestic height. So this was it; she felt like the old adventurers setting foot on virgin land. This was to be her home for the next two years or more. When they disembarked and she put her feet onto English soil, she said to herself, "I have done it. Life will improve."

Her decision was to stay optimistic. Briefly, her mind went back to... Not to mention the name. She had done it, and robbed him of his greatest ambition to put his feet onto English soil. A sadness fell over her to think of all the people who had suffered for this ambition. Well, sera, sera; whatever will be, her future in the hand of the almighty.